BROTHER WEST

Selected Books by Cornel West

Hope on a Tightrope: Words & Wisdom

Democracy Matters: Winning the Fight Against Imperialism

The Cornel West Reader

Restoring Hope: Conversations on the Future of Black America
(edited by Kelvin Shawn Sealey)

Keeping Faith: Philosophy and Race in America

Race Matters

*Prophesy Deliverance! An Afro-American
Revolutionary Christianity*

*The American Evasion of Philosophy:
A Genealogy of Pragmatism*

Prophetic Fragments

*The War Against Parents: What We Can Do for America's
Beleaguered Moms and Dads* (with Sylvia Ann Hewlett)

Jews & Blacks: Let the Healing Begin (with Michael Lerner)

Please visit: Hay House USA: **www.hayhouse.com**®
Hay House Australia: **www.hayhouse.com.au**
Hay House UK: **www.hayhouse.co.uk**
Hay House South Africa: **www.hayhouse.co.za**
Hay House India: **www.hayhouse.co.in**

BROTHER WEST

LIVING AND LOVING OUT LOUD

A MEMOIR

CORNEL WEST

with David Ritz

SMILEYBOOKS

Distributed by Hay House, Inc.

Carlsbad, California • New York City
Sydney • London • Johannesburg
Vancouver • Hong Kong • New Delhi

Library of Congress Cataloging-in-Publication Data

West, Cornel.
Brother West : living and loving out loud / Cornel West with David Ritz.
  p. cm.
ISBN 978-1-4019-2189-7 (hardcover : alk. paper) 1. West, Cornel. 2. West, Cornel—Political and social views. 3. African American intellectuals—Biography. 4. African American scholars—Biography. 5. African American college teachers—Biography. I. Ritz, David. II. Title.
E185.97.W56A3 2009
378.1'2092—dc22
[B]   2009009735

Hardcover ISBN: 978-1-4019-2189-7
Tradepaper ISBN: 978-1-4019-2190-3
Digital ISBN: 978-1-4019-2677-9

13 12 11 10   5 4 3 2
1st edition, October 2009
2nd edition, September 2010

Printed in the United States of America

For my precious parents
Clifton and Irene West

And my beloved brother and sisters
Clifton, Cynthia, and Cheryl

CONTENTS

AUTHOR'S NOTE

This is a work of nonfiction.
Conversations have been reconstructed
to the best of my recollection.

I'm a bluesman in the life of the mind,
and a jazzman in the world of ideas.
— **Cornel West**

PART I

A SHILOH BAPTIST KIND OF BROTHER

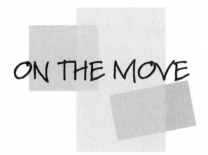

ON THE MOVE

PLANE'S DUE TO TAKE OFF in a few minutes. Awfully tight here in the coach compartment of the big 747, but, as the O'Jays put it, "money can do funny things to some people," and my money's been funny for years, so coach will have to do. Coach is cool. It's a blessing to be on this plane at all. Blessing to be alive. Blessing to be on this journey of love.

I take my phone from my vest pocket and call my blessed mother in Sacramento.

"Off to see Zeytun," I tell Mama. Zeytun is my eight-year-old daughter who lives in Bonn, Germany.

"You give that beautiful child a kiss for me, son."

"You know I'm going to do that. Stay strong, Mama."

I look around the cabin and see that just about everyone is equipped with a laptop computer. Everyone except me. Haven't caught up with the high-tech world of the instant Internet. I have a bag full of books and a writing pad. A good pen is all I need.

It's enough to bring along volumes of the poets I love best—John Donne, John Keats, Walt Whitman—and the philosopher Søren Kierkegaard, whose questioning approach to the deep notions of existence and knowledge help keep me halfway humble. It's enough to scratch out my ideas on the pad, enough to drift off to sleep and dream unremembered dreams that quiet my mind and relax my body.

A week in Bonn with my precious daughter Zeytun. I can't wait to see her and give her a hug. Midday walks along the Rhine and thoughts of Karl Marx, who attended the ancient university in this very city and whose attraction to Jesus as a teenager attracted me to him as a graduate student intrigued by the ethical dimensions of feeling and thought.

At the end of the week, it's back to Princeton. This is my sabbatical year, but I'm returning to my home university for a joyous occasion: "Ain't that a Groove": The Genius of James Brown Conference, the first such academic assembly to take the Godfather seriously, that funkafied genius whose "Get Up Offa That Thing" lifted me high during low days at Harvard. I give the keynote address. I acknowledge that JB is integral to the formation of my spirit and my soul. I say that, like all of us, James was a featherless two-legged linguistically conscious creature born between urine and feces. Like all of us, he was born out of the funk and, like the great Victorian novelist Thomas Hardy, he was still-born. JB was abandoned by both parents, saved by an aunt, raised in a brothel, and yet, through it all—or because of it all—the man managed to transform social misery into artistic delicacies of the highest order. His funk raised us and renewed us. His funk got us through.

I'm getting through.

I'm pushing on.

I'm a bluesman moving through a blues-soaked America, a blues-soaked world, a planet where catastrophe and celebration—Frankie Beverly and Maze call it "Joy and Pain"—sit side by side. The blues started off in some field, in some plantation, in some mind, in some imagination, in some heart. The blues blew over to the next plantation, and then the next state. The blues went south to north, got electrified and even sanctified. The blues got mixed up with jazz and gospel and rock and roll. The blues got on the radio, got in the movies and went all over the world. The blues had to grow.

Like the peerless Russian writer Anton Chekhov and the matchless Irish author Samuel Beckett, the bluesmen sing of real-life, here-and-now experiences of tragedy and comedy even as they offer up help. They offer up strategies for survival. They share their coping skills. They get us to dancing and laughing, rapping and exposing the hypocrisy of a soulless and sanitized civilization.

Bluesmen aren't sanitized. Bluesmen aren't deodorized. Bluesmen are funky. Bluesmen got soul. The great blues artists—Toni Morrison, Louis Armstrong, B.B. King, Sterling Brown, Koko Taylor, Marvin Gaye, Aretha Franklin, Lil' Wayne, Alvin Ailey, Curtis Mayfield, Giacomo Leopardi, Sarah Vaughan, Gwendolyn Brooks, Bruce Springsteen, Muriel Rukeyser, Savion Glover, Bob Marley, Bob Dylan, Thomas Hardy, Ella Fitzgerald, August Wilson, Mary J. Blige, Jacob Lawrence, Federico Garcia Lorca, Duke Ellington—fight the good fight by doing what they can and moving on.

But what does it mean to be a bluesman in the life of the mind? Like my fellow musicians, I've got to forge a unique style and voice that expresses my own quest for truth and love. That means following the quest wherever it leads and bearing whatever cost is required. I must break through isolated academic frameworks while, at the same time, I must build on the best of academic knowledge. I must fuel the fire of my soul so my intellectual blues can set others on fire. And most importantly, I must be a free spirit. I must unapologetically reveal my broken life as a thing of beauty.

I try to give heart to intellect by being true to the funk of living. For me, this can only be seen through the lens of the cross and realized in the light of love. This is the reason that I greet each person struggling through time and space in search of love and meaning before they die as brother or sister no matter what their color. I affirm them as brother or sister to acknowledge their human struggle and suffering. It's not simply a greeting that Christians reserve for other Christians, or even an acknowledgement reserved for and between black people. Both are too narrow.

In a dark world, this means making pain and sorrow my constant companions as I engage in an endless quest for healing and serving others. If I can touch one person—you, holding this book right now—to examine the funk and the capacity to love in your own life so that you become more truly you at your best, then I will not have labored in vain.

So I try to fight the good fight and keep moving on. I'm flying down to Venezuela where, in Caracas, a brother is introducing me to a huge community audience as "Hurricane West." He says,

"I call the good professor Hurricane West because when the force comes through, everything and everyone is unsettled. After you feel the impact, you will never be the same."

I'm moving on to New York to catch a few plays. I have this burning passion for Broadway theater and especially the musicals of Stephen Sondheim. I'm also going to drop by the Oak Room at the Algonquin Hotel and catch Sister Maude Maggart, one of my favorite new cabaret singers. Then on to Atlanta to catch up with Clifton Louis West, my super-talented thirty-one-year-old son, a gifted novelist, poet, and hip-hop artist, who's also acting in a play. When he puts his mind to it, Cliff does it all. And it'll also be wonderful to spend some time with my beautifully mild-mannered and sharp-minded grandson Kalen. I thank God for him.

Back in Princeton, back in my bedroom that is a fortress of books and records, I'm fortified by long listening sessions with the sanctified music of John Coltrane. Trane: another celestial genius whose sacred voice gives me hope. And by hope I mean blues-inflicted hope that is morally sound; hope learned and earned in the harsh realities of daily struggle; hope that remains on intimate terms with death; hope that is life-renewing and opposed to the cheap optimism of market-driven America where Disneyland is sold as heaven on earth.

Three days later I'm in Los Angeles, helping to inaugurate a black arts center. I talk about the miraculous and ongoing rebirth of a people who, inspired by their artists, preachers, teachers, actors, singers, dancers, painters, writers—bluesmen, blueswomen—have overcome the social death of slavery, the civic death of Jim Crow and Jane Crow, the psychic death of self-hatred, and the spiritual death of despair.

Back to New York for the *New York Times* Arts and Leisure Weekend, where I was interviewed by the prophetic and courageous Frank Rich. This "Political Dialogue" in which I lambasted Imperial America was televised by C-SPAN. I turned a spotlight on the Ice Age of Indifference that casts a cold eye on the least of these, the most vulnerable among us—the orphans, the elderly widows, the relatively helpless children, and goes on to embrace poor people, working people, people of color, victims of violence, domestic or international. One wants to look at the world continually through the lens of those people you want to be in solidarity with. This solidarity is manifested best by being part of activities connected to the worlds and experiences of the least of these.

On the long flight to Japan, where I've been invited to lecture at several universities over several weeks, I consider how deficient I am in deep knowledge about the country I'm about to visit. I've been on a steady diet of books on Japanese history, culture, philosophy, and religion, but there's no doubt that I'm marked by a certain parochialism. Like everyone, I bear the limitations of the province from which I've emerged. And yet in Tokyo, when I respond to a question from a Japanese sister, when I say that we find out who we are on the most profoundly human level only when we stand before the dead bodies of our loved ones, the good sister breaks down. Her dad has just died. The provinces of our pasts converge. Grief binds us.

Off to New Orleans, where grief is still palpable. More talks, a college, a church. Someone asks if I'm a lapsed Christian. "Lord, no! I'm a believing Christian," I say. "But my faith can be renewed by lapsed Christians like the author Samuel Beckett. Even as Beckett wrestles with despair, his compassion comes through, and his compassion inspires me to feel more deeply for others."

Back to Princeton, back to Germany—I see precious Zeytun every six weeks—a quick lecture at Yale, a listening party for my new spoken word CD in L.A. I'm on Bill Maher's *Real Time* with Mos Def and next morning I'm on the first plane out. Minneapolis for two days, North Carolina for a day.

Bluesman singing for his supper.

Bluesman born of a blues people trying to serve all people a healthy portion of no-nonsense, stick-to-your-ribs blues.

Bluesman recognizing the fact that the blues is rooted in gutbucket funk. A true bluesman commands respect but doesn't give a damn about respectability.

Bluesman connecting on the college circuit but also working to connect with those the incomparable Sly Stone called "Everyday People" or the magnificent James Cleveland called "Ordinary People."

Bluesman considering the nature of this new song, this attempt to explain himself—and his calling—to everyone.

"We want to get to know the real you," says my dear brother and closest friend, Tavis Smiley. "The real Cornel."

I admit it: I've never taken the time to focus on the inner dynamics of the dark precincts of my own soul. Like St. Augustine once said, I'm a mystery to myself.

"Well, explore the mystery," says Brother Tavis. "Just tell us who you are. Just lay it out." Where to start?

The plane's landing in Sacramento and, praise God, I am one grateful Negro! Haven't been home in months. Going to see Mom! Going to see my dear sisters, Cynthia and Cheryl! And going to get to witness the ordination of my hero, my beloved brother Cliff, as deacon in the church of our childhood, Shiloh Baptist. What an honor!

Sitting in the pew next to Mom, I see tears streaming from her eyes as her oldest son stands before the congregation wearing the red tie symbolizing his deaconship. It's a beautiful thing. And sitting there, I'm experiencing a beautiful feeling. I realize that when all is said and done, I'm a Shiloh Baptist kind of brother. This is where I grew up and this is where I've returned. These are my roots, my righteous beginnings.

It is in this holy sanctuary, surrounded by family—those present and those gone off to Glory—that I understand where my story starts. It starts in this church.

JANUARY 1, 1961

I CANNOT POSSIBLY CONCEIVE OF two brothers being any closer than Cliff and Cornel West. I followed him every minute of the day from sports to music to church. He taught *me* how to read when *he* first learned how to read. The way *he* walked and talked and related to people was the way *I* wanted to walk and talk and relate to people. He was my model in every sphere of life. On the streets and in the classrooms and sanctuaries of our childhood, the West brothers were indivisible and inseparable. Cliff was my model in every sphere of life. In fact, he made history as one of the first black kindergarten students enrolled in Topeka, Kansas after the 1954 Supreme Court decision, *Brown v. Board of Education of Topeka*.

Over the Christmas holidays Cliff said, "Time for us to get baptized." We made the decision together, two brothers on a mission.

I thought about it. Thought about how, for years, I'd been watching my daddy's daddy, the great Reverend Clifton L. West, Sr., come to deliver guest sermons at our church. He was a pillar of strength and a man dedicated to service. For years I'd been sitting under the teaching of our own deeply loved minister, Reverend Willie P. Cooke, whose humble person-to-person pastoring could bring the most cold-blooded sinner to salvation. We decided to make Jesus our choice on Christmas Day and to be faithful unto death with baptism on New Year's Day. We vowed to never forget it.

We never have.

I was seven, Cliff was ten. I was seized by a spirit and, owing to the gravity of the decision, trembled with joy. I decided to love my way through the darkness of the world. We decided to go under the water. Even then I had a good sense of what it meant. We were making a choice. We were choosing the kind of love represented by a Palestinian Jew named Jesus whose hypersensitivity to the sufferings of others felt real and right. A lifetime later, it still feels real and right.

My parents sat there beaming. Their boys were following the same path as their parents and their parents' parents. Following Jesus was no small matter in the West household. I remember someone asking, "Do you have pictures of Jesus all over your house?"

"We don't have to," I said. "We have Jesus in our hearts."

This declaration, made arm in arm by two young black boys in Sacramento, California, in the early days of what would be one of the bloodiest and most disturbing decades in American history, would gain momentum and meaning as their bodies grew and their minds blossomed.

Jesus Christ at the center.

Jesus Christ as model and motivator, Jesus Christ as moral instructor, Jesus Christ as source of unarmed truth and unconditional love.

But that love, no matter how powerful and life-altering, was accompanied by other emotions far less ennobling.

THOSE WERE YEARS WHEN I was called Little Ronnie—Ronald is my middle name—and for Little Ronnie rage was perhaps the main ingredient. Like morning thunder, rage came early and rained over the first part of my life. I'm not sure I can explain it entirely. Psychological theories won't do. I'm unable to name the cause of this restless anger that led to the violent behavior marking my childhood and troubling my parents to no end.

Little Ronnie was, in short, a little gangsta. When it came to confrontations of any kind, Little Ronnie was always up for big drama. Facing the most formidable opponent, he just wouldn't back down. As a little kid, his hands were sore from fighting. He'd take on kids older and meaner and, more often than not, he'd prevail.

What were his motives for such outlandish behavior? Hard to say. He certainly wasn't angry at his folks. Fact is, he adored them. Mom was a schoolteacher, a remarkably energetic woman with a rare gift for teaching young children to read. She would make her mark as a legendary educator. She taught first grade, became a principal—the first black person in both roles—and when she retired, so great was her contribution that the Irene B. West Elementary School was named in her honor.

Mom was in perpetual motion, a woman of dynamic intelligence, grace, and dignity. She was a quiet storm of charitable work and extraordinary instruction. Because of her sensitivity for children, it's no surprise that her oldest son Cliff became a model student. You might assume the same for Little Ronnie, whom she showered with endless love and affection. But I'm afraid you'd be wrong. Little Ronnie was out of control.

Dad tried his best. And Dad, the sweetest and gentlest of men, was always cool. When he entered a room, his smile lit it up. He worked at McClellan Air Force Base for thirty-six years buying and selling parts for fighter jets, and was the most popular guy on the base. He was a college grad and, as an active Alpha, was also the most popular brother in his fraternity. (Later I, too, became an Alpha man.) Everyone loved Clifton L. West, Jr.

Nothing flustered Dad, not even Little Ronnie's rebellious antics. Like Lester Young, the poetical laid-back saxophonist who floated over the beat like an angel floating over fire, Dad never got flustered. Mom might call Dad during the day and tell him that Little Ronnie had messed up again, gone after some kid in his class for God knows what reason. Mom would put me on the phone.

"Little Ronnie," Dad would say, "when I get home, have the strap ready." He'd arrive home, cool as a cucumber, give Mom a kiss—"How you doin', baby?"—and then turn to me. "Boy, when you ever gonna learn?" After the whipping, he'd hug me and say, "Hope this is the last one." Then we'd eat dinner and he'd watch sports or his favorite shows, like *Bonanza* or *Gunsmoke*.

No, I wasn't rebelling against Mom and I wasn't rebelling against Dad, who headed Shiloh's social outreach program and, along with the other fathers, like Mr. Peters, in our neighborhood, created our Little League and built our ballparks with their own hands. When it came to my parents, I harbored no anger. Then, what was it?

In second grade, our teacher was Miss Silver, a lovely woman, who simply couldn't deal with so many bad Negroes. Little Ronnie was the baddest of the bad.

"Where's your lunch?" kindly Miss Silver would ask my classmate Linda.

"Mama forgot to pack it," Linda would answer.

But I saw that every single day Linda's mama forgot to pack her daughter a lunch. That was a funky situation. Shouldn't have been. Linda needed to eat. So when I saw Bernard strolling into the classroom, a boy big as a barn with a lunch bag stuffed with goodies, I had to jump the brother, beat him up, and give some of his food to Linda. Drove poor Miss Silver crazy.

Miss Silver, though, had it easy compared to Mrs. Yee, my teacher in the next year. I loved Mrs. Yee, but Mrs. Yee and I had the worst encounter of my childhood. Happened in 1962 when I was nine.

"Students," said Mrs. Yee, "please rise for the Pledge of Allegiance."

Everyone got up—except me. I didn't move.

"Please rise, Cornel," she said. I still didn't move.

"You heard me, Ronnie."

I heard her, but I wasn't rising. Even at that age, I had issues with America. Most of my fights had to do with bullies beating on weaker kids. Yet Mrs. Yee wasn't a bully—she was a sweet woman who also happened to be pregnant—and she wasn't preying on the weak. But she was insisting that I pledge allegiance to a flag that stood for some things I didn't like. Her request stirred up ugly memories of racist treatment of my family in Jim Crow Texas during the summers and the piercing story of how my great uncle was lynched and his broken body was left hanging, wrapped in the American flag. In my little boy's mind, I saw saluting the flag as an insult to my family and an imposition on my free will. If I didn't want to pledge allegiance to the flag, I didn't have to pledge allegiance to the flag.

"You *will* pledge allegiance to the flag!" she demanded, coming over to me and slapping my face. Something snapped inside me. Her slap stung and, just like that, I socked her in the arm. *Hard* in the arm. She ran out of the room and came back with the principal. Principal had a paddle and went after me. My partners and I jumped the principal until he had to back off. It was practically a riot. The principal expelled me.

When told what had happened, Mom wept. Dad gave me the whipping of my life. And when that was over, I decided I had to leave. I had to run away from home. I packed my little bag and started leaving the house when Cliff saw me.

"What happened?" he asked. I told him about hitting the teacher. I said that to me the flag stands for a nation that treats us bad. I went on about how when we visited our grandparents over the summer we had to sit in the balcony of the movie theater, unable to sit on the ground floor where the white kids sat. I said that our dad and uncles fought for our country but our country didn't treat them right.

"Well, all that's true, baby bro," said Cliff, "but where you off to?"

"Away."

"Away to where?"

"Far away."

"What's that gonna do?"

"I don't know."

"When you get back, you just gonna get a worser whipping."

I thought about what Cliff said, but I left anyway. Went down to the street to stay with a friend and his folks. But then a funny thing happened. My friend and his brothers ran around the house doing whatever they wanted. For some reason, that didn't sit well with me. I disliked being there because their household had no rules. Rules, I realized, could be good, and often came from a place of love. So that very evening I took my little bag, went back home and, as Cliff predicted, got a worser whipping.

My rage, my antagonism, my aggression.

Why, where, and how?

Maybe I saw myself in some heroic Robin Hood role. I'd notice that poor kids came to our school without lunch money. Others had money to spare. So I forced the haves into giving to the have-nots. If anyone resisted, I'd beat them until they forked over their nickels and dimes. In the fighting itself, I turned into an unapologetic brute.

Mom would try to reason with me: "It's not your responsibility to distribute the money among your classmates."

Dad would try to reason with me: "You might think you're helping some of these kids, but doing it by hurting others makes no sense, son."

Reason, though, didn't calm the storm raging inside me. Besides, it wasn't just the money issues that triggered me. Big kids who teased littler kids got me just as incensed. I took it personally and beat up the big kids as if they had been picking on me. Every week my parents were given reports of a new incident, another fight, some classmate whose nose I had bloodied or even broken. In one encounter, I pinned a boy down on the ground and rubbed sand in his eyes. His whole family came after us. Were it not for Dad's super-cool diplomacy, the thing could have blown up into full-scale warfare. Other times, I came close to actually killing some of my adversaries. I was a dangerous thug.

Only big brother Cliff could restrain me. That's because big brother Cliff could handily kick my behind—and did so whenever I was out of control.

For all this bullying of the bullies, I wasn't a big kid. In fact, I remained small until I went off to college. I wasn't a kid who harbored negative feelings about my family. Not only did I feel deep love for Mom and Dad, but I had mad love for my grandparents as well.

Dad's dad was Reverend C.L. West, Sr., pastor of the Metropolitan Baptist Church in Tulsa, Oklahoma for forty years. A small, handsome man, he was a tower of strength and a paragon of Christian compassion. His life was all about self-sacrifice and spiritual growth. His drive to break through the boundaries that would imprison most men was extraordinary. Born in Hamburg, a hamlet outside Alexandria, Louisiana, he went through grade six only to learn that's where the black school stopped. But Grandpa couldn't be stopped. He walked, hitch-hiked, and rode borrowed bikes into Alexandria for six years straight years until he earned a high-school diploma.

One summer, I couldn't have been older than four when Grandpa took me and Cliff, along with Mom and Dad, way out into the fields to meet his dad. This was my great-grandfather, James West, and his wife. They were sharecroppers and former slaves. I was fascinated by their grace, dignity, and old ways but was frightened by their frail appearance. They looked like skeletons, ghosts from a God-forsaken past.

After marrying Grandma Lovie O'Gywn, Grandpa moved to Tulsa when my dad, the baby of their children, was an infant. Granddad got a job as a bellhop in an upscale hotel while Grandma, the most elegant of women, built up her culinary skills to the point where she was catering for the governor of Oklahoma. These were some highly motivated folk. University of Tulsa wouldn't admit even the most motivated Negro, though, so Grandpa held down his hotel job as he commuted to Langston University, an historically black land-grant school located about a hundred miles from Tulsa, where, in true West fashion, he didn't leave before graduating. Later Grandpa and Grandma Lovie divorced—she told me that she never wanted to be married to a preacher—but both remained an integral part of my life when we visited Tulsa every summer.

Big Daddy—Mom's father—was one bad brother. Born in Crowley, Louisiana, he chose to be maladjusted to injustice. Big Daddy was my kind of black man. Looking back, hearing how he talked back to whites that disrespected him, I'm amazed that he lived a long and fruitful life. He lived without fear or apology. When accused of miscegenation—his Creole wife was often confused for white—he scoffed at his accusers so threateningly that they thought it best to back off. A churchgoer and believer, he also told the deacons where to go when they chastised him for operating a liquor store. "I just don't work in the store," he'd say. "I *own* the store. Don't toil for nobody but myself." He carried a piece and would lovingly crush a motherhucker for unduly messing with him or his family.

When Mom was three, her mother complained of a bad tooth. During the day, the pain became unbearable and Big Daddy took his wife to the only hospital in Crowley. The sole black doctor was working elsewhere that week, and no white doctor would touch my grandmother. She was told to wait outside on the steps. The infection spread and within a day or two she passed. She was

15

thirty-one. Enraged, Big Daddy could not be contained. Fearing for his safety, his friends urged him to leave town. That's how he wound up in Orange, Texas, just across the border. Of his seven children, five would go to college. His second wife, T'Rose, was a loving force in all our lives.

Mom went off to Fisk University in Nashville, where she met my father in August 1949. By year's end they were married. She was seventeen, he was twenty-one. Dad had gone into the Army after high school to benefit from the GI Bill. There was no other way to pay for college. He served in Guam and Okinawa for two years, then showed up at Fisk, where he became a member of the service-oriented Alpha Phi Alpha fraternity. He was a star basketball player who, even with his average height, could dunk the ball authoritatively.

But the Army called him back and sent him to Fort Hood near Killeen, Texas. Meanwhile, Mom, who had given birth to Cliff in 1950, returned to college at Dillard University in New Orleans. When Dad was transferred to Fort Bliss, way out in El Paso, he wouldn't dream of going without his family. Consequently, Mom's college career, just like Dad's, was cut short. Fort Bliss is where I was conceived, and Tulsa, Oklahoma, home of my father's preacher daddy, is where we moved after Dad's stint was up.

I was born in Tulsa on June 2, 1953. But University of Tulsa still refused blacks, so my folks' next stop was Topeka, Kansas. For two years we lived on the campus of Washburn College where Dad earned his degree.

Around the time of the birth of my sister Cynthia in 1955, Dad found work at the Forbes Air Force Depot. When the depot closed, he applied for a teaching job in Washington, D.C. His credentials were superb and he was quickly accepted. The letter of acceptance, though, had one proviso. They demanded a photo of Dad before giving the final word. He sent the photo and the final word came back: *Sorry, Mr. West, no job.* They had presumed anyone that qualified had to be white.

My father was always a favorite in the workplace, and the senior officers at Forbes recommended him to three other bases: one in Alabama, a second in Pennsylvania, and a third in Sacramento.

My parents knew California had the superior educational system, so they chose Sacramento.

Before we left Topeka, though, one incident from over a half-century ago continues to haunt me. On a sunny Sunday afternoon, the West family—Mom, Dad, Cliff, Cynthia, and myself—were out for a drive. For no good reason, the police pulled Dad over. He was told disrespectfully by an officer to get out of the car. The officer then looked in the car and called Mom the b-word. My cool, calm, and collected dad exploded. The next thing we knew, Dad was being hauled off to jail. Back home, Mom comforted us with prayer. "Just trust in the Lord," she said. "Your father will be home soon." And he was.

We moved to Sacramento in August 1958. Shortly after my sister Cheryl was born in 1959, Mom went right back to college. No brothers have ever been more devoted to and appreciative of their sisters. Cliff and I adored Cynthia and Cheryl. Cynthia, our oldest sister possessed incredible sensitivity and undeniable compassion. She was a member of the California State Hall of Fame in gymnastics. Her heart was always overflowing with laughter. Like all the West kids, she excelled in school.

Cheryl was our cherished baby girl. Early on, she followed her own path. That meant pursuing her deep love for animals. Her extraordinary ability to identify with others was always an inspiration to us. She enacted and embodied a tremendous empathy.

The West family looked like this: Corn and Cliff on one side, like white on rice; Cynthia and Cheryl on the other side, like wet on water; and Mom and Dad the loving bond holding us all together.

BY THE EARLY '60s MOM had her degree in education and was teaching first grade in the Elk Grove school district. She had a heart and gift for teaching young people to read. I have no doubt that her heart was broken time and again when she saw how her second son was unable to control his violent temper. Teachers complained; parents of kids I attacked complained; and in the instance when I struck Mrs. Yee, the school principal himself brought the news of my expulsion to my mother. Given my love and respect for my parents, you would think I'd find a way to curb my fury. But Little Ronnie could not and would not listen to anyone. For reasons that remain mysterious to this day, Little Ronnie was born to rebel; the kid was primed to slug it out with anyone he considered an oppressor.

In consideration of Little Ronnie's knuckleheaded nature, drastic measures had to be taken. Given their deep intelligence, my folks responded by turning to the solution they understood best: education. Seeing that I was already an advanced reader, Mom made certain that I take an IQ test for gifted children. When I received a score of 168, I was placed in the Earl Warren Elementary School, an institution dedicated to dealing with gifted children. That's where I met my close friends: Brother Gary Schroder, of German extraction, and my Japanese-American brother, Randy Arai. Two loving teachers, beautiful white sisters named Nona Sall and Cecelia Angell, took me under their wings and taught me to fly. I immediately skipped the fourth grade and was put in the fifth. When I graduated I received the highest award, the American Legion Medal.

That's when my change arrived.

WHEN SAM COOKE SANG "A Change Gonna Come," he expressed the centuries-held hope of black folks trapped in a country that considered them subhuman. Sam's song was played in millions of households, especially the West household at 7990 Forty-eighth Avenue in the Glen Elder section of Sacramento. To this day I consider myself a Glen Elder-styled Negro. Glen Elder was cool. Our neighborhood was populated by solid working-class blacks. Fact is, Dad was the only man on the block who wore a white shirt and tie to his job.

Sam Cooke's "Change" brought with it a certain hard-earned sense of possibility tempered by reality. "I was born by the river in a little tent," sang the singer, "and just like the river I've been running ever since."

The West family had been running. Running from Texas and Louisiana to Oklahoma and Tennessee to Kansas and now out here to California. We'd been running after that change. My people saw that the best way to realize that change was schooling. So when one school shut us out, we'd run after another. Running was in our blood, and literal running became a big part of how Brother Cliff and I got over.

But back in the day when my rage got me into so much hot water most parents wouldn't know what to do, Mom and Dad knew *just* what to do.

"Give this child more books," they said. "Give him more trained teachers. Give him tougher lessons. Challenge his little mind. Keep him busy learning new things. Keep him intellectually stimulated and all that violent business will soon fall by the wayside."

And it did.

And when I say, "Thank you, Jesus, for giving my folks the wisdom to push for my change—and push in exactly the right direction," I mean it from the bottom of my heart.

MY CHANGE

THERE WAS THE SPIRITUAL CHANGE brought on by my baptism. Jesus Christ's spirit surely entered my soul. Concurrently, there was the educational change brought on by a new school that stimulated my hunger for new facts and ideas.

The spiritual change had been anticipated by what had happened at my christening. Mom recently told me the story:

"Christenings are usually not that memorable," she said. "The infant is carried to the front of the church, the pastor prays over the baby and the family returns to the pew. But yours was different, Cornel. It happened at Paradise Baptist in Tulsa. That's the church Grandma Lovie attended. Well, son, as soon as your father and I carried you up to the altar where Reverend Branch began his blessing, something happened—something I've never seen before or since. The Holy Spirit just took over. Everyone began to shout. Reverend Branch himself started shouting—'This child is anointed! This child is anointed!'—and then the choir started singing, 'Jesus Be a Fence All Around Me.' The celebration couldn't be contained. Reverend was preaching about how 'Jesus *will* be a fence around this child every single day of his life, oh yes, He will!' Even after we returned to our seats, the rejoicing and praising and hallelujahs grew louder and louder. It was a phenomenon that none of us could explain."

A few years later, in the same city of Tulsa, my grandfather, Reverend West, had me stand up in his Metropolitan Baptist Church and asked the choir to sing that same song, "Jesus Be a Fence All Around Me."

"Jesus will protect this boy," said Granddad. "Jesus will guide him throughout his life."

Somewhere in my unconscious soul I hold these memories. The memory of my baptism, of course, is clearly conscious, as is the memory of my unconscious christening, my very conscious choice to be baptized, and switching to a school that would redirect my energy from fighting to learning were the major turning points in my young life. I cannot overstate the importance of my relationship to Jesus Christ and my relationship to books in developing my character. The Living Word of an outcast carpenter—fully human yet fully divine—and the written words of hundreds of authors, believers and nonbelievers alike, came together in the early years of my childhood. I did not look for contradictions between the secular and sacred, though those contradictions existed. I merely soaked it all in. I drank it all in.

My foundation consisted of three powerful elements: family; the Socratic spirituality of seeking the truth; and the Christian spirituality of bearing witness to love and justice. If the child is father to the man, then the Cornel who grew out of Little Ronnie was produced by a Christ-centered paideia. *Paideia* is an ancient Greek word that literally means "education." When we use it today, it means a deep education that connects you to profound issues in serious ways. It instructs us to turn our attention from the superficial to the substantial, from the frivolous to the serious. Paideia concerns the cultivation of self, the ways you engage your own history, your own memories, your own mortality, your own sense of what it means to be alive as a critical, loving, aware human being.

Even as a little kid I was deep into paideia. Every week I'd run to the bookmobile that came to our neighborhood and leave with a pile of books that reached halfway to the sky.

"You gonna read 'em all?" the librarian asked with a smile.

"Yes, ma'am."

"We're having a contest," she said one Friday. "The child who reads the most books in a weekend gets a little ribbon." By Monday I'd read seven books. I got the ribbon.

I also got the benefit of living in a black community filled with love and care. Today they call it a 'hood. But back then, it was a sure-enough *neighbor*hood, with ties of empathy and deep bonds of sympathy. What a joy to wake up in the morning and run the streets with my brothers Irvin Durham, Roland Office, Leon Lewis, Ricky Peoples, and Don Brown! When Mom ran out of milk, sugar, or salt, all I had to do was go to Mrs. Burton, Mrs. Durham, Mrs. Stuckey, or Mrs. Knight, and everything was all right.

When I think of those early days, my mind also goes back to the home of Mr. Alfred Carr, father of my dear friend William. He was an early militant proponent for black dignity. He had copies of the Black Muslim newspaper, *Muhammad Speaks,* and the *Autobiography of Malcolm X.* He'd speak nonstop for hours on black history and black resistance. His arguments were powerful. And though I am a Martin Luther King, Jr. kind of brother, the fiery passion for racial justice and deep love for black people found in the often misunderstood lineage from Malcolm X to Minister Louis Farrakhan will always be a part of me.

That's when, even at this early age, the question kicked in: is it possible to love oppressed people and not be a fanatic for fairness?

That same warm love I experienced in Glen Elder was there when I visited Aunt Pang, Uncle Nick, and Aunt Lilly in Texas and Uncle Earl and Aunt Tiny in Oklahoma. These were mighty loving folk.

And even though I was a serious child who struggled with the most profound paradox of all—certain death in the face of joyous life—I was moved mightily by other passions: I loved sports, I loved music, and, at an alarmingly early age, I loved girls. Sports, music, and girls ruled my young world.

Once I got past the urge to take on every bully in sight, I found myself walking more steadily in Brother Cliff's footsteps. Cliff wasn't just a good athlete. He was a *great* athlete who, before our childhood was over, would wind up in the record books. Many big brothers ignore or even terrorize their younger siblings. Not Cliff. Big Cliff was an encourager, a born teacher, and blood-loyal protector. As a model of discipline and devoted training, he not only gave me something to work for, he helped me get there.

And because Cliff loved music—he has a beautiful singing voice and, as an adult, would also develop into an accomplished songwriter—we shared that love virtually every hour of our lives.

The musical love was present in our home, in our neighborhood, and in our church, where a young genius named Sly Stone, playing a ferocious organ, showed up at Shiloh Baptist with the Northern California Mass Choir. This is the same Sly who'd become a deejay on the soul station in the Bay Area and later turn his Family Stone into a pillar of forward-thinking funk.

The music that Mom and Dad played at home had an edge to it, a cool intelligence and sophisticated take on grown-up romance. I missed the sophistication but I could feel the salty sensual attitude emanating from these stellar sisters. It was Dakota Staton's singing 'bout "The Late, Late Show," Dinah Washington making her existential observation of "What a Diff'rence a Day Makes," and Gloria Lynne's bittersweet anthem of irony, "I Wish You Love."

Every generation, of course, must find its own musical truths, and ours came largely out of that group of '60s artists who profoundly shaped the way we moved through childhood. We were blessed that Mrs. Reed, the mother of one of our neighborhood friends, was a music lover who ran to the store to buy the freshest Motown hits. Not only was Mrs. Reed a deep lover of soul music, but she also believed in sharing the love. She loved when Cliff and I came and danced to the music. I was only nine, for example, when The Contours tore it up with "Do You Love Me." Something about the song's spirit made me crazy. Something about the groove got me to dancing like a half-pint Jackie Wilson, busting moves that amazed guys twice my age.

By then Cliff was moving into his teen years and dating a bevy of beautiful sisters. When Cliff would go to those garage parties, he let me tag along. He recently reminded me of those days.

"You couldn't grow up the way we did and not be aware of style," said Cliff. "You couldn't ignore what it meant to be cool. Cool, of course, had to do with how you spoke, how you walked, and how you talked. But cool essentially had to do with how you handled your space. That concept became clear to me as a boy, and it became clear to you, Corn, at a very early age. Man, you were always ahead of the curve. Those garage parties were your first showcase. That's when we'd shut the doors, screw in a red light bulb, and crank the phonograph loud as it could go. It looked like a teenage version of that Ernie Barnes painting for Marvin Gaye's *I Want You*.

"We'd throw on The Contours, whose spoken intro had us tingling with anticipation:

You broke my heart 'cause I couldn't dance,
You didn't even want me around.
And now I'm back, to let you know I can really shake 'em down

"When the groove dropped, you'd grab a girl four or five years older than you and go to town. You'd show her all your moves. No one had hip action like you, Corn. Remember this line?

I can mash potato
I can do the twist
Now tell me, baby
Do you like it like this?

"That was the line that got you spinning like a top. You were the star attraction. You were the show, bro. The best parts were when we threw on the slow jams—like The Dells' 'Oh, What a Night!' Smokey Robinson and the Miracles' 'You've Really Got a Hold on Me' or Brenda Holloway's 'Every Little Bit Hurts.' That's when one of those older sisters—one of them stacked brickhouses—would ask you for a dance. You wouldn't hesitate, Corn. You'd just knock it out, grinding up on her like nobody's business. Everyone would be busting up. My partner would come up to me and say, 'Your brother know how to handle that?' I'd say, 'Right now he's just going with nature.' You always loved those bow-legged gals. The cats would say, 'You haven't lived till you've seen Corn grind on a bow-legged honey.'"

Quiet as it's kept, as a kid I actually made a little money winning dance contests here and there.

MY SEXUAL AWAKENING CAME EARLY, and it was beautiful. Those first instances of intimacy were especially sweet. I realized that, beyond the physical pleasure, the girl/boy bond was a glimpse into a poetry not unlike the songs of Curtis Mayfield, another towering figure from my childhood who continues to inform my soul to this very day. It was Curtis's magical song called "Gypsy Woman" that became the underscore for another major moment in my pre-teen years. That moment, in opposition to the life force I found in the funk of music and the fun of dancing, was linked to the death force. Looking back from an adult perspective, I now call it the death shudder.

THE BRIDGE

THE BRIDGE WAS A METAPHOR, a symbol of racist neglect. It was also a symbol of the fragility of life and the easy fall to death. But the bridge was also literal. It was the path that I was forced to cross over to get to elementary school every morning.

The white kids came from the north and their road led directly to school. But we black kids approached school from the south. To get to the school building, we had to walk over a rickety bridge that looked like something out of *Raiders of the Lost Ark*. The bridge was always on the verge of collapse. Down below was Elder Creek, where rushing water ran over jagged rocks. Not only was the bridge on its last legs, it didn't have rail guards and wasn't wide enough for both a car and a pedestrian. If you were walking over the bridge and a car happened to come roaring by, you'd either be run over or thrown into the creek. It was a heavily trafficked road, so nearly every day I'd face the frightening challenge of trying to run over the bridge before an approaching car reached it first. Even then I knew that if white kids had been required to use the bridge a city ordinance would have quickly passed, either widening it or appointing a crossing guard. The city had no concern for the well-being of its black kids.

I envisioned myself falling off and cracking my skull in half. In the words of Kierkegaard, it was with fear and trembling that I imagined being struck head-on by a speeding Chrysler Imperial. The death shudder got all over me. What is the death shudder? I experienced it as a deep anxiety or dread connected to the overwhelming fragility of life in the face of death.

Cliff tells me that I came face to face with my terror at an early age: "There's a defining moment that shows you what you're made of. The bridge was your moment. You were only five years old, but you did what the big kids were afraid to do. You were an incredibly brave little dude. You made it to the other side."

And it wasn't just the bridge that had me shaking and tripping and thinking about this notion of here today, gone tomorrow. Though I had accepted Jesus into my heart, it was not my nature to dwell on literal notions of heaven and hell. In fact, when my Sunday school teacher, the wondrous Mrs. Sarah Ray, posed the question, "If there is only one place left in heaven, would you take it?" my answer was, "No."

"Why in heavens not?" asked Mrs. Ray.

"Because I'd have to do the Christian thing, and the Christian thing would be to let someone else pass into heaven first."

Mrs. Ray was amazed. "And you'd choose to fall into hell, Cornel?"

I just assumed that Jesus had promised to be with me even until the end of the world. So I just stand on his promise. I have always believed that ours is in the trying; the rest is not our business.

So what was "nonexistence" really about then? What did it mean to lose consciousness? Years later when I was a seventeen-year-old at Harvard, my tutor Robert Nozick, a superb philosopher, helped assuage my shudder by saying, "Life after death is no more problematical than life before life. What do you think it was like before you existed? You were born in 1953, Cornel, but what was it like for you in 1952? That year, 1952, was certainly not a problem for you. In the same way, neither will you have a problem during the year following your demise."

As a child, I didn't have the benefit of Professor Nozick's wisdom; the death shudder would not leave me alone. In years to come, it would manifest itself differently. I'd later learn that certain figures with whom I felt deep rapport—Martin Luther King, Jr. among them—had also entertained the notion of nonexistence. As I said, the shudder came early to me—perhaps as early as age six—but to call it total fear would be a misrepresentation. Yes, dread and terror were involved, but also perplexity. Exploration. Where does nonexistence take you? What does it mean to be stripped of your own consciousness? How do we live with the idea that we are always tantalizingly close to death? At any moment the bridge can collapse.

On the other side of the bridge, and perhaps on the other side of the death shudder, was another symbol. This symbol had a name—Delores. Delores lived in the first house when you crossed over. She lived with her mother and, to my eyes, Delores was the most beautiful girl in the world. She had black hair and brown eyes, and when I listened to Curtis Mayfield and his Impressions singing "Gypsy Woman," I knew he was talking about Delores:

From nowhere through a caravan around the campfire light
A lovely woman in motion with hair as dark as night
Her eyes were like that of a cat in the dark
That hypnotized me with love
She was a gypsy woman

As a kid, I didn't even know what a gypsy was, but whatever she was, Delores fit the bill. I was drawn to her mystery. I was attracted to her shyness. She seemed unknowable, and yet I was moved to know her. Then why couldn't I muster the courage to say anything to her? Lord knows I was an aggressive dancer. I pursued puppy love all the time. But Delores, who lived just on the other side of the bridge— which is to say, on the other side of death—was deeply different.

Delores existed as a young girl, but she was also an idea. She stopped the shudder. She stopped my heart. She took my breath away. She seemed to say, *In this world where death is always imminent, always threatening, always frighteningly possible, I can make you happy with a simple smile.*

Then there was Eliot's smile.

Eliot Hutchinson was a schoolmate, a beautiful brother with a sunshine disposition. Easy-going brother, help-you-out brother, fun-to-be-with brother. Eliot wasn't a gangster and Eliot wasn't a bully. Eliot was cool people. Eliot got along with everyone, growing up with all of us, dancing, playing sports, joking, doing his homework, and living his life. Then tragedy struck. Eliot got a brain tumor and, just like that, cancer consumed him. Eliot died.

I'll never forget Eliot's funeral. The level of grief was extraordinary. The pain on his parents' faces is something that still lives with me. The wailing, the crying out to God, the casket in the ground. Death came home to Glen Elder. Death took Eliot. And I couldn't help but wonder—*Why not me? Who gets to live and who gets to die?* I had no answers. Wasn't enough to say, *God is in charge and we can't understand or question God.* Jesus was real and Jesus was love, but why couldn't Jesus's love have kept Eliot alive? The fact that my friend fell without warning or reason haunted me. Eliot's death seemed so absurd it created a surd—a gaping hole—in my understanding of life. It excited a certain panic in my way of thinking and feeling. It sucked all the meaning and rich sublimity out of being alive. It had me fixated on this dead-end notion of nonexistence. For the first time, I understood that most common of expressions—*I'm scared to death.*

Yet I cannot characterize myself as a frightened child. As fascinated as I was by death, I was still deeply in love with life as it was lived in the black neighborhoods of Sacramento, California in the fifth and sixth decades of the twentieth century. I was deeply in love with life because I was deeply in love with music and girls and sports. I can't overemphasize the role of sports. Because both Dad and Cliff were superb athletes, I was inclined to excel as well. I had no compunctions or conflicts about running out on the baseball diamond, putting on a glove, and fielding those hot grounders to second base until I absolutely perfected my double-play move. In fact, my father, along with our neighbors—other black men involved in their sons' lives—built those diamonds with their own hands and organized our leagues themselves.

But how did the fiery passion for competitive sport and its breakneck energy coexist within the soul of a boy preoccupied with questions of mortality?

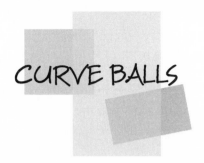

CURVE BALLS

THE IMAGES COME AT ME like curve balls. They do not arrive straight over the plate. They twist, they drop, they change direction. They hop, skip, and jump all over the place . . .

I'm running. I'm born to run. I'm following in my brother's footsteps—I'll never catch Cliff or match his achievements—but I'm running nonetheless. Coach says I have talent in the two-mile and I'm starting to win meets here and there. The schedule is crazy. Dad gets us up and we run five miles.

Earlier in my life, I was running back home, grabbing my bike and heading out to throw my paper route. I threw the *San Francisco Chronicle*, the *Sacramento Union,* and the *Sacramento Bee.* I was bicycling like a madman 'cause the dogs were waiting for me. Man, the dogs were mean. The Rottweilers, the Dobermans, the angry-hungry-killer-foaming-at-the-mouth mongrels going after me like I'm their sure-enough breakfast. After school, I was still running, running to my piano lessons. My teacher, Mrs. Crawley, said I had talent and a good shot to get into the junior orchestra. I felt a natural affinity for the classics. Loved me some Beethoven. Loved me some Mozart. Kept practicing—played violin as well—and even made it as first violin concert maestro, winning a statewide competition against some of the baddest kids in San Francisco and L.A.

Man, I'm running.

Running hard. Still trying to catch Cliff.

Cliff is a champion athlete. Cliff has aspirations to be the first black man to break the four-minute mile. Cliff and Dad take me to the backyard—there's lots of land and empty lots in the suburbs of Glen Elder—and teach me baseball. Comes naturally. Even develop a curve ball.

"That's a mean curve you got, bro," says Cliff. "The thing just falls off the table. Keep working and no one will be able to touch that thing."

I keep working. Mrs. Reed's sons—Raymond and Duane—are my constant playmates who help me hone my skills. My pitch gets meaner. Batters keep falling. At age 8, I strike out every twelve-year-old in sight. At age twelve, the sixteen-year-olds can't touch me. Cliff and Dad put me at second base.

"No one's got eye-hand coordination like you, Corn," says Cliff. "You can make it to the majors if you wanna."

I just wanna keep running. Coaches encourage me. Dad and Cliff keep pushing me on. When the rainstorms come and I can't run or play ball outside, Cliff and I make up little imaginary baseball leagues using yellow pencils as bats and toothpaste caps as balls. We invent track meets using dice to get the runners going.

Dad's running us to San Francisco's Candlestick Park to see our heroes, Willie Mays and Willie McCovey and Hal Lanier, my role model as a second baseman. These are Giants.

"My boys are giants," says Dad. "Giants in spirit. My boys have the hearts of lions."

I'm going. I'm running. Mom is running to teach at school every day, brimming with enthusiasm for teaching the young kids to read. Every night before we go to bed she's reading us poetry. I'm reading about Teddy Roosevelt who went to Harvard—hey, that gives me an idea: I wanna go to Harvard—and I'm relating to Teddy because, although he's running throughout his life, he loses his breath, like me. We both suffer with asthma.

Asthma is frightening. Like the bridge over jagged rocks and the Rottweiler looking to bite off my backside, asthma threatens my life by cutting off my breath. Gotta stop. Can't run. Start choking. Start panicking. Hate it when the asthma hits. The asthma keeps me from moving on. It's keeping me from gaining ground. It's got that death shudder falling all over me. What am I going to do about the asthma?

Orange, Texas. One hundred degrees in the shade. We're visiting Mom's people. I'm waking up in the middle of the night, choking, feeling close to death's door. Cliff wakes up with me, gets me a glass of water, helps me catch my breath. But I see the fear in his eyes. I see the fear in Mom's eyes the next morning when I get an asthma attack at breakfast.

At sundown, Cliff and I take a little jog around the neighborhood, just to stay in shape. I'm feeling a little better, but the lack of breath is always on my mind. We stop at a little convenience store to get some Kool-Aid.

"You seem to be breathing okay, bro," says Cliff.

"For now," I say, "but that asthma thing ain't going away."

A sister buying white bread overhears our conversation. She's a middle-aged woman with a kindly air about her.

"If you suffer from asthma, son," she says, "you best pay a visit to Madam Marie."

"Who's Madam Marie?" I ask.

"She's got some remedies."

"What kind of remedies?" Cliff wants to know.

"She can explain them," says the kindly woman. "I can't. All I know is they work."

"She a God-fearing lady?" asks Cliff. "She a Christian?"

"She's different. I'll give you her address. If you decide to go by, say Miss Johnson sent you. She saved my boy when he was just about your age."

That night Cliff and I tell Big Daddy, Mom's father, what happened. Remember—Big Daddy is a deacon at the Mount Zion Missionary Baptist Church.

"That's a voodoo lady," says Big Daddy. "No grandson of mine's gonna have nothing to do with no voodoo lady."

"What's voodoo, Big Daddy?" I ask.

"It don't come out of the Scriptures," he answers. "Ain't got nothing to do with what we believe."

That night Cliff and I talk it over.

"Hate to go against what Big Daddy says," I reflect, "but this asthma thing is getting no better. None of the regular treatments work. You think the voodoo can hurt me, Cliff?"

"I'll come along with you to make sure it doesn't."

Madam Marie is a big woman who lives in a little one-room shack. She's got strange things hanging from the ceiling—roots and peppers and beads. I tell her that Miss Johnson sent me.

"I see you don't breathe right," she says even before I explain my ailment.

"Yes, ma'am," I say.

"I have a cure."

"How much will it cost?" asks Cliff with a hint of skepticism in his voice.

"If you got a little money, that's fine. But money or not, baby, I'm giving you the cure."

With that, Madam Marie gets up, takes a pair of scissors, and cuts a big tuft of hair from the back of my scalp. She leaves me looking something like a monk.

"Follow me, son," she says.

Cliff and I follow her down an alley to where a long fence separates us from an open field. She stands me in front of the fence. Then she takes the tuft of hair she has cut, gathers it together with a rubber band, and glues it to the fence.

"Stand up straight," she says.

I stand straight and listen as she speaks words that I don't understand. A whole lot of conjuring goes on. She removes the hair and speaks some new words, just as incomprehensible as the first ones. I remain standing for several minutes. The tuft is placed back on the fence. I look out of the corner of my eye and see Cliff looking as if to say, "These folks are clean out of their minds!"

"Bless you, son," says Madam Marie. "You'll never have problems breathing again."

And I never have.

I didn't delve deeper into the mysteries of voodoo. I didn't question Madam Marie and I didn't try to explain what happened to anyone. In fact, when I got back to Big Daddy and he saw my bald spot and heard what happened, I caught hell. Always protective of me, Cliff tried to take the blame and said, "It was my idea." But I told the truth and said it was my decision.

As the days and weeks and months went by, as I found myself free of even the smallest sign of an asthma problem, I was not tempted to abandon the love ethos of Christianity for voodooist practices. I did, however, see myself moving in a more ecumenical direction. I began to understand that answers to problems—physical, emotional, and spiritual—often require enquiries that go beyond the confines of a narrow dogma.

As to why the conjuring worked, I still have no idea.

OUR SUMMERS IN TEXAS AND OKLAHOMA were important times. These were, after all, the territories of my immediate origin, places where the countrified nature of my people—and of me—was nurtured. Just as much as California, Texas, and Oklahoma represented home.

The home of Grandma Lovie in Tulsa was especially impressive. As a result of her catering skill, she was a good earner who put her money into interior décor. Her house was immaculate. The silver was polished, the linen freshly laundered, her upholstered furniture spotless. I loved being there. Grandma gave me a feeling of well-being, not only because her beautifully appointed home offered security—the security that results from achievement against all odds—but because she was also deeply charitable. She fed the poor and cared for the downtrodden.

Yet she was also stern. When, for example, I disobeyed her by climbing a tree in her backyard and breaking a branch, she angered quickly.

"Get me a switch from the tree, boy."

She took the switch and struck me. As the blow came down, I turned. That's when Grandma Lovie inadvertently caught the side of my eye with the switch. It stung like crazy and left a permanent scar. If I had turned a fraction of an inch more, I might have lost the eye. Grandma Lovie cried out in remorse. "Lord Jesus!" she said, "I didn't mean to do that." For the rest of her life she never stopped apologizing.

COACH COULDN'T STOP APOLOGIZING. I understand that it wasn't his fault, but, on some fundamental level, I remained shocked. This is another childhood blow that became clear years later. I'll explain in a minute.

I was barely a teen. I was committed, like Brother Cliff, to becoming a champion runner. I was swept up by the Shiloh Baptist sermons of Reverend Cooke. I was swept up by the sounds of Jr. Walker's "Shotgun." I was slow-dancing with the girls to Barbara Mason's "Yes, I'm Ready" and Smokey Robinson's "Choosey Beggar." In fact, some of the girls told me I looked a little like Smokey. I was also into Arthur Schopenhauer, the German thinker born 220 years ago who said that art was more important than reason or logic in understanding life. Man, I related. I knew that Marvin Gaye's "Stubborn Kind of Fellow" was more than just a song. When the Impressions sang about "Keep on Pushing" and "People Get Ready," their words, like Schopenhauer's or Kierkegaard's, resonated deep within me. When Mom and Dad had taken us to hear Martin Luther King, Jr. speak at Sacramento's Memorial Auditorium—that was back in 1963 when I was ten—I was spellbound. I felt him. I felt *it*. I felt the rhythm of righteous speech. He was, like a song, pushing us on.

Early at Will C. Wood Junior High, the teachers were pushing me on. While I made the varsity baseball team as a seventh grader and won the Inspirational Trophy in football, I also was reading biographies of Albert Einstein and fell in love with the fact that, for all his scientific brilliance, he played the violin. Just for the heck of it, I started writing books. At twelve, I wrote a 250-page history of Canada. At thirteen, I wrote a 180-page history of Mexico City. These were not books of any insight or analysis. They were simple accumulations of facts placed in chronological order and rendered in storytelling form.

I was running, running, running.

"You were running so hard," Cliff recently reminded me, "that you once got into my stash. I'm not sure I was such a good role model for you, Corn. I might have had Dad's cool, but Dad never used his cool to seduce women. He was a one-woman man.

He knew about what the psychologists would later call 'healthy boundaries.' But man, I used that cool for all it was worth. And it was worth a lot of girls. They dug that cool. Fact is, there were several girlfriends I was juggling at the same time when, out of nowhere, still another one popped up. We'll call her 'V.' I said, 'Corn, if V calls, tell her I'm not home.' Sure enough, V called and you gave her my message. But then you started chatting her up. Next thing I know, bro, you're going out with V!"

"But no, Cliff. That happened only after you broke up with her."

V was definitely ghetto fabulous.

COACH BILL MAHAN LOVED THE West brothers. He was our biggest booster and our cross country coach. When Dad couldn't take us running, Coach would show up at six AM and take us on ten-mile treks. Coach had gone to Stanford, where he earned a master's degree in history. He was a progressive white brother. At one point, he gave me Upton Sinclair's *The Jungle,* a novel that introduced me to the horrors suffered by workers exploited by unchecked capitalism. Coach and I discussed it for days.

"Here's another book," he said, giving me *Uncle Tom's Cabin.* "You'll hate it, Corn, but I think it's important that you read it."

I didn't hate it.

"Why not?" asked Coach. "I was sure you'd hate the stereotypes."

"I saw Tom as somehow trying to be Christ-like," I said.

Recognizing my voracious appetite for the written word, Coach gave me books far beyond my reading grade level, such as the renowned American historian Richard Hofstadter, who wrote about anti-intellectualism from a subtle progressive perspective. A lifetime later, my first public lecture would take place in the classroom of Coach Mahan—turned Professor Mahan—at Sacramento City College. The topic? Hofstadter's classic treatment of anti-intellectualism.

Back when I was still a kid, Coach was also determined to teach me how to swim.

"It'll increase your strength," Coach said, "and help your stamina when you run. There's a swimming pool in the apartment complex where I live. We can practice there."

When we arrived, the pool was being used by a half-dozen white people. I didn't pay them any mind. I was dead-set on learning to swim. But the moment Coach and I got in the pool, every last swimmer got out. I mean, those folks fled! I looked at Coach and Coach looked at me. I didn't understand it. I had showered that morning and brushed my teeth. What was going on here? No matter. Coach gave me my lesson, and an hour later we got out. While we were leaving, maintenance arrived and began to drain the pool.

"Why are you doing this?" Coach asked indignantly.

"The manager just told me to clean out the pool."

"Is this when you usually do it?"

"No. It's not due for a draining for another week."

"Did the manager tell you to wait to drain until after we got out?"

"Yes."

With that, Coach went in and told the manager that he was moving out of the complex. "You hurt me," he told the manager, "and you hurt my student. You should hang your head in shame."

NEGATIVE CAPABILITY

I HAVE A LIFELONG LOVE for John Keats, the greatest of the English Romantic poets who lived during the nineteenth century. His uncanny ability to create beauty with words touched my soul. I was still quite young when I read the letter Keats sent to his brother in 1817. In it, he wrote about "negative capability," which he explained as the quality "when a man is capable of being in uncertainties, mysteries, doubts, without any irritable reaching after fact and reason." I was drawn to this idea because so much of what I experienced as a kid, teen, and young man seemed shrouded in mystery.

Even the basic story that had been passed down from my grandparents to my parents to me was clearly mysterious. If I read a biography, for example, of Theodore Roosevelt, I was told where he was and what he did every year of his life. But the four biblical accounts of Jesus's life don't do that. The narrative is sketchy, the vast majority of his growing-up years undocumented. At times, Jesus expresses uncertainties and doubts. In the Garden of Gethsemane he falls to the ground and wants to know if God will let him out of this jam. On the cross, he cries out that worrying blues line, "My God, my God, why hast thou forsaken me?"

None of this made me challenge the power of Christ-based love. I lived with people who modeled that love—my mom, my dad, my brother, my sisters, my grandparents, my preacher. They modeled humility. In their own way, they washed the feet of those they served, just as Jesus washed the feet of his disciples. But at this critical juncture in my life I also knew what Keats was talking about. If Jesus Christ could express his uncertainties and doubts, then the English poet was pointing me in the right direction. I didn't have to resolve every contradiction or inconsistency. When I read the poetry of Walt Whitman, I could understand why he answered the question, "Do I contradict myself?" with "Very well then I contradict myself. I am large, I contain multitudes."

Because I was considered precocious, I was asked to deliver sermons during the junior church service. I tried to avoid it, not because I felt incapable, but because it meant missing a sermon by our pastor, Willie P. Cooke. Cooke was not bombastic, although he would have Holy Ghost visitations during his sermons. He was not intellectual. He was sincere. He loved to talk about the litany of love. He started each sermon by quoting Psalm: 121 "I will lift up mine eyes unto the hills from whence cometh my help. My help cometh from the Lord." Later in my life, when I began speaking in churches, I followed his lead and started with those same wonderful words. He was a man of deep discernment and genuine charity. He was humble. He wasn't interested in hellfire and he wasn't interested in self-aggrandizement. It seemed right that he was a carpenter as well as a preacher. The only other preacher who came close to Reverend Cooke's depth of spirit was Reverend Dr. J. Alfred Smith, the renowned pastor of Allen Temple Baptist Church of Oakland, California. As an adult, I've been blessed to speak and preach many times in his church.

Back in my childhood, I remember that my first sermon in junior church focused on Jesus as the "water of life." I took it from John 4:14. I worked it hard. I compared the pure water of Christ to Kool-Aid—one can sustain you, the other can't. The congregation got to rocking and I got to rocking even harder. If my desire to hear Reverend Cooke hadn't been so keen, I'm sure I would have worked up more sermons. I had some rhetorical gifts and I liked the inspiration it gave to others. But I have never received the calling to preach. I am neither licensed nor ordained as a minister. I see it as a sign of God's wisdom that I was never chosen to be a pastor. I have tremendous respect for that calling. But I know that, as a preacher, I would fall far short of the mark. Ironically, many people do believe that I'm a Christian minister simply because I speak in a preacherly style. But the simple truth is that I'm a Christian bluesman in the life of the mind and a Christian jazzman in the world of ideas.

As a child, Cooke's beautiful soul kept calling me. I also loved the way he called on the deacons to serve the parishioners. Deacon Hinton was our designated mentor. He was childless and treated me and Cliff like sons. Lord, this man was a loving soul! He was a chauffeur who drove for white folks. Every summer he'd make sure to take me and Cliff to the picnics put on by his rich employers. We were the only blacks in attendance. It was like something out of *The Great Gatsby*, F. Scott Fitzgerald's classic novel about social yearning and spiritual malnutrition. Strangely enough, though, Cliff and I didn't do a lot of yearning. We were too happy running around the great manicured lawns and gardens of the wealthy. We won all the foot races. Played ball with the kids. Asked if we could borrow their mitts. "Hey, man," we'd say, "nice glove you have here. Mind if I use it?" "No, go ahead." It was an easy rapport. Deacon Hinton carried us to these picnics every year of our childhood. We developed friendships and allowed the social graciousness of the occasion to wash over us. And I believe that we, being the children of Irene and Clifton West, brought some social graciousness of our own.

SOME OF THE RESIDENTS OF FLORIN, a white district on the other side of Glen Elder, were not especially gracious. Between our neighborhood and Florin was Black Hills, a large landscape of open fields overrun by weeds. Black Hills was the demilitarized zone. Mom and Dad, for example, never ventured into the area while Cliff and I fearlessly charged full steam ahead. We liked Black Hills because it was raw and wild and rabbits ran free. We'd take our BB guns and our dog and hunt down the hares. Didn't matter to us when we got close to Florin. But to some folk it mattered a lot. When one white man spotted us, he sicced his ferocious Rottweiler on our mutt. When we tried to rescue our dog, the guy pulled out a gun and told us to stay put. Somehow our dog escaped, and so did we. Cliff and I might have been able to take the guy, but we were too smart to challenge his pistol. A week later, though, when our dog was healed, we went right back into Black Hills, figuring it was just as much our territory as anyone else's.

Yet the real racial integration of my school life didn't happen till junior high. I was placed in advanced classes, just as Cliff had been. And just like Cliff, I was often the only black student in the college placement classes. Cliff was a school leader and became president of the student body. Three years after Cliff, I was elected to the same office. Naturally that meant we were able to win over white kids, since whites comprised the vast majority of the student population. I was voted Most Likely to Succeed, Best Scholar, and Most Popular.

IN 1967, WHEN I WAS FOURTEEN, Mom and Dad made a big decision. They saw a house that they liked in South Land Park, an all-white middle-class suburb, and decided to buy it. We would be the first blacks in the neighborhood. The home represented an upgrade. It gave us more space and was located on a quiet street. Cliff, my sisters, and I were excited—though we hated to leave Glen Elder. It was something nicer than what we were used to, and we were up for the adventurous move.

The adventure got ugly.

When the white neighbors heard that we were coming, they panicked. They decided to stop us, as in Lorraine Hansberry's classic play, *A Raisin in the Sun*. They had a series of meetings in which they concluded that the only way to keep us away was to pool their money and buy the house out from under us. But Mom and Dad were organized and efficient professionals. They had made certain that the mortgage papers were in order, the i's dotted and the t's crossed. The house was ours. When the neighbors saw that the financial tactics wouldn't work, they got down and dirty. They went to threats. Nasty notes in the mailbox. Ugly phone calls.

Dad reacted in typical Dad fashion. He didn't answer their name-calling with names of his own. He didn't threaten them back. He didn't get a gang of his friends together and come back with a show of force. He simply put on his coat and tie and began going door to door to all our neighbors. He'd knock politely and when the resident responded, he said, "Just want to introduce myself. I'm Cliff West, and my wife and I, along with our four kids, have moved into that house just down the street. We're hardworking folks and are pleased to be able to live in such a nice part of town. We intend to be good neighbors, and I want you to know if there's anything that we can do for you, all you have to do is ask. It's a pleasure to make your acquaintance."

The neighbors were disarmed. Dad's kindness would unnerve the unkindest person around. The threats and the ugly calls stopped, but that didn't mean that we were given welcome baskets and warm apple pies. We hardly heard a "good morning." Rarely did we see a friendly smile. The vibe was cold as ice.

"Don't matter," said Dad. "We're here to stay. Let the people react however they react."

One man, though, reacted with love. His name was Tom Hobday. He was a white brother—I call him the John Brown of our neighborhood—who immediately saw that the West family was up to good. He befriended Dad. When it was time for the Golden West Track Meet, Mr. Hobday extended us a personal invitation.

"I wasn't good enough to enter," Cliff recently remembered. "In my junior year, my best time in the mile was only 4.37. But not only did Hobday insist that you and I go to the meet, Corn, he used his position as head of the sponsoring organization to introduce us to the Grand Marshal, Jesse Owens. After the meet, Jesse came to our house for dinner. Man, that was the thrill of thrills! When he asked me about my time in the mile and I told him, he said, 'Son, I see something in you that makes me think next year you'll be in this meet and win it. I see a champion in you.' His words were so strong and his heart so sincere I couldn't help but believe him. And sure enough, next year I won the national and state championship. I ran a 4.09." It is still a Kennedy High School record forty-two years later.

Having Jesse at our dining room table was really something. I asked him about Germany in 1936. That's when he won four gold medals at the Summer Olympics and, in the process, undercut Hitler's hateful nonsense about a superior Aryan race. In the course of our conversation, though, I learned something else: It wasn't the fact that Hitler didn't shake his hand that bothered Jesse. It was how he had been ignored once he got back home. For all his record-breaking honors, for all the glory he brought to the United States, Jesse Owens was not acknowledged by the president or invited to the White House. Roosevelt ignored him, and so did Truman.

"I never even got a congratulatory telegram," he said.

CLIFF ATTAINED FAME HIS SENIOR YEAR in high school by winning practically every meet he entered, and setting new records to boot. His victories were so spectacular that he was on the front page of the daily paper. California's governor, Ronald Reagan, took note and invited Cliff and his family to the State Capitol for a congratulatory luncheon.

I need to put this in context.

It was 1968. Only a year earlier, the Black Panther Party, formed in nearby Oakland by Huey Newton and Bobby Seale, had marched to this same State Capitol to protest a bill that would prevent a citizen from carrying a loaded weapon in public. The Panthers showed up armed, their weapons in full display. They wore black leather jackets and black berets. The police arrested Seale and some two dozen others. That was May. In October, Huey Newton was charged in conjunction with the slaying of a police officer in Oakland.

The party newspaper, *The Black Panther*, had a profound influence on me. Their articles on social and political history opened my eyes and triggered my curiosity. They dealt with issues that other publications flat-out ignored.

As Dad drove us down to meet the governor, I was thinking of another issue: Reagan had backed the 1966 bill that would have killed open housing. Open housing allowed us to make this recent move up to South Land Park. Reagan had supported all sorts of Jim

Crow measures that would have, in the minds of some, kept us in our place.

But Reagan was a charmer, an ah-shucks-so-great-to-have-you-here kinda guy. We Wests possessed charms of our own. When the governor was introduced to me and he started complimenting Cliff, I said, "Yes, sir, I know. There's no one like my big brother." But when Reagan started telling me how liberal he really was—how he had been a brave pioneer in integrating radio—I had to speak up. I had to tell him that, yes, we were good Christians and we appreciated the honor of being invited to this occasion; and yes, we appreciated all his efforts in integrating radio (even though everyone is invisible on radio); but no, we were not supporters; and yes, I did applaud the activities of the Black Panther Party in trying to educate our own people.

"Well, I can respect that," the governor said.

This was my first encounter with an establishment power figure of this magnitude. I learned a lesson. Such figures often have a begrudging respect for someone who speaks his mind. They respect candor. At the same time, that respect doesn't alter their ideas. They still dismiss you.

A successful athlete understands that the preparation for competition requires total concentration. The rest of the world falls away as you focus on the most important thing in the world at that moment—winning.

It was 1968, the same year Cliff was invited to the Capitol by Governor Reagan. We found ourselves running in an early spring track meet. Kennedy vs. Sacramento High. It was guaranteed to be a spirited contest. On the day of the meet we were both absolutely focused, promising to leave everything we had at the finish line. And, Lord knows, we did. The euphoria of youth can be a bubble nearly impossible to burst. Even after the final event was over and the public address announcer had announced the final tallies. Even when he added that he had a very important announcement. Even as we began to register what it was he was trying to tell us. Even as we were about to be shaken to our very core.

In Memphis, Tennessee, Martin Luther King, Jr. had been assassinated.

What?

How?

Not possible.

Incredible.

A rumor.

No, a fact.

It happened.

The man is dead.

Now nothing makes sense.

Why am I getting up every morning and running five miles? Why am I training night and day? What's the point? Who cares who hits the tape first? Who cares if the honor of my school is upheld? Who cares about some silly foot race? What does it all mean anyway?

My life up to that point revolved around winning every track meet and getting an "A" in every course. Now those goals didn't seem to matter. Hitting the tape no longer mattered. Acing the history paper no longer mattered. Not when they shot down Dr. King like a dog.

Next day Cliff and I quietly joined a protest. Saying nothing, we marched out of school. Hundreds of us simply got up and left. We didn't have to explain. Actions spoke louder than words. Everyone understood.

I'm not sure I understood. I was reading, reading, reading. I was running, running, running. I was going to church, I was praying alongside my parents, I was mourning the loss of Dr. King, I was feeling an anger and outrage that was hard to control. But did I actually understand the way the world was moving? No, sir. I had to rely on Keats's "Negative Capability." I had to remind myself, as the poet had reminded me, that the goal is to chill in that state of "uncertainties, mysteries, doubts, without any irritable reaching after fact and reason."

Music helped the most. Marvin Gaye spoke to me with "Ain't That Peculiar." Sam & Dave said, "Hold On, I'm Coming." But, oh, Lord, James Brown shut the whole thing down with "Cold Sweat." Far as I was concerned, that was the existential statement of the decade. It was the groove of life. It was the paradox of para-doxes and the dance of dances. It caught the fury and lit the fire, and, most of all, it kept us dancing.

THE REST OF 1968 WAS CRAZY. Because Cliff had gotten national recognition for his running, coaches from all over the country were looking to recruit him. Every week another famous track coach was in the house, trying to sell Cliff and Dad on his school. O.J. Simpson came up and personally flew Cliff down to L.A. to sell him on USC. We were all glad, though, when Cliff decided on the University of California at Berkeley. That meant big brother would be close by. Dad drove us up there practically every week-end so we could see Cliff run. We never missed a meet. It was wonderful to see my brother competing—and winning—at such a high level. It also brought me into brief contact with a whole new world of social unrest.

That world—the antiwar white college protestors as opposed to the black civil rights protestors—was foreign to us. I remember Cliff talking about how his roommate at Berkeley, a Jewish broth-er from the Bronx, had introduced him to a far-out guitar player named Jimi Hendrix.

"He'll blow your mind, Corn" said Cliff. And he did.

That was cultural information about a radical black artist com-ing from a radical white brother. Things were changing, and they would change even more dramatically as I entered high school.

High school was heavy for several reasons. My political con-sciousness, especially after the assassination of Dr. King, was raised. My political involvement intensified. And so did my leadership position. First time I ran for president of the John F. Kennedy stu-dent body I was a junior. It turned into a funky affair. Those op-posing me stuffed the ballot box and rigged the results. The school was only 10 percent black so they figured no one would care if the black guy lost. But because I was the overwhelming favorite, lots of people cared—so much so that they started talking about going to war with the cheaters. They were talking violence. Cries of "Right On! Right On!" were being heard as "Riot! Riot!"

They were waiting for me to give the word to go to war. I had to think about it. I was tempted. These were fiery times, and I was enflamed enough to see the school go up in flames. But I couldn't. I didn't see where it would do any good. Fact is, I saw it hurting the cause. It wasn't that I wasn't angry. Man, I was furious. The way they stole the election was cold-blooded. At the same time, though, busting some windows or busting some heads didn't make sense. So I got the most radical folk together and told them, "Hey, we'll get 'em next time. We'll watch the ballot boxes like hawks. We'll make sure it's done on the up-and-up." And special friends like Rick Delgado and Joanne Palmi helped sustain me.

And we did bounce back. Senior year I was elected president.

Throughout high school—and even a little earlier—I started hanging out at the Black Panthers party headquarters in Sacramento. Our proximity to Oakland lent our local Panthers extra passion. Huey and Bobby were around. I liked kicking it with those brothers and sisters because I recognized the legitimacy of their anger. I also recognized that they were saying things that needed to be said. I learned from their newspapers. I saw them as radicals disillusioned with the system, but I also saw them as servants. I saw them as brothers and sisters who loved their people.

At the same time, I had deep differences with the Panthers. I noticed, for example, that every time I'd go to their headquarters to hear a lecture or panel discussion, there was a poster or a piece in the newspaper featuring "handkerchief-head nigger of the week." Without fail, the guilty party was a minister. Now many of these so-called ministers *were* pimping the people, no doubt about it. But I'd tell the Panthers, "Brothers, how come y'all don't have no lawyers or doctors or accountants on your posters? Why always a preacher?"

The Panthers liked me because they saw I was student of black history. Even as a young teen I had read Martin and Malcolm. And I knew the work of Frantz Fanon. They encouraged my reading but always criticized my Christianity.

"Black Christianity," they'd argued, "is a source of oppression. This is a party of freedom fighters—and atheists."

I dug the freedom part, but could never get with the atheism. Besides, the Panthers, for all their good intentions, were caught in a paradox—and I'd be the first to run it down to them.

"Y'all be knocking the church up in here," I'd say, "but every time I come 'round you got Aretha on the box. You got Marvin, you got Curtis, you got Stevie. You got James Brown."

The Panthers would laugh and say, "We ain't going nowhere without Brother James."

"I hear you," I'd say, "but these are church folk. They were raised Christian and stayed Christian. Way I see it, the music that's driving your revolution is Christian music. Now ain't that something!"

"They're Christians who've been led astray."

"But their music is leading *you*. And under their music is the love of God."

"Who doesn't exist."

I'd come back with, "Well, his music sure exists. And you're supporting it. And it's supporting you."

These discussions got hot, but my feelings about the Panthers stayed warm. I stayed close to the party, even if the atheism requirement kept me from joining. I liked the black leather outfits and the cool berets; even got me a black leather Panther-styled jacket of my own. But it would take a whole lot more than a political organization sporting hip outfits to separate me from Jesus, especially when the right-here right-now reality of Jesus's spirit was such a palpable force in my own family.

I would discuss the Panthers with my mom and dad who, most naturally, had their reservations. I'd explain to my parents that, even as Christians, we could learn from the Panthers. "We Christians," I'd say, "are backwards when it comes to the social analysis of capitalism."

Mom and Dad were open-minded enough to accompany me to a lecture by Eldridge Cleaver. Cleaver had just published *Soul on Ice*, a hot book in the black community, and I was hoping he'd make a good impression on my folks. Unfortunately, the brother was off the wall. His entire talk was aimed at the sisters. He told them to hold back all sexual favors until the brothers became bona fide revolutionaries. If the brothers didn't support the party line, the brothers didn't deserve no loving.

I was flabbergasted. Eldridge spent the entire hour talking about employing sex as a recruitment ploy. Dad looked at me as if to say, *Is this Negro crazy?*

I think he was. I think that the Panthers, even though they would continue to influence me in high school and college, suffered from the absence of a spiritual base. The more I read, the more I realized that black revolutionary nationalism didn't work for me. No nationalism did. My understanding of Jesus Christ went like this: Everything comes beneath the cross—nationalism, tribalism, patriotism, networks, even kinships. The cross is that critical juncture where catastrophe defines our condition and offers salvation, not in the name of a specific ideology or theology, but in the simple name of love. It is love that saves us from the tyranny of chauvinism and its many manifestations.

A CONCRETE EXPRESSION OF THE TRUTH of love happened to me during a field trip to an Indian reservation. I had never seen such abject poverty in the face of children. These red brothers and sisters were living in squalor. It was shocking and heartbreaking. Right then and there, I promised that I would never forget the suffering of indigenous people—I would never allow black suffering to blind me from the suffering of others, no matter what color, culture, or civilization. I was saved from the mistake of devaluing other people's suffering. Later in life, I would never give a speech about the struggle for freedom without acknowledging the dignity and determination of Native Americans.

ANY WAY YOU LOOK AT IT, I got radicalized in high school. Glenn Jordan, Kenneth Jones, Melissa Lawson, and I formed SETIMA, a black student group to uplift the community. Forty years later, it's still going.

Some of the issues raised by the Panthers got to me and still do. Lack of black studies, for example, was something I couldn't ignore. I was learning my people's history on my own, not in school. The curriculum was pathetically outdated and white-washed. I hooked up with other student leaders throughout the city. We joined forces and demanded black courses. We said that black students as well as whites should be reading *The Autobiography of Malcolm X* and *Blues People* by LeRoi Jones. We had big meetings with the superintendent and argued our case in front of the Board of Education. When our case wasn't accepted, we went on strike. All over the city, the boycott was implemented. For the most part, the high schools were deserted. Our strategy worked. The administrators wanted to meet with us again. They conceded. Yes, black studies were important. Yes, black studies would be inserted into the curriculum. I was a witness to how intelligent protest can cause real change. The lesson wouldn't be lost on me.

I KEPT RUNNING. One year I ran the two mile in 11:22; by end of the season I had set a city record by running a 10:28. In the same meet, Cliff set a city record for the one mile: 4:22. When I ultimately got my time down to 10:12, I was notified that it was one of the fastest ever run by a fourteen-year-old. Cliff and I had gone against the grain by excelling in cross country. Blacks were supposed to set records only in sprints and long jumps. We liked taking it to a whole different arena.

So there I was, burning up the track and burning the midnight oil, reading books like they were going out of style. I was still holding down that first chair violin for the orchestra. I couldn't read enough about the lives of the classical composers. I was reading philosophy like other kids read comic books—not to impress anyone, but to feed my soul. The philosophers were the ones who grappled with the big questions. They knew about the death shudder. They were asking, what's real and what's not? To paraphrase Keats, they would haunt my days and chill my dreaming nights.

On weekends, when I wasn't running, I was looking for dance partners. Smokey's "More Love" hit deep. That was the song that led to beautiful loving. Smokey's deep. Smokey knows how to pit the comic against the tragic. He understands the paradoxes faced in life and love.

Senior year was tremendous. I won meets, won academic awards, won the hearts of a few wonderful girls, especially the marvelous Margaret McBride. My confrontations with the officials who ran the schools made me realize that anyone could—and should—be questioned, as long as the questioning is based on hunger for knowledge and deeper understanding of what's right and wrong.

I graduated in June of 1970. The start of a new decade for the country, the start of a new life for me. When I applied and was accepted into Harvard, there was a huge celebration. This was a first for a Glen Elder brother. My people were proud and happy to gently push me on. I liked the push. I liked the thought of heading off to a part of the country I had never seen. Knew nothing about Boston or Cambridge or Ivy League schools. I did know, however, that Harvard had teachers who knew all about the books I'd been reading—and that excited me. I knew that the Panther Party was all up and down the East Coast, and that excited me as well. I felt like I could make the connections. Felt like I could make it.

Naturally I was a little nervous. I knew kids from fancy prep schools would be taking the same courses that I would. I knew they'd be more prepared. I also knew that my own experience had been limited. Sacramento wasn't New York, Boston, or L.A. When I looked over the incoming freshman class, I saw I'd be meeting students with famous last names. Some spent their summers touring Europe. Some had already published poems or started political magazines in their high schools. It was daunting.

But I felt ready. I had felt ready for Harvard, in fact, since I had read that Theodore Roosevelt and John F. Kennedy had gone there. I was too naïve to see the obstacles in front of me. I had too much support behind me to worry about failing. I hated leaving home but I loved leaving home. California was home—Mom, Dad,

Cliff, Cynthia, and Cheryl. Shiloh Baptist was home. Reverend Cooke was home. John F. Kennedy High was home. I was secure and happy at home. I had people rooting for me at home.

But home wasn't enough. I remembered that even Jesus had to leave home and follow his calling. Jesus said turn from your own kinfolk and do what you got to do. In a sense, I was doing that. I was following what seemed to me a mandate to grow in wisdom and love. My folks were loving enough—and sophisticated enough—to realize that I had to go. Mom reminded me of that song, "Jesus Be a Fence All Around Me." She said, "That's your song, son. That's your protection. That's the reason you never have to be afraid."

And I wasn't.

PART II

A PHILOSOPHER WITH A GROOVE

ALBERT EINSTEIN AND MALCOLM X

MY FATHER BROUGHT ME TO HARVARD. When we flew to Boston, it was my first plane trip. When we drove to Cambridge, it was my first look at the oldest university in the country. I had seen it only in books. The college dated back to 1636, and some of the buildings looked it. The place was imposing.

Dad dropped me off at the dorm and said, "I'm going over to Roxbury to see where the black folk live."

Three hours later he came back and said, "They got some problems over there. When you get settled here, son, go over and see for yourself. Don't want you to get lost up in here. Far as Harvard goes, the competition will be rough, but you'll do fine. God gave you a good mind. We don't care if you make all A's. Three C's and a D will keep you here. Know this, son—you're loved and respected by the people who know you best, the people who raised you. Just remember that I'm more concerned with the kind of person you are than the kind of grades you get."

After a few days at the Holiday Inn on Massachusetts Avenue, Dad said that it was time for him to go. We hugged, and he was gone.

Alone. For the first time. Me on one coast, my family on the other. More excited than scared, I hit the books like a madman.

Then Harvard said, "We know you're a terrific cross-country runner. We want you to go out for the team."

I said, "I didn't come here to run. I came here to read. Came here to learn. I'm through with running."

Scholarship said, "We're paying part of your college costs, but you have to work."

I said, "I'm used to working. Work don't scare me none."

Work meant cleaning the toilets two hours a day freshman year—we called it dorm crew—and delivering mail at Mather House in later years. No problem. I loved campus. Loved the library. Had never seen anything like it. The stacks went up to the ceiling and I was ready to climb on up to the very top. The course offerings were staggering. I wanted to take them all at once. I jumped in with Hebrew. Had to learn that language. Jumped in with philosophy, the heaviest subjects taught by the heaviest professors. But I also took Dad's advice and went out to see what was happening in the neighborhoods.

I hooked up with the local Black Panther Party. Still wasn't going to join because I still wouldn't—and never will—turn from Jesus. But I liked their breakfast program for needy kids and got up early every morning to go over there and pitch in. That's something I did for the length of my undergraduate career. It was more than serving those wonderful children hot meals. Because of the inferior schools they attended, the kids also needed tutoring, especially in the area of African American history. I was honored to help.

And talking about serving in the name of Jesus, I also made sure to join the Pleasant Hill Baptist Church in Dorchester, a congregation that in some ways gave me the feeling of Shiloh. I got there through their pastor, my dear brother Reverend Boykin Sanders, a Ph.D. candidate who was in my Hebrew class.

"Corn," he said, "I was just appointed to lead this church, but I could sure use some help."

"You mean like teaching Sunday school?"

"I mean like revamping the whole Sunday school program. I want you to be superintendent of our educational division."

"Man, I'm too young for something like that."

"Youth is what the church needs. You have sound biblical knowledge and you have a righteous Christian attitude. The kids will love you. What do you say?"

What could I say? Boykin became my dear brother and Pleasant Hill became my church home away from home.

WHEN I WENT HOME TO SACRAMENTO that Christmas of my freshman year, I hooked up with Glenn Jordan, my close friend who had been president of Sac High the same year I served as president of Kennedy. Glenn had fought with me for Black Studies back when we were seniors, and then gone off to Stanford. Naturally, we compared notes about our first months in college.

"Corn," said Glenn, "there's a man at Stanford who's changed everything for me. He's everything I want to be."

"Who is he?" I asked.

"St. Clair Drake. He's amazing. He's inspired me like no one else. He's a black intellectual conversant with any idea you can throw at him. At the same time, Corn, he's filled with humility. His fundamental aim is to connect the life of the mind to the struggle for freedom. He's grounded in the struggle for black freedom, but he's also a universalist who embraces all people. He's a professor. And that's what I intend to be. A professor."

At that moment, something clicked. Something turned. Something changed. I had entered Harvard pre-law, mainly on Mom's suggestion. But I really hadn't given it much thought. I hadn't really considered a major or, beyond that, a vocation. Until now. Now, in a moment that I can only call transformational, I was feeling the miraculous passion that professor St. Clair Drake had passed on to Glenn.

A teacher. A professor. Connecting the life of the mind to the struggle for freedom. That was it. That would be my life. And just as on that day in the winter of 1961 when, with Brother Cliff, I committed to the gospel of Jesus Christ, on this winter day of 1970 I committed to the vocation of teaching. From that time forward, I have never veered from either commitment.

THERE WAS PHYSICAL AS WELL as intellectual growth during my early years at Harvard. I unexpectedly grew several inches taller. It was a strange feeling to shoot up so dramatically in such a short period of time.

There were other forces at work. I'm thinking of two powerful forces in particular that opposed one another. I was drawn to both.

There was the force of my fellow students—Paul Nichols, Leonard Wallace, and Clyde Dorsey, to name only three—and there was the force of my teachers. The truth is that I loved both groups, even as they found themselves in nasty conflict. Sometimes I felt caught in the middle, but mostly I felt fortunate to be exposed to such a wealth of ideas and an assortment of extraordinary people. I spent the majority of my time with students like myself—young men and women, many of whom were black, swept up by the emotions and politics of the time. We opposed the cruel and tragic war in Vietnam. We marched for civil rights. We protested Harvard's investments in corporations who backed corrupt regimes. We demanded a voice in determining our curriculum. I maintained a strong solidarity with my brothers and sisters of all colors who, more than any generation in the history of American higher education, were skeptical of the system. We were activists who understood the critical importance of asking tough questions and not budging until we were given answers that made sense.

The old ways were falling, and understandably many—in fact, most—of the faculty were put off by the assault. Their entire lives had been invested in a traditional hierarchy and a fixed canon of knowledge. They felt obligated to protect their turf. Yet, in some instances, they also reached out to young students who showed promise. Of course, I was only too happy to engage my teachers in more than a classroom relationship. I would visit them during office hours and often go to their homes. I had never before lived in a community of intellectuals. I loved the stimulation. If you'd asked me which I liked more—Curtis Mayfield's superfunky new jam called "Superfly" or hanging out with Professor Martin Kilson to discuss the history of political development in the black community—I'd say, "It's a tie."

Kilson was a wonderful man who'd become the first black professor to secure tenure at Harvard. He had all sorts of problems with the student protestors during my undergraduate career, but he also became my trusted mentor. He was a man of the mind but also the heart. Beyond his encyclopedic knowledge of history and politics, he had great love for poetry. Kilson took me to his vacation home in New Hampshire where I spent weekends with his loving wife Marion, a Ph.D. in anthropology. It was idyllic. I had never known anyone with a country house before, much less a black man. There was a roaring fireplace, lovely paintings on the walls and books everywhere. That's when I read the poetry of T.S. Eliot, Ezra Pound, and Elizabeth Bishop. My mother had read us poems all during our childhood. Mom introduced us to the lyricism of Rudyard Kipling and Henry Wadsworth Longfellow. But modernism, with its dark turns and enigmatic irony, was new to me. I embraced it. I cherished being in this privileged setting.

When springtime came, Kilson and I took walks in the woods. The first blades of grass were breaking through. Little green buds were popping up on the branches of ancient trees. The air was fragrant with wildflowers and the sky filled with puffy clouds.

I mentioned that my friend Glenn Jordan was studying with St. Clair Drake at Stanford.

"Drake is my hero," said Professor Kilson. "There is no one I respect and admire more."

I loved learning that the link between Kilson and Drake was now linked to my friendship to Glenn. I told my professor about my commitment to teaching.

"You'll be a wonderful teacher, Cornel," said Kilson as we hiked along a well-trodden trail. "You have as much academic potential as any student I've ever taught, but you're wasting your time."

"How so?"

"This Panther Party business is juvenile. They celebrate violence and are set on a course of self-destruction."

"I disagree with them on many issues," I said, "but on other issues they have something to say. We have a rich dialogue."

"Your association with them will deter you."

"Deter me how?" I wanted to know.

"Deter your ability to excel in the academy. Your style is too black for the academy. That's the style you've adopted from the Panthers. The Afro, the black leather jacket..."

"I had this style back in high school."

"Which is when you met the Panthers. Right?"

I had to laugh and agree before adding, "The style you're seeing really doesn't belong to the Panthers. It belongs to my granddad, and my dad, and especially my brother Cliff. Cliff's the one who schooled me on style."

"But there's an aggressive style of political action, especially in the Black Student Association, that is too immature. I just want the best for you. And getting swept up in a political movement that will have small consequence in the future isn't good thinking."

Professor Kilson was a profound thinker and he had a special love for Negroes. Who was I, a seventeen-year-old kid, to challenge him? I respected his scholarship, respected his position at Harvard, respected his place as an accomplished black man in the white world of academia. I also respected how he showed me respect. The man never talked down to me. When he discovered that I held a different view than his own, he argued energetically but never condescendingly. I wrote a long paper on the Black Panther Party in Kilson's famous course, Social Sciences 132—and he gave me an A!

As the faculty–student wars heated up in the early '70s, Kilson would find himself in a tough position. Because he opposed a separate department for black studies—after all, he had worked to assimilate into the university's structure, not to separate from it—the radicals sometimes called him an Uncle Tom.

I was with the radicals. I thought the creation of black studies required official recognition and considerable resources. But to insult Kilson would be as painful as insulting my own father. Far as I was concerned, he had paid the dues to tell the news. His news was different than mine. From where I was sitting, it looked like old news. But he was entitled to say what he had to say without being ridiculed. Unfortunately, this was an era of ridicule, one generation looking to shame another.

My focus stayed on the studies, not only because the studies held me spellbound—I loved learning Hebrew, for example, and reading the Hebrew scripture—but I had my scholarship to maintain. Keeping in mind, though, what Dad had told me about caring for my people, I decided, beyond my work at Pleasant Hill Baptist, to do a prison outreach. Seemed like the brothers and sisters behind bars needed to know that those of us on the outside—and especially those of us fortunate enough to attend college—cared about them. They needed to be taught, just as we were being taught.

ON CAMPUS, THERE WERE SOME marvelous students—such as Sylvester Monroe and Karl Strom—who gave me a sense of family and home. In my dorm room, I hung two pictures on the wall: Malcolm X and Albert Einstein.

"How come those two?" asked my roommate James Brown—not the singer but the extraordinary brother who would become an outstanding national sportscaster. Beautiful brother.

"Well," I said, "Einstein's probably the baddest scientist of the past hundred years and Malcolm inspires me."

"Aren't you more of a Martin man?" asked James.

"I am, but one doesn't cancel out the other. I'm loving them both, just the way both of them loved us."

"Talking about a lovin' brother," said James, "Muhammad Ali is talking on campus tomorrow."

"What?" I didn't know.

"You been too busy cleaning those toilets."

"What time is he talking?"

"Noon," said James.

"That's toilet-cleaning time."

"Well, I know Valerie's going," said James, referring to a girl I was crazy about. "Once the Champ gets a look at Valerie, you will be out of the picture."

"That's another reason for me to go," I said. "I got to protect Valerie."

James laughed and left.

I couldn't sleep that night. I had to see the Champ. I viewed Ali as the athletic equivalent of Dr. King. He had big love for his people. He had big courage. He thought beyond narrow nationalism and conventional views of patriotism. Mainly, he represented his own view of integrity. He did what he had to do. He spoke the unvarnished truth. When he said that no North Vietnamese had ever called him a nigger, that made sense. When he said he had nothing against the North Vietnamese people, that made even more sense. He had reached the pinnacle of celebrity in the paradigm of American sports, and then turned that paradigm on its head. He converted to Islam out of conviction. Even devout

Christians like my dad loved Ali for his guts and honesty, not to mention his skill. I had to see this brother in person. Like Richard Pryor, and Dizzy Gillespie, he was a free black man of the highest order.

That meant lying. So I lied. I told my supervisor that I'd do my noontime toilet-cleaning. Except that I didn't. I took the bucket and mop and hid it in my room while I went down to see Ali. The man was magnificent. His mind was razor-sharp and you best believe his razzle-dazzle poetry brought down the house.

Back at the dorm, my supervisor spotted me.

"Been looking around," he said, "and it seems like you didn't do what you said you would."

I hemmed and hawed.

"Ali?" he asked.

"Ali," I answered.

"I understand."

Under my breath, I said, "Thank you, Jesus."

SUMMER AFTER MY FRESHMAN YEAR, I went back home. Overjoyed to see the family, I was also filled with the spirit imparted by Professor Kilson. If I had a fire under me, Professor Kilson fanned the flames. Through papers I wrote for him, I had become a Fellow of the Institute of Politics (a forerunner of the Kennedy School of Government). That would later allow me to spend some time in Maine and work for the election of Margaret Chase Smith as well as George McGovern.

This early political experience led me to the campaign of Daniel Thompson, who was looking to be the first black city council member in Sacramento. Thompson and I had deep trust of each other, and I helped strategize his race. My approach wasn't all that effective because the good man lost. Eventually, though, he'd triumph and break the color barrier in my hometown. Decades later, I was delighted to support the first black mayor of Sacramento, Brother Kevin Johnson.

Political campaigns are one of the moments in American culture where my fellow citizens are most open to democratic awakening. So my involvement has not only been to support a candidate but also to lay bare a vision and analysis as a form of democratic paideia (education) as my part in the campaign. From the campaign of Daniel Thompson to Barack Obama, I thrive on the excitement of sharing my perspective on where we are now and where we need to go as a nation.

Back in the day, though, working on Daniel's campaign wasn't enough for me. I also had a grant from the Kennedy School at Harvard to write a book about organizing the black political community. I dedicated it to Skip Slaughter, the father of Phyllis, the wonderful woman who had married my brother Cliff.

The most exciting moment of the summer, though, came through my friend Glenn Jordan. Professor St. Clair Drake had commissioned Glenn to work on a project on African religion and philosophy. Glenn, in turn, contracted me to help him. As a result, I would actually get to meet the great man. Talk about a thrill. Talk about a life-changing encounter!

Glenn and I drove over to Palo Alto, and there he was, the professor himself—rich brown skin, soft brown eyes, big ol' fro. By then, of course, I knew his credentials: In 1945, he had written, along with Horace R. Clayton, a seminal book called *Black Metropolis: A Study of Negro Life in a Northern City*. At Roosevelt University in Chicago, he'd started one of the first departments of African American Studies. The summer I met him, he was about to initiate a similar program for Stanford. In social sciences, where black folk were often marginalized or flat-out excluded, Brother Drake placed his people front and center. He asked the right question: How do we react and respond in an urban system that tries to marginalize us?

He treated Glenn and me like sons, spending countless hours dialoging, pointing us in subtle intellectual directions while displaying a mind free of prejudice and predictability. He told me of his admiration for Professor Kilson, and assured me that I could have no better mentor. Being in Drake's presence, my commitment to teaching was reinforced: *This is who I want to be. I want to be a professor like St. Clair Drake and my mentor, Martin Kilson.*

That same summer, my family drove to Tulsa to visit another exceptional man, my father's dad, the Reverend C.L. West. When he asked me about Harvard, I told him about my Hebrew course. He was pleased and proud.

"What other books are those professors telling you to read, Corn?" he wanted to know.

I mentioned the modern theologian Paul Tillich. With that, Granddad got up, walked into his library and returned with a well-worn copy of Tillich's *Dynamics of Faith*, a text I had read at Harvard. Granddad handed me the volume and just smiled, as if to say, *I might be a country preacher down here in Oklahoma, but I know what's happening.*

R.E.S.P.E.C.T.

1971. SOPHOMORE YEAR AT HARVARD. I was the kind of student who followed my curiosity. If a course interested me, I was going to take it. Professor Preston Williams, for example, taught a famous course in Christian ethics for graduate students only. I wasn't bothered being the only sophomore in the class. Nor was Preston Williams. I received an A–. At the end of my term paper, he wrote a note urging me to do graduate work and become a professor, a validation that meant the world to me. I then suggested that I turn my term paper into a larger project entitled *A Stroll Through a Theologically Inclined Mind*. A few months later, I delivered a 110-page manuscript to my surprised professor and his delightful wife Connie, herself a Ph.D.

Meanwhile, the storm brewing over racial politics, on campus and off, kept gathering strength. The storm was coming whether we liked it or not. Rallies, protest meetings, all-night rap sessions in the dorm. Questions were raised. Answers were challenged. Everyone was restless. Everyone was on edge.

The Nation of Islam was coming to Harvard, and we black students were curious, eager, and excited to see what George X, the minister representing the Honorable Elijah Muhammad, had to say. We packed the hall.

The minister began speaking. He was an articulate and intelligent man, but when he referred to Malcolm X as a "dog," I was startled. Though Malcolm had been shot six years earlier, his murder still felt painfully close. The minister's speech went on, and then, for no apparent reason, he found it necessary to call

Malcolm "dog" a second time. I was about to say something, but my friends, seeing I was agitated, restrained me. There were hefty Fruit of Islam guards, the paramilitary wing of the Nation, stationed at all the doors. I swallowed hard and let it pass. But when the minister went out of his way to call Malcolm a "dog" for the third time, I couldn't take it. I jumped up and spoke my mind.

I said, "Who gives you the authority to call someone who loved black people so deeply a 'dog'? You better explain yourself."

"Young man," the minister said, seething with rage, "you best be careful. You're being highly disrespectful and impudent."

"Being disrespectful of character assassination is nothing I'm ashamed of."

"I demand that you apologize."

"For what? Ain't nothing to apologize about," I said.

"Young brother," the minister fired back, "you'll be lucky to get out of this building alive. And if you do manage to slip out, you'll be gone in five days."

"Well, if that's the only response to my challenge, then I guess you're just going to have to take me out."

From there, it got only worse. The crowd went dead silent. They figured me for dead meat. I figured I had probably gone too far, but I said what I felt. I realized Malcolm's shortcomings, but his life, his writings, and the development of his character, had taken on—and still retain—heroic grandeur. I knew he was wrong to have castigated the Honorable Elijah Muhammad in public. Discretion demanded otherwise. And God knows, following Malcolm's lead, I had hardly been discreet in castigating George X. But when the Four Tops sang "I Can't Help Myself," they might as well have been talking about me.

When the minister's lecture finally ended, everyone looked around at me. I stayed in my seat while my friends talked to the Fruit of Islam, saying this wasn't the place for violence. My friends cooled off the situation to where they could escort me out, but for the next week I went underground. I kept moving around from dorm room to dorm room, staying with various friends who had my back. I was afraid to attend class. When I walked around campus, I had my friends with me. Everyone was uptight. For as long as I was on the Nation's most wanted list, I didn't get a good night's sleep.

Finally I had to do something. I couldn't afford to miss any more classes. I had to step out and decided to take matters into my own hands. I knew a brother at Harvard who was in the Nation. He lived at Quincy House and was among the most prominent Black Muslims on campus. I showed up at his room, knocked on the door, and simply said, "Hello."

"Brother West," he said when he saw me standing there. "This is unexpected."

"We gotta talk," I said. "This is getting crazy."

"From where I'm sitting, I think you've already talked too much."

"You may well be right, but I'm here to listen to your point of view."

"From the Nation's point of view, you disrespected one of our ministers, just as Malcolm disrespected the Honorable Elijah Muhammad. Do you realize what Minister Muhammad meant to Malcolm?"

"I do," I said. "I've always believed that there's no Malcolm without Elijah. Elijah's love for Malcolm was deep, rich, and resurrecting. I've never denied this. But you all be calling the brother a dog, and I can never allow that. Not in public. That's a level of disrespect that's too much."

"Our platform and our philosophy are sacred to us," said the brother.

"I understand that, but you can see where I'm coming from."

"Yes, but are you able to feel where *I'm* coming from?"

The brother had a point. At first our dialogue was tense, but when I kicked back a bit and allowed myself to listen—and listen from the heart—we started connecting. Ultimately, we had a wonderful conversation. But that was only possible when I tried to put myself in his shoes. Wasn't that I changed my mind or that he changed his. It was just a matter of giving each other space to be heard. After a couple of hours of exploring each other's backgrounds, we got closer. Empathy overwhelmed anger. By the end of the evening, the brother assured me that all was cool. I no longer had anything to worry about. Mutual respect was in place.

My incident with the Nation raised my profile and was one of the reasons I was elected co-president with Kevin Mercadel of the Black Student Association. In that capacity I invited prominent speakers. At the top of my list was Imamu Amiri Baraka, a seminal man of letters, a revolutionary black nationalist, and a mesmerizing poet. I had the high honor of introducing him.

I read off his many credits and praised him to the sky, saying something about democratic socialism and the European cultural tradition that had helped shape us all. Well, when Baraka came to the microphone, he turned on me like I was Satan himself. He said it was insulting to be introduced by a two-bit Eurocentric wrong-headed boot-licking pseudo-Marxist slave to Western thought. Meanwhile, as he went on, I was thinking to myself, *Lord have mercy, what is wrong with this Negro?*

Anyone who knew me understood that I always gave props to the European minds and hearts that inspired me. But Baraka didn't know me. He was digging deep into his black nationalist bag. Any whiff of European appreciation coming from a black man made him crazy.

We spoke afterward and I argued my position. I think Baraka was taken aback by an eighteen-year-old who came on so strong, but when he saw I could hold my own, he reluctantly offered respect. I explained that I look for intellectual riches wherever I can find them—America, Africa, Asia, Europe. "Wise men and women have emerged from every culture and country," I said, "and I don't want to cut off any source of strength." Baraka warned me about the dangers of European thinking. I argued for the advantages of universal thinking. We went back and forth, didn't really get anywhere, but decades later we became friends. In fact, when Baraka's son ran for the City Council in Newark, I spent a day knocking on doors for him. I was eager for Ras Baraka to serve as a critical contrasting voice for my dear brother Cory Booker, whose mayoral candidacy I had strongly backed.

DURING MY UNDERGRADUATE YEARS students at Harvard took protest to the highest level yet—we staged the biggest strike in the history of the university. Black students took over the president's office to demand Harvard divest its holdings in Gulf Oil, a colonialist exploiter and amoral force in the international marketplace. Our militancy paid off when the president finally agreed.

Ferment continued to brew over recently inaugurated black studies departments coast to coast. The old guard of African American intellectuals could not accept the concept. John Hope Franklin, a black scholar who stands as one of America's supreme historians, had received his Ph.D. from Harvard in 1941. From his endowed position at the University of Chicago, he refused to be associated with black studies. Like my dear brother, the scholar Nathan A. Scott, Franklin shared the views of my mentor, Professor Kilson. These monumental figures had invested a lifetime in the prevailing disciplinary division of knowledge.

They resented Ewart Guinier, Jr., who had been appointed the first head of Harvard's Department of Afro-American Studies. Guinier was certainly not a scholar—he didn't even have a Ph.D.—but he had forged a distinguished career as a trade unionist and political activist. He'd gone to Harvard as an undergraduate where he'd been spit on by white students and barred from the dorms. He'd gone through discriminatory hell and had little use for the Harvard administration. That, of course, made him a favorite of many student radicals. With his enormous white Afro and tough-minded anti-establishment attitude, Guinier was beloved by the students.

I could understand why the old guard reacted so strongly against Guinier. Their scholastic structure was under attack. Despite my love for many of those venerable professors, I opposed the old guard. I stood with my fellow students, convinced then—as I am now—of the need to break down the old paradigm that tended to marginalize black humanity.

"**CLIFF,**" I SAID, "**YOU AIN'T GONNA** believe this, man."

"What's wrong, Corn?"

Cliff knew something was wrong because I hardly ever called from college. We couldn't afford it.

"Calling you from jail, bro."

"Jail!"

"The Cambridge police took us. We down here now, right across the street from the City Hall."

"What happened?"

"Accused of rape."

"Rape!"

"Me and my two roommates. They hauled all three of us down here."

"Corn, I can't believe it."

"Girl down the hallway got raped. Said it was a black dude. So they just came by and arrested us."

"I'll get a plane right now," said Cliff. "I'll be there in the morning."

"Don't do that, man. Let me see if I can get it worked out first. None of us touched the lady, so there's no evidence of any kind."

"Is she white?"

"She's white."

"Then the police don't need no evidence. I'm catching a plane."

"Stay put for a day or two, Cliff. And don't say anything to Mom or Dad. I don't want them worrying."

"You know a lawyer?"

"We'll get someone to help us. But if you don't hear from me in a couple of days, then head on out here."

I had good reason to worry. This was the first year the Harvard dorms were coed. The idea of men and women living on the same floor was worrisome to some. The idea of black men being close to white women was even more worrisome to others.

My roommates and I, all black brothers, found ourselves in the lockup, no questions asked. We demanded a lawyer, but the lawyer didn't come around in time to spring us for the night. We were given no information except that we were suspects in a rape charge. Didn't matter that the woman said she was raped by one man. All three of us were being held.

We each could account for our whereabouts when the rape happened. Our innocence was absolutely provable, but when you're sitting in a cold jail cell, you start thinking about the jacked-up cases involving so-called sexual assaults by black men on white women. You start worrying that, no matter the facts, the system is designed to hang you. You work your head off in high school; you get good grades. Against all odds, you make it into Harvard and then, just like that, you wind up spending your young life in prison for something you didn't do.

"They can rig this thing anyway they wanna," said my roommate, Brother Paul.

"They probably already have," said my roommate, Brother Lenny.

"This is some funky stuff," I said.

I hardly slept that night, and when I did, nothing but nightmares.

In the morning, we were called into an office to face the girl. We knew her and she knew us. She looked frightened and confused. As terrified as I was about what could happen to me and my friends, my heart went out to her.

The white detective doing the interrogation was strong-minded and insistent. His questioning was harsh.

"You sure you were raped?"

"Yes."

"And you're sure it was a black man?"

"Yes."

"Was it these men?"

"It was only one man."

"Well," said the detective, "was it *one* of these three?"

She swallowed hard before answering. Only a few seconds passed, but, man, it felt like a lifetime.

"No," said the lady.

We exhaled.

"You sure?" asked the detective.

"I'm sure."

"I'm not sure you're sure," said the man. "I think you're afraid. These guys can't hurt you anymore."

"They never did hurt me."

"I want you to close your eyes now," said the detective, "count to ten and then open them again."

She closed her eyes, counted to ten, and opened them.

"Okay," he said. "Take a deep breath and look around. These guys live right down the hall from you. They've been watching you. They've been studying you. They have access to you. I know these kinda guys all look alike, but study them, study them good."

She studied us. Again we held our breath. Again, this woman spoke the truth. "They didn't do it," she said.

Yet the more she exonerated us, the more the detective pushed her. For a third time he asked her to reconsider her assessment, and for a third time she held fast. Much to the chagrin of the Cambridge Police Department, we were released. And we were so glad that the white sister told the truth. Her example convinced me even more how sublime the courage to bear witness to truth and justice can be.

WHAT'S GOING ON: LUDWIG WITTGENSTEIN AND/OR AL GREEN?

EDUCATION AT HARVARD HAD TO do with learning the masters. My masters were the world's leading philosophers who wrestled with the questions of how to live. I devoured books for breakfast, lunch, and dinner. Though I read voraciously, I like to think I also read critically. In the great Socratic mode, I was taught to question, question, question. But if the thinker was astute, if his ideas were original and his explanations eloquent, I could vigorously question and still remain fascinated.

Early on, I didn't embrace a Cartesian tradition or dream of transparency. That's the thinking that says reasoning leads to indubitable certainty. I embraced a sense of history, like Hegel or Marx, so that all reasoning is contextual—yet truth does exist even if we never fully reach it.

Now thinkers like Hegel and Marx had subtle minds. Their critiques demand careful study. And naturally I believe that critical energy, applied to any body of information, can unearth some truth. But for every unearthing, you don't find absolute truth— you find another fallible truth, and then still another. That's because each revelation is tied to another concealment. You reveal what's been concealed, only to repeat the process into infinity. Enlightenment has no end. The paradoxes are never resolved.

In 1971, at age eighteen, my paradoxes went unresolved. At age fifty-six, the same is still true. I was excited about discovering my calling. I had to teach. I still have to teach—teaching as I had been taught—with loving passion for uncovering and recovering vital knowledge and wise insights that lead to intellectual clarity and moral growth.

The knowledge and insights could be found in textbooks, but they were also just as powerfully present in music. The music contained the paradoxes, expressed the paradoxes, and exploded the paradoxes with such a sense of heightened joy and rhythmic wonder that all we could do was dance the night away.

It was in 1971, working and studying and dealing with an America in the throes of massive confusion, that I heard Marvin Gaye's *What's Going On*. It was everything I wanted, everything I needed. It was the ideological/theological feast of funk that got me—and countless others, black and white, yellow and brown—through these years of uncertainty and fear. Marvin worked with uncertainty and fear. They were his emotional clay. He molded them into things of lyrical beauty. His answer to the profound question "What's going on?" was in the imagery of his songs. Police brutality. Ghettoes ravaged by drugs. Boys going off to die in an unconscionable war. A planet ravaged by greed and waste. A political landscape of hopelessness. Yet hope comes. Hope emerges from his gut-bucket black Christian faith, a faith powerful enough to transcend the sins of his own Christian father and have Marvin believe—believe to the very end of his life—in the transformational miracle of love seen from the cross. Like Marvin's ethereal suite of songs, that love does not deny calamity or scandal. It sees injustice, just as Jesus saw injustice, as a worldly reality to be transcended through a funky faith. Marvin calls this faith the "Wholy Holy." It's nothing more or less than the love ethos, the love that lasts forever, the love that leads us from darkness to light.

So I was listening to Marvin, I was listening to Stevie telling us *Where I'm Coming From*, and then, at the start of my junior year at Harvard, I was listening to the Spinners singing about "How could I let you get away?" when I spotted this brown-eyed angel. I had to ask her to dance. We took off—mind, body, and spirit—and the Spinners were working it out, the Spinners were saying it for me: "Girl, I'm kinda glad you walked into my life." The Spinners were bringing us closer together, Philippe Wynne whispering in this girl's ear, "It takes a fool to learn that love don't love nobody." The Spinners breaking into "Mighty Love."

This sister had style. Beauty. Brilliance. She was a knockout. I was smitten and smitten bad. One dance led to another. She was a freshman at Radcliffe and her name was Mary Johnson. Years later she'd become the first black woman to earn a Ph.D. in sociology from Harvard. But on that night of nights, when fate smiled and the planet tilted in my direction, she was just a young thing, filled with promise and boundless energy. Soon she'd become the most important woman in this stage of my life.

That night, after the dance, I walked her back to her dorm. She asked me what courses I was going to take in this, my junior year.

"I'm going to take eight courses each semester so I can graduate a year early."

"That's crazy," she said. "I've never heard of that."

"Harvard hasn't either, but I've got to do it. My sister's going off to college and Mom and Dad are running out of money. If I graduate early with high grades, I can get a full scholarship to graduate school. That way next year will be free."

"And Harvard is letting you do this?" asked Mary.

"At first they said no. As a philosophy major, I'd be required to take a year-long junior colloquial *and* a year-long senior colloquial. Those couldn't be squeezed into two semesters. But as it turns out, I've taken most of the courses required for a major in Near Eastern Languages and Literature—Hebrew, Aramaic, Mesopotamian thought. So I've switched majors. This year all I have to do is take sixteen courses and write a thesis in Near Eastern Languages and Literature."

"*That's all?*" Mary laughed.

"That's all," I assured her. "In my heart, I'm a philosophy major. That's my fundamental intellectual identity."

"How can you be accepted into a graduate philosophy program if you're not a philosophy major?"

"That worries me, but maybe they'll take me anyway."

"Just because you're cute?" she asked slyly.

"No, but by then I'll have a cute girlfriend, and she'll be able to convince them of my worth."

"Really, Cornel, how are you going to pull it off?"

"I really don't know."

"So you're making it up as you go along," said Mary.

"A bluesman in training," I said. "We're moving through any way we can."

THAT WAS THE YEAR I FELL for Mary Johnson, fell in love so completely I hardly knew what hit me. I loved falling in love and the feelings it gave me. I loved loving a woman as strong and determined as Mary, loved seeing her absorb everything Harvard had to offer, loved having an intellectual companion and a lover who liked James Brown almost as much I did. Life reached a new level of happiness. I took the sixteen courses in those two semesters and passed with flying colors. I knew I had to keep moving so I applied to Princeton's Ph.D. program in philosophy—then considered the best in the world—and was accepted on a full scholarship.

There's one moment in that final undergraduate year that I'll never forget: I was all set to go out and see Al Green at a nightclub in downtown Boston. He was hot as he could be with "Tired of Being Alone" and "Let's Stay Together." There's no way I was going to miss my favorite soul balladeer. On my way out of the door, though, I just happened to flip open the first page of a book I'd picked up earlier in the day. It was *Wittgenstein's Vienna* by Allan Janik and Stephen Toulmin, a depiction of the cultural world of Ludwig Wittgenstein that included classical composers Johannes Brahms and Gustav Mahler, and historical sociologist Max Weber. It wasn't that I forgot about Brother Al—no one could ever forget Brother Al—but this dang book was absolutely riveting. I tried to stop reading, but couldn't. Wittgenstein's courage and genius got to the core of who I was and wanted to be. I never did get to Al Green's show, but Wittgenstein's performance in the text was astounding.

WHEN I GRADUATED MAGNA CUM LAUDE in three years, the Sacramento paper ran a long article on me with a big picture. They went over to interview Dad. They told him they needed thirty minutes to ask a battery of questions about how he had raised his children. But Dad being Dad broke it down beautifully. He said, "I don't need thirty minutes. Fact is, I don't even need one minute. I can give you the answer in four words. *Be there for them.* Give your children all the time they need."

"That's it?" asked the reporter.

"That's it," said Dad. *"Be there for them."*

And he was. He always was.

DAVID HUME AND
ARTHUR SCHOPENHAUER IN
THE BROOKLYN NAVY YARD

I WAS KNEE-DEEP SURE-ENOUGH all-the-way in love. Mary Johnson had won my heart. I had won hers. We were so tight that the summer after I'd graduated, she invited me to live in her family house in Springfield Gardens, a quiet section of Queens. Her Dad, who had traveled the world, liked me. He saw me as his potential son-in-law and hooked me up with a desk job at the Brooklyn Navy Yard. I did the clerical work assigned to me each day in a hurry, giving me enough time to study and concentrate on the two figures who were saying the most to me: Schopenhauer and Hume. The two men were linked: Schopenhauer, the only great German philosopher who could read English, actually wrote a long introduction to Hume's philosophy. Of course I'd been reading Schopenhauer since childhood—Schopenhauer who put will over reason and mystery over fact; Schopenhauer who dealt so profoundly with the questions of sadness and sorrow. I kept his essays and aphorisms under my pillow.

That summer I found myself writing little Schopenhauer-styled notes to myself. "What's the point of living?" "Why not see what nonexistence is all about?" "When this consciousness ends, what does the new consciousness look like?" "Do I dare step into the void?" "Is there a void?" I didn't fall into depression. I was happy with Mary and eager to get to graduate school. There was no reason to be depressed. And yet these thoughts of nonexistence rattled through my daily thoughts.

These were not suicidal thoughts as is normally understood—the usual despair that accompanies that state of mind was not

present. No, it was nothing on par with the mental health cri-
ses that others have faced. Rather, I was curious to see whether,
when these lights go out, other lights come on. I'd been entertaining these thoughts since I was a kid back in Sacramento. But the
thoughts never turned into action because of a singular insight:
The thoughts were narcissistic. They involved only me and my
philosophical query. I thought of the people I would hurt—Mom
and Dad, Cliff and Cynthia and Cheryl. Mary would be devastated. So would my friends. So I stopped the notes and put away
Schopenhauer. But not for long. To this day, Schopenhauer remains one of my closest companions.

David Hume became an even closer companion. Hume's still
my man. Gotta teach a course on him at least once every two
years. Gotta have his books by my bedside. Gotta keep reading the
brother. He is the finest philosophic mind in the English language.
Back in the summer of 1973, I was preparing for an oral exam at
Princeton in September. Even though they had admitted fourteen
of us to the graduate program, they reserved the right to weed out
four or five if we didn't do our summer preparation. That meant
choosing one legendary philosopher and not only absorbing his
entire work, but all the scholarship on him as well. Hume was my
choice cause there's no one like him.

Hume was a Scottish genius who lived in the eighteenth century. I started out with his *A Treatise of Human Nature*, written when
he was in his late twenties. At twenty-seven, he had a nervous
breakdown. I related to his intensity and eagerness to know. He put
down religion. He even put down conventional knowledge. He said,
"Reason is, and only ought to be, the slave of the passions, and can
never pretend to any other office than to serve and obey them."
He was an iconoclast who questioned fearlessly. His book, *Dialogues
Concerning Natural Religion,* published after his death, is the most
profound critique of any religious faith. His atheism challenged my
faith but never destroyed it. He understood dread—he himself had
experienced the death shudder. David Hume was a soul brother.

Mary Johnson was a soul sister. I was so head-over-heels that
one Sunday afternoon I invited her to ride the subway into Manhattan with me.

"Where we going?" she asked.

"You'll see, baby," I said.

I waltzed her into St. Patrick's Cathedral on Fifth Avenue, dropped to my knees, presented her with a ring and said the words for the first time in my life (though, I hasten to add, not the last): "Will you marry me?"

The lady smiled and said yes.

It was August. That was the summer Sylvia had her "Pillow Talk," Marvin was telling us, "Let's Get It On," and Gladys and her Pips were saying, "Neither One of Us Wants to Be the First to Say Goodbye." It was a romantic time, a sexy time. I had found love and love was going to last.

"This is it," I said to Cliff over the long-distance line. "I asked and she accepted."

"Congratulations, my brother," said Cliff. "Sure you ain't moving too fast?"

"Wanna move even faster," I said, thinking of graduate school coming up and wondering how many courses I could take. Reading over the list, I wanted to take 'em all.

WE OPERATE ON DIFFERENT TRACKS at the same time. New experiences energize us. New possibilities excite us. Fresh romance warms our hearts, thrills our imagination, animates our dreams. These are the positive blessings of a life fueled by love. Yet our essential duality can never be denied. Christians consider Jesus Christ the most divine creation to ever walk the earth. Yet his full divinity coexisted with his full humanity. At times he doubted, at times he cried, at times he felt abandoned, alone, even traumatized.

I entered graduate school a blessed man. Arriving at Harvard with less than a superior high school education, I caught up, caught on, studied hard, and graduated in three years. I got into Princeton, where I was fortunate enough to have Londoner David Lumsden, an extraordinary philosopher, as my roommate. My dear brother Eugene Rivers was a frequent visitor. My fiancée back in Cambridge was everything I had ever wished for in a woman. I was so crazy for Mary Johnson that I did not spend a single weekend in Princeton.

(If truth be known, even today, as I long to enjoy the beauty and idyllic pleasures of my New Jersey community, I'm a bluesman and have yet to spend one single weekend at home.)

Every Thursday morning, I'd catch the bus for New York City and at the Port Authority Terminal would change buses for Boston. I was teaching a course at an adult education school that was stimulating. I was taking courses that were stimulating. I was running around in my usual manner, up half the night reading books, making notes, writing papers. You'd look at me back then and say, "This brother's on the go. This brother's got energy to spare. He's moving fast, he gives out positive vibes." You'd be right, but you'd also be unable to explain why, in this very same period, I experienced a series of blackouts that seemed to indicate that, beneath the surface, darkness loomed.

Several of these blackouts came at or around the Port Authority Bus Terminal in midtown Manhattan. One time I found myself flat on my face on Forty-second Street. I had no idea what happened. Afterward, I thought of the wonderful line spoken by Blanche DuBois, the American Hamlet, in *A Streetcar Named Desire*, that masterpiece by the white literary bluesman Tennessee Williams: "I have always depended on the kindness of strangers." Were it not for strangers who picked me up and helped me to the first-aid station, I could have easily been robbed, beaten, or left for garbage. This was, after all, a time when the crime rate was out of control and the city was swimming in squalor.

Another time I blacked out on the bus itself. When I came to, I found myself being attended to by an older white woman who, with the help of two men, had picked me up off the floor of the aisle where I had collapsed, gathered up all my books and placed a wet towel on my brow.

"You must be quite an accomplished young man to be reading books of this caliber," she said, pointing to those thick philosophical tomes I carried with me. "But you best see a doctor and have a thorough checkup."

Doctors and checkups have never been high on my priority list. In fact, since high school I haven't engaged in a single athletic activity. I haven't once set foot in a gym. I say that not out of arrogance. Obviously, exercise is vital. As with everyone, exercise would do me good. But my absorption into the life of the mind, together with a commitment to political action, has been so complete that I've eschewed such training.

During graduate school, I got my workouts on the dance floor. You'd find me at the discos. This was the grand period of Parliament, who had transmogrified from Funkadelic and was tearing it up with "Up for the Downstroke" and "Chocolate City." Later, of course, the funk got thicker with "Give Up the Funk (Tear the Roof Off the Sucker)," and "Flash Light," not to mention the ethereal Aqua Boogie (A Psychoalphadiscobetabioaquadoloop)." I hadn't lost my love of dancing first triggered by Mrs. Reed, our Sacramento neighbor whose devotion to early Motown got me spinning like a top.

This was also the glorious period of the Maestro, Barry White, whose soaring orchestral flights of fancy were anchored by deep-bottom grooves that had us half-crazy. "Never, Never Gonna Give Ya Up," the Maestro declared. "Can't Get Enough of Your Love, Babe," he swore. "Let the Music Play." As the music played, as I danced my existential blues away, as I lost thoughts of entangled philosophical systems, I found myself at one with pure motion. Barry elevated the funk—gave sheen to the funk—without abandoning the funk. That was his artistic mission. He understood on the deepest level that the funk can be a springboard for beauty. Funk faces brutal reality and reflects its raw consequences. But in doing so, funk is transformational, even redemptive. Funk is liberating. In the funky dance, we express outrage at our human (and political and economic and social) condition, even as we transcend it, even as we get high-up on something low-down, even as we celebrate the catastrophic human condition—which is to say, the certain death of the flesh—by following the mantra first set down by Funkadelic: "Free your mind and your ass will follow."

And yet after a long evening of such freedom, after a super-stimulating night at a New York City disco where Archie Bell and the Drells' "I Can't Stop Dancing" and "Tighten Up" had me whirling and The Main Ingredient's "Spinning Around (I Must Be Falling in Love)" and "Everybody Plays the Fool" had me grinding, I left the disco feeling fine.

Then why, right there on the streets of midtown Manhattan at three o'clock in the morning, did I black out?

I hadn't been feeling faint. Hadn't been drinking. I don't drug. I'd eaten sufficiently. And yet I was gone. When I came to, I saw that a group of late-night revelers were caring for me. Once again, good Samaritans were seeing me through.

After a number of these dark episodes I went to the doctor. The man said, "I don't see anything wrong with you. You're just going too fast."

I'd told him about the number of courses I was taking and my nonstop weekend trips out to see Mary Johnson in Massachusetts.

"I've always moved this fast," I said.

"Well, it's time to slow down."

"I can't."

"You must."

I didn't.

I still haven't.

I WENT THROUGH GRADUATE SCHOOL at Princeton in philosophy, still grappling with the questions, still racing through books and sociopolitical platforms, still searching and questioning, still unable to pinpoint the source of my blackouts. There was so much new light in my life coming from the knowledge of my professors. And yet the darkness did not abate.

Mary and I drifted apart. She was accepted into the London School of Economics where she would earn a master's degree. Ironically, even before I had written my Ph.D. thesis, I had won a Du Bois Fellowship to study philosophy back at Harvard. Mary and I were two ships passing in the night.

We would write. Occasionally we would speak by phone, but the distance did us in. By 1975, we were no longer a couple. Samuel Beckett said it best. His insight into the human effort to get things straight would follow me throughout life.

Try again. Fail again. Fail better—that's how Beckett saw it.

It's a deep thought, and one that's helped shed light on what happens when a relationship falls apart. Then there's that Saint Augustine statement that keeps haunting me, the one that says that he's a mystery to himself. I ain't no saint, and my life sure hasn't moved toward celibacy, but I relate to Augustine's humility. I fell for Mary. I saw myself living the rest of my life with Mary. I was overwhelmed with the warm feelings that come with romance. I thought I had surrendered to those feelings, but maybe not. Maybe the circumstances of my life proved greater than my devotion.

At the time, Eddie Kendricks, former high tenor for the Temptations, sang a song that said it all for me: "Tell Her Love Has Felt the Need." I remember playing it for Mary. In soaring falsetto, Eddie sang, "Tell her love has the felt to the need to leave her . . . I could never be what she wants of me."

The song is heartbreakingly beautiful. Images abound: a woman is awoken at dawn, sunshine warms her face, the morning breeze blows her tears away. She dreams of a wedding, she dreams of children, she dreams of a home filled with love and a husband who never leaves her side. That's the life she wants, the life she desires and deserves. In the words of the song, however, "But my life is like a ship that sails."

MY LIFE HAD SAILED. I *had* received a calling so powerful it required obedience. I knew I had to keep reading, keep thinking, keep teaching in as many ways and in as many places as possible.

A formulation was taking shape in my mind and heart: that the centrality of vocation is predicated on finding one's voice and putting forth a vision. All three are intertwined: vocation, voice, and vision.

I view vocation in stark contrast to mere profession. Vocation cuts deeper. I also contrast a voice with an echo. True voice doesn't imitate or emulate prevailing paradigms. The notion, for example, of staying within restricted categories would never work for me. My voice, by its funky blues character, cuts across the disciplines.

The radical uniqueness and sheer singularity of voice are connected to the depths of our soul and the love that abides therein. In the greatest scene in the greatest play in English about love,

Shakespeare's *Romeo and Juliet,* Romeo approaches Juliet in the dark and gives voice to his soul, despite his despised name. Juliet replies, "My ears have not yet drunk a hundred words/Of thy tongue's uttering, yet I know the sound." Or as Nick Ashford and Valerie Simpson, those rhythm-and-blues love poets, would say, "I'd know you anywhere."

As I reflect on the eternal art and sudden death of the incomparable Michael Jackson, it is clear that there are profound joys and unbearable sorrows that accompany being true to one's calling. The comfort is in the knowing that by giving one's heart and soul to uplift others through one's art, one's vocation, voice and vision are fulfilled. As a blues philosopher, Michael Jackson is my true soul brother.

Contrary to that unforgettable moment in line 607B of Book Ten in Plato's *Republic* where philosophy quarrels with poetry, I believe philosophy must go to school with poetry and music. In short, like Nietzsche, we need dancing philosophers, Socrates with gaiety—poetic thinkers philosophizing under a funky groove.

I come from a blues people whose anthem is, "Lift Ev'ry Voice and Sing." The connection between unique vocality and empowering visionary practice is profound.

A vision is not a stare. A stare is flat. A vision is vital and vibrant. A vision is biblical: without a vision, people perish. Our job is to keep people from perishing.

My vision was surely based on my black Baptist foundation. It had everything to do with Jesus Christ's mandate to love extravagantly and radically, but it also went in a dozen different directions. I didn't see a precedent for this calling. I wanted the maximum degree Princeton had to offer, but I knew I wasn't born to be a conventional professor. I believe in on-the-ground education. For years, I taught adult ed. And yet I knew those venues weren't enough. I also taught in the prisons and churches and neighborhood schools.

I have found prisons to be both liberating and depressing institutions, where my soul is elevated and challenged. Be it at Sing Sing in New York, the city jail in Boston, the correctional facilities in Bordentown, NJ, or the juvenile detention center in Jamesburg, NJ, I am inspired when I speak and teach at those places where my brothers are incarcerated.

One of the most moving moments, I experienced during my teaching was when a prisoner simply asked me, "What was the source of hope for someone with a life sentence in prison?" I replied, "We all have a death sentence in space and time and there are many outside the prison walls whose hearts, minds, and souls are in profound and permanent bondage. So there is a sense in which a wise and courageous person can be free with a life sentence in prison, just as others can be unfree walking the streets of New York City. My fundamental aim is to touch the souls and unsettle the minds of people be they in prison, classroom, church, or on the block."

During this time I began writing, but not in any traditionally academic way. And when I needed to find an expression of the complex romantic anguish I was facing, I turned not only to Brother Shakespeare, but also to Brother Eddie Kendricks who said, "Tell her love has felt the need to leave her."

I knew what that meant, and I didn't know what that meant. I knew that in leaving Mary Johnson I had not stopped loving her. I love her to this day. Love of her led me to leave her. But some other kind of love, whose dimensions were beyond both description and comprehension, was fueling my feelings and moving me in directions that I hadn't anticipated. I had found love. I had lost love. Love of my calling was pushing me on.

THE BIG BLOCK

THEY CALL IT ABD. All But Dissertation. If it sounds like a disease or psychological disorder, well, dear brother or sister, that ain't far from the truth. I suffered with ABD for years. I raced through my graduate work at Princeton with enthusiastic dedication. Philosophy was my meat and potatoes, and I was blessed a little later in this period to study with the greatest philosopher of the latter part of the twentieth century, Hans-Georg Gadamer. This brother was so heavy it was ridiculous. Lived through the hell of the Third Reich without supporting Nazism. Survived to write, among other major works, *Truth and Method*, one of the most profound books written in any language on any subject. The man lived to be 102. When he lectured, he never used a single note. Like a master jazz musician, he spun the words out of his spirit. He improvised magnificently. He was the Count Basie of philosophy. He was the architect of twentieth-century hermeneutics, a fancy word that refers to the ways we use to interpret texts, especially religious texts. His follow-up to *Truth and Method* was an examination of Paul Celan, the finest post–World War II poet in Europe, a Jew from what was then Romania. The follow-up blew the minds of Gadamer's fellow philosophers. Philosophers just don't knock out a complex work of theory and then devote a volume to understanding some poet. For traditional scholars, one doesn't just follow the other. But Gadamer saw it was a continuum. To others, Gadamer's leap seemed crazy. To me, it seemed right. I was doing some leaping of my own.

I was also leaping from philosophy to poetry. Truth was in metaphor, uncertainty, ambiguity, the beauty of the blues, words and thought mixed in the muddy waters of raging literary seas. I got back to Harvard as a philosophy graduate student, but I could never be a straight-up philosopher. I had been granted membership in the first class of Fellows of the W.E.B. Du Bois Institute not for any distinguished academic work I had written, but because my former Harvard mentors, Martin Kilson and Preston Williams, used their power to get me in. They just liked me and figured I'd thrive in that environment. They were right, even if I found myself heading in a different direction.

The direction was toward literature. All I wanted to do was read novels, and Russian novels to boot. I started jonesing for every nineteenth- and early-twentieth-century Russian novel ever written. Those were the bad boys who really understood the blues. They broke down the blues better than anyone. Talkin' 'bout Pushkin, Gogol, Turgenev, Dostoyevsky, Tolstoy—the heavy hitters who, from their strong moral base, wrote sagas about our tragic condition as people, the complexities of personality, the exploitations of society, and the scandalous intersection where indifferent history collides with human passions.

I didn't want to write my Ph.D. dissertation. I wanted to write literature. I had a notion of realizing an intellectual performance that would sing like Sarah Vaughan and swing like Duke Ellington. In fact, it was during this time that I wrote a short story. I got the title from Earth, Wind & Fire. "Sing a Song" is a jazz-fused piece of fiction fixated on Duke's death. (Ellington had died only a year earlier in 1974.)

It's a barbershop-based story peopled with hustlers and pastors. It's got the new music of the day—Teddy Pendergrass singin' 'bout "Wake up ev'ybody, no more sleepin' in bed...no more backward thinkin'...time for thinkin' ahead"—and P-Funk screaming "We gonna turn this motha out!" It reflected my love of musical geniuses like Isaac Hayes, David Porter, Kenneth Gamble, and Leon Huff. It's got the narrator going to a club where he paints a picture that had been burning in my mind for years: "People of all sizes and shades of the Negroid spectrum filled the misty, sweltering room. Flashing fluorescent multicolored lights shone just bright enough to see who was wearing what and who was with whom. The floor was filled with banana-skin females dancing with jet black men and chocolate-colored women dancing with paperbag-brown males." This was a scene that Ernie Barnes would paint for the cover of Marvin Gaye's *I Want You*. This was a story about the clash of generations, the young losing its connection with the best of the old, the old losing its connection with the fire of the young. The narrator, who was once a musician, was losing his hearing and had to make a vocational decision. Should he become a jazz intellectual in the world of ideas? He says, "Watching the vivacious dancers, I could see my former Self. There I was, fingerpopping and ass-twitching. But I also could see me now through my former Self. There I was, wall-flowering and analyzing." The narrator is caught between the world of observing and the world of acting. Doing. Dancing. Singing a song.

At age twenty-two, I wanted to act on the stage of life. I still do. I wanted to do, and dance, and sing a simple song. The simple song was about death and rage and love and music and ideas of justice and freedom. The song had to include the distractions and disruptions but, to be effective, it had to be simple because the blues are simple. Yet, at the same time, as B.B. King, King of the Blues, once wrote, "The blues are a mystery, and mysteries are never as simple as they look."

So here's how my life looked in the mid-'70s:

I was sad over breaking up with Mary, glad about being at Harvard, and, in spite of my usual eager get-ahead-get-the-degree attitude, getting nowhere on my dissertation. Those Russian novelists kept calling me. I even started a literary salon devoted to reading those texts. I had a crib on 888 Massachusetts Avenue where my partners and I discussed a different Russian novel every week. Man, was I obsessed! Didn't want no English novels and didn't want no German novels. Forget Proust and Joyce. Later for Cervantes and Victor Hugo. I'm not saying those writers didn't turn out books we'll be reading for centuries to come. But I just didn't want to read them or re-read them in 1975. I had to have Turgenev every dang time. When it came to plays, my man was Anton Chekhov, whose understanding of the human condition is rivaled only by Shakespeare and Sophocles. Chekhov is the deep blues poet of catastrophe and compassion, whose stories lovingly depict everyday people wrestling with the steady ache of misery and yearning for a better life. As I grew older, only Franz Kafka inhabited the same literary stratosphere as Chekhov.

Others in our literary salon in Cambridge got tired of my Russian-only policy and made me stretch out. Ultimately we let in a little James Baldwin. We got to a little Ralph Ellison and we couldn't ignore Brother Richard Wright. The only non-black non-Russian whose work we analyzed was Thomas Pynchon. We devoted a chunk of time to *The Crying of Lot 49* and *Gravity's Rainbow*.

The literary salon had an impact on me beyond the books we read. It was during this period that I toyed with the idea of becoming a writer—a serious novelist. In fact, I started an ambitious novel that, if it found form, would contain all my philosophical musings in dramatic fashion. I toiled on the book, looking to the Russians for literary inspiration and to the transcendent corpus of Mahalia Jackson, Sarah Vaughan, Louis Armstrong, and Stephen Sondheim for musical inspiration.

Of course, I was also teaching. Won't ever forget my first day as a teaching assistant for a course taught by Stanley Cavell, one of the philosophical geniuses of our time, and Martha Nussbaum, a young creative classical philosopher. Martha was brand-new on the Harvard faculty while Stanley had been there for twenty years. He was a Wittgenstein man, but the brother could teach anything from "Antigone" to the films of Fred Astaire. When I entered the classroom, two students were already there. "You better bring in more chairs 'cause this is a popular class," they told me. They presumed I was the janitor.

"Cool," I said. I went and got more chairs, waited for the others students to file in and then went to the lectern and started teaching. The young brothers nearly died. They fell over themselves apologizing. "Hey, man," I said, "we all got our stereotypes." We wound up being friends.

MY DEAREST FRIEND IN GRADUATE SCHOOL was Brother Larry Morse, the last of the Renaissance men. His novel, *The Sundial*, is the best literary depiction of life at Howard University. Larry is also a trained economist and one of the finest minds in American business. Through Larry, I met Henry Coleman, who happened to be teaching economics at Tufts. "Corn," Henry said, "you got to meet this sister who's running the black house at Tufts."

Turned out her name was Hilda Holloman, and, believe me, Brother Henry was right. Hilda was off the hook. Brilliant woman, beautiful woman, loving woman, seriously Christian woman with a highly developed critique of Christian dogma. She'd gone to Spelman as an undergraduate and was the first black woman to be working on a Ph.D. in philosophy from Tufts. She was writing papers on Descartes.

Tufts is just down the road from Harvard, and it didn't take long for us to meet. The connection was instantaneous. We had worlds in common. She'd come to the philosophy classes that I was conducting as a teaching fellow; she became part of our literary salon. Soon she became part of my life, night and day. Hilda had a singular style and wonderfully supple mind. We could talk all night. And then some nights we didn't need to talk at all. I saw my future, at least my domestic future, as having everything to do with the fabulous Hilda Holloman.

There was an excitement in my relationship with Hilda where the sexual, intellectual, and spiritual all came together. She and I met in 1975, and on January 1, 1977, we married at her parents' home in Atlanta. Brother Cliff was my best man. Mom also flew in, but my father and sisters didn't make it—the cost of travel was too much.

It was a beautiful wedding. I saw a beautiful future. I saw children and I saw domestic stability. I saw myself settling down into a long and loving relationship with one woman and one home, much as my Mom and Dad had created in my childhood home.

Another beautiful thing happened. I'd been offered a job at the Union Theological Seminary in New York, one of the finest such institutions in the world. There was no place I'd have rather been. Union is the oldest nondenominational seminary in the country. The finest theological minds had taught there, including Reinhold Niebuhr and Paul Tillich. The Christian theologian Dietrich Bonhoeffer had studied there before being martyred by the Nazis in World War II. So had Adam Clayton Powell, Jr. Black liberation theology, as expressed in the work of the incomparable James Cone, blossomed at Union.

So when Union offered me a teaching job with the understanding that I'd complete my Ph.D. thesis, long overdue at Princeton, within a few months, I accepted. Man, I jumped at the chance. For a prophetic Christian like me, Union was as close to academic heaven as I was ever going to get. Hilda was willing to make the shift from Tufts to Columbia graduate school, where she could continue her philosophy studies. Meanwhile, our child was due that August.

How well I remember arriving in New York in September to start my job at Union's facility on 122nd Street. I was blessed to be offered the office of Reinhold Niebuhr, the spiritual volcano and intellectual hurricane of his time. The room was immaculate and the desk was bare except for two letters addressed to me.

The first was from Professor Nathan A. Scott, Jr. of the University of Chicago. My black brother, Nathan, was the leading religious scholar of modern literature, a former student of Niebuhr and a Ph.D. from Union and Columbia. When I was in graduate school, I had attended his Noble lectures at Harvard on my favorite contemporary English poet, W.H. Auden. I was so inspired, I asked him whether we could have a cup of coffee and keep talking. The professor was gracious enough to say that, although he had plans that evening, he would meet me the next morning at six o'clock in Harvard Square. I was there at 5:45 AM, eager to pursue our discussion. Professor Scott arrived with a smile, and we talked for hours. Now, looking at his letter on the desk, I had to wonder what was on his mind.

It turned out to be a heartfelt warning. Nathan was convinced that I was making the mistake of my life. According to his perspective, the Golden Age of Union was over and the school had been taken over by leftists. I put down the letter with a sigh.

The other envelope had a return address from Drew University. It was from George Kelsey, the renowned Christian ethicist. Kelsey was the first black professor to teach religion in a predominantly white university. He had taught Martin Luther King, Jr. at

Morehouse. Like Dr. King, Kelsey was shaped by the godfather of all twentieth-century black religious scholars, Howard Thurman. "Dear Professor West," wrote Kelsey. "Words cannot express my delight at your appointment at the historic Union Seminary. May God bless you as you keep alive a rich Christian heritage."

Later that day, I felt compelled to make a neighborhood pilgrimage that included two stops. The first was to the home of Lionel Trilling, a giant among the public intellectuals of his day. The second was to the home of Ralph Ellison, the grand novelist of his generation. I made this sacred trek with my newborn son in my arms.

Nothing thrilled me more than the birth of Cliff on August 9, 1977. He carried the name of my brother and father and grandfather. What a blessing to have a son! And how wonderful, back in 1973, to have a nephew—my brother Cliff's son—named after me. Cornel, alongside Erika, Phillip, Phyllis, Kahnie, and Briana, have made me the proudest uncle in late modernity. Just as later in life my grandson Kalen and my godchildren Brian, Ruby, Emma, and Langston bring joy to my heart. My son Cliff's lovely wooden cradle was given to us by the celebrated freedom fighters Robert and Janet Moses. I had met Robert in Cambridge when he returned to Harvard from Tanzania to complete his Ph.D. in philosophy. I viewed this brother as the most courageous and compassionate leader in the Civil Rights Movement, with the sole exceptions of Martin Luther King, Jr., Ella Baker, Stokely Carmichael, and Fannie Lou Hamer. His Algebra Project, which teaches poor young people mathematics as a form of literacy and cultural liberation, operates to this day from Cambridge, Massachusetts, with branches across the country. I loved putting Cliff to sleep in this cradle that symbolized the intergenerational struggle for freedom.

Robert Moses is one kind of spiritual colossus. At Union, I was about to embark on an adventure with another spiritual giant, a man whose friendship would sustain me for two tumultuous decades to come.

BROTHER WASH

WE MADE QUITE A PAIR. Wash looked like James Cleveland *after* the picnic. And I looked like an undernourished Smokey Robinson.

Wash was James Melvin Washington, ordained preacher and Professor of Church History at Union. He was unique. Big man, big heart, big intellect. Wash came out of Knoxville, where he grew up materially poor and spiritually rich in the Baptist tradition. He'd been a boy preacher who got the calling early—at sixteen he was leading the 126-member Riverview Missionary Baptist Church in Lenoir City, Tennessee—and spread the Word every single Sunday of his life. After graduating from the University of Tennessee, Jim was accepted into Harvard Divinity School, where he earned a master's in theology. Then on to Yale, where he wound up with two more degrees, including a Ph.D. He'd been teaching at Yale when Union called him down to New York. I'd met Wash years before in Cambridge, but we didn't tighten up until we hooked up at Union. From then on, we were inseparable.

I loved the man for many reasons. Some folk have a spark of divinity—from time to time you can see the Jesus in them. Wash didn't have a spark—he had a fire that warmed everyone he met. You saw the Jesus in him as clearly as you saw his dark loving eyes. For all his extraordinary erudition, Jim Washington was first and foremost a down-home brother who never—not for an instant—betrayed his country roots. Fact is, he was countrified as cornbread, and yet could delineate the most complex theology text with the precision of a surgeon. His mind was amazing. I related to him as I have related to few other men. After Cliff, Jim became my closest friend in life. Perhaps the thing that brought us closest together was the way in which he married his deep Baptist faith to his vast intellectual sophistication. In other words, for all his Socratic questioning and powerful curiosity, for everything he had learned about every conceivable theological system, for all his understanding of the metaphysical subtleties of religious thought, he still believed in the Jesus of his mama and his mama's mama. He still called that Jesus real, still prayed to that Jesus, still preached Jesus's love every chance he had.

For both me and Brother Wash, following Jesus requires a radical child-like sense of faith and wonder, and a mature effort to pick up our cross and bear the cost. This is not to be confused with a childish dogmatism that trumps mystery or a will to power that celebrates worldly success at the expense of spiritual integrity. For us, Constantinian Christianity produces people well-adjusted to injustice and well-adapted to indifference. Prophetic Christianity produces people maladjusted to greed, indifference, and fear. We vowed to love our crooked neighbors with our crooked hearts. We believe that if the kingdom of God is within us, then everywhere we go we should leave a little heaven behind.

Jim called Dr. King his contemporary religious hero. He looked to James Baldwin's *The Fire Next Time* and James Cone's *Black Theology and Black Power* as inspirations and said that he "discovered in existentialism a certain secular celebration of the inevitability of marginality." He called "spiritual malaise the root cause of the social callousness that has befallen too many segments of African America." And we both considered Karl Barth the grand Christian theologian of the twentieth century.

The central question with which Jim grappled was unjustified suffering—the problem of evil. Why would a benevolent, all-knowing and all-powerful God permit such pain on any people? He and I didn't approach the dilemma theoretically, however. In the end, we saw the answer as the conclusion of a practical Aristotelian syllogism. It was all about action. It was all about the practice of faith. As in the novels of Dostoyevsky, your life becomes your response. Your response doesn't take the form of a written-down, reasoned-out argument. Your response becomes the quality of your day-to-day behavior. The question doesn't go away. It remains powerful and daunting. But the fact that there is no reasoned-out answer doesn't turn you cynical. You live with the reality that the question remains, a challenge to your mind and your heart. You can't bring back the bodies that died in the Atlantic Ocean during the slave trade. You can't reconcile a tidal wave wiping out an entire city with the notion of a sovereign God. You can't equate catastrophe with the human condition—but you can, following the teachings of this particular Palestinian Jew, do what you can to help the least among us.

For Christians, serious faith begins when we experience the sweet shipwreck of the mind and the bittersweet cracking open of the heart. As George Santayana noted, "Religion is the love of life in the consciousness of impotence."

Both Wash and I shared a Christian worldview that conformed to what we saw as here-and-now reality. To be human is to call for help. We saw birth itself as a catastrophe: you're thrown in space and time to die. The flesh fails. Then the question becomes simple—how you gonna cope? Life is shot through with contradictions and incongruities. But that doesn't mean that any ol' life is acceptable. On the contrary, it means there's a big distance between a holy fool and unholy fool. Robin Hood and Alexander the Great were both gangsters, but consider the difference between them. As the Reverend Al Green once preached in his "Love Sermon," that's the distance "from heaven to earth."

The intellectual rigor that Wash brought to bear on his Christianity—together with the tremendous historical and theological knowledge accumulated during a lifetime of disciplined study—was inspiring. Appropriately, his classic text is *Conversations with God: Two Centuries of Prayers by African Americans*. Covering some 235 years, the prayers selected by Wash begin in 1760. He has the sensitivity to recognize the most spiritual words uttered by our people. Jim never placed the mind above the heart—not in the prayers he picked, not in the life he led—and the book remains by my bedside, even to this day. It reminds me of the good times spent with Wash, his beloved wife Patricia, and his lovely daughter Ayanna.

Wash and I had a special bond. When we arrived at Union, we had both been told by white men in authority that we would never gain tenure. We didn't believe them for a minute. We didn't believe them for a minute. Wash and I promised each other that Union would have no choice but to tenure us. We would out-write, out-publish, and out-shine anyone in the country.

There was a third brother in our triumvirate, Jim Forbes. Together, we were the Three Musketeers of Union Theological Seminary.

The Reverend Dr. James Alexander Forbes, Jr. was not only a distinguished professor of preaching at Union, he became the first black Senior Minister at the Riverside Church on the Upper West Side of New York City. This is the magnificent gothic church, the tallest in America, built by John D. Rockefeller in 1927. It's interdenominational—Baptist and United Church of Christ—and known for its progressive policies. When they installed Brother Forbes, though, they'd never heard preaching like that before. Jim was called the "preacher's preacher" for good reason. No one could touch his eloquence. No one could dispute his scholarship. He expressed the mystery and magnificence of Christ's abiding love in a way that broke down color lines, political differences, and economic barriers. When it comes to giving the Good Word, Jim has the big gift.

Riverside had always been a bastion of white liberal Christianity. Before Forbes, William Sloane Coffin had been Senior Minister. He was another giant. Yes, indeed. Brother Coffin was the man who said, "The devil's always suggesting we compromise our high calling by substituting the good in place of the best." Brother Coffin liked to suggest that it's the devil in every American that makes us feel good about living in a country so powerful. Love of country is fine, but why should love stop at the border? Brother Coffin was quick to say that we're all capable of the extraordinary. His formulation was that extraordinary people are ordinary people who do ordinary things extraordinarily well. Coming from an extraordinarily rich family, he gave up much to become a preacher. At the same time, as the predecessor to Forbes, Coffin embodied many of the typical positive characteristics of a white liberal Christian.

Forbes, though, had been a lifelong Pentecostal. He had to become a Baptist before assuming the senior pastor role. He did so, even as he retained the passion of his original faith. When his graceful wife Bettye and son James and I use to see him up there in that high pulpit, among the European architectural ornamentation of that church, preaching in his own poetical style, it was a beautiful thing. When we hooked up in 1977, Brother Forbes was forty-two, Brother Wash was twenty-nine, and I was twenty-four. In fact, I was the youngest person to be appointed a professor in Union history—and I still hadn't written my Ph.D. thesis.

Hilda reminded me of my neglect. It bothered her to no end, and I can understand why. In her mind, instead of running off to these academic conferences, I should have been concentrating on getting that degree. My energy, though, was focused on being an active member of this Union faculty, at the time the most prestigious gathering of black religious scholars in the country. Their company thrilled me. Their conversation inspired me. I knew I was where I needed to be, reading and teaching. My mind was growing, my understanding of the black spiritual experience being broadened by the mere fact of spending so much time with these men.

I remember going with my colleagues to a conference at Yale. It was a big-time gathering of the most celebrated theologians in the world. When I walked into that hall with my brothers—James Cone, Jim Washington, and Jim Forbes—man, I felt like we were the Dramatics walking on stage at the Apollo. We were the Spinners. We were the Temptations at the top of their game.

Back in New York, I was also teaching at the prophetic Reverend Herbert Daughtry's House of the Lord Pentecostal Church in Brooklyn. We had a Timbuktu Learning Center—led by Charles Barron, A.G. Miller, Reverend Clarence Brown, and Karen Daughtry—where I taught the community folk something of the history of Christianity. This commitment, which continued for years, was especially important. It was during those lectures that I realized I could abandon my notes. In fact, using notes hindered my ad-lib style and my ability to riff. It wasn't until the early '80s, when I taught at Haverford College, that I found the confidence to speak without notes in an academic context. I've been freestyling ever since.

Meanwhile, 1978 came around, and this Negro still wasn't producing nothing. By the end of the year, Union was saying, "Brother West, we're giving you one more year, and if that blessed thesis of yours isn't written, you're out."

Hilda got more uncomfortable.

"Just sit down and write the thing," she said.

"Were it that easy, baby," I said. "I'm not feeling it right now."

"Well, *make yourself feel it,* Corn."

"It don't work that way."

"How about our future and our child's future? The way you're procrastinating, it's hard for me to believe that you're ever going to take care of business."

Hilda had every reason to register her anxiety. To her credit, she was always emotionally honest with me and let me know that, as a provider, I wasn't thinking the way I should have been thinking. What *was* I thinking? Well, I was always thinking of kicking it with Wash. Wash was my man. We had nonstop all-day all-night rap sessions, running down everything from the works of Toni Morrison to Plato's *Republic.* Wasn't nothing Wash didn't know.

Meanwhile, I was up to my neckbone in politics and philosophy. I was writing for and attending the biweekly meetings of *Social Text,* a leading left-wing journal led by Fredric Jameson, Stanley Aronowitz, Richard Wolfe, Stephen Bronner, and Sonya Sayres. I was working on *Boundary 2,* the first postmodern journal the country had ever seen, headed by the grand critic William Spanos, whose deep love for America's greatest writer, Herman Melville, I share.

I was contributing to the leading Marxist journal, *Monthly Review,* led by the legendary political economists Paul Sweezy and Harry Magdoff.

I was also working with Edward Said. Edward was an uncompromising and inspiring humanist, a professor at Columbia and a towering public intellectual of late-twentieth-century America. As a Palestinian American, he was an absolute original. I cherished his friendship. I also cherished the time I spent sitting at the feet of the world-changing Pan-African scholar and activist Professor John Henrik Clarke.

I also was an early participant in the seminal Society for the Study of Africana Philosophy, headed by Howard McGary, Al Prettyman, Lucius Outlaw, Leonard Harris, and Bill Lawson. John Rajchman and I co-edited *Post-Analytic Philosophy*, a highly influential text that's still in use today.

And as if that was not enough, I attended monthly meetings of the Columbia University religion group led by Peter Finch, Wayne Proudfoot, John Cuddihy, and Hans Jonas. I also participated in the renowned Yale theological group headed by Hans Frei, David Kelsey, and George Lindbeck. And I was a part of the Process Theology group led by my brothers John Cobb, Schubert Ogden, and David Griffith. And at the point of near exhaustion, I was deeply immersed in the Columbus Circle of American Literary Scholars led by my dear brothers Sacvan Bercovitch, Werner Sollors, and Quentin Anderson.

Man, was I ever ripping and running in the life of the mind, not only smitten with ideas but absolutely overwhelmed with intellectual curiosity!

I CHERISHED MY FAMILY—my dear wife Hilda and our precious son Cliff—but the husband-wife relationship had reached a point of no return. Hilda wanted more stability. My career path—if, in fact, I had a career path at all—was too circuitous. She could not support my intellectual wanderings. She wanted to move back to be near her family in Georgia and take Cliff with her. Had to face the fact: This dream of mine, this idea that, like Mom and Dad, my marriage would last a lifetime had come to an abrupt end. My marriage wouldn't last three years. Rough stuff.

When it was time to leave, Cliff clung to me like his life depended on it. He kept crying, "Daddy! Don't go, Daddy!" I went, crying along with my son.

I was painfully torn between my responsibilities as a dad and my calling as an intellectual bluesman. The torment of this civil war inside my soul would darken and shorten my days.

The blues took on new meaning. Like the song said, "Blues too deep to go away. These blues, man, they here to stay."

MOONLIGHT
OVER MANHATTAN

THERE WERE CERTAIN DANGERS INVOLVED in sleeping in Central Park in 1979. Crime was still on the rise. But there were certain spots, between the thick grove of trees and lush expansive lawns, where I could spread out my blanket, rest my weary head, look up at the heavens and, regardless of the crazy circumstances that brought me here, enjoy some peace of mind.

The summer weather was mild and the night breeze cool. The air was clear. The moon was full, the sky flooded with stars. My mind was flooded with thoughts.

How in the name of reason had I wound up here?

When I got my Reno divorce from Hilda, the judge saw I was making $503 a month and told me to give her $383. That meant I had $117 to work with or, to break it down further, $29.25 a week.

In my head, I kept hearing Johnnie Taylor singin' 'bout, "It's cheaper to keep her."

Brother, I got the blues.

When we split up, even before Hilda went to Atlanta, I gave her the apartment we were renting. That meant I had no place of my own. When I started looking for a place, the security and first month's rent were more than I could handle. Rather than hit on friends for a loan, I figured it might do me good to relax in the great outdoors until I could plan my next move.

When it came to money planning, I didn't do well. I didn't want to fight with my ex-wife who was the prime caretaker of our beloved son. I didn't want to fight with anyone. At the same time, by giving her practically everything and keeping little for myself, I set a pattern that would last for . . . well, maybe forever.

On those two nights, out there on the grass of Central Park, cuddled up in my sleeping bag, there were times when I had to laugh. Here I was, graduate of Harvard and Princeton, student of philosophy, lover of literature, professor-on-the-rise, and broke as the Ten Commandments. Now ain't that something. Maybe it was then when the bluesman shuffle started playing inside my brain. Maybe it was then when I heard the rhythm, the rhyme of the song, the stars overhead spelling out the story: Your baby's gone. Your money's funny. You ain't got no home. Nobody loves you but your mama and—as B.B. King says—"she could be jivin', too."

But, oh, never never my loving and loyal mama, B.B.! She is my rock forever! There's humor in those statements. There's pain. That's the comic tragedy of the blues. You tease the situation for what it's worth. You comfort yourself with a joke a two. You close your eyes and hope no one mugs you during the night. You wake up and move on—teaching at Union, putting a few bucks together to rent a little place uptown. See what happens next.

ONE OF THE BIG BOOKS OF 1979 was *Black Macho and the Myth of the Superwoman* by Michele Wallace. I read it and loved it. I viewed it as a brilliant and brave critique of black nationalism and black sexism. Back in 1973, Michele and her mom—the celebrated and innovative artist Faith Ringgold—had been founding members of the National Black Feminist Organization. I knew that Michele had come out of the heavy-duty intellectual climate of New York's City College. I wanted to meet Michele, so I invited her to my class at Union.

I remember the moment when she walked through the door. The instant I saw her, I said to myself, *Lord, have a-mercy! It's gonna be a thang!* And Lord knows it was. Michele was magnificent, a different kind of sister than any I had encountered before. She'd been shaped by the kind of rich but existentially ambiguous subculture of the Jewish intelligentsia. After college, she had gone to the *Village Voice*, where that same sort of heavyweight cultural environment continued to sharpen her mind. I had met few black women who had emerged from this background. As a writer, thinker, and social critic, Michele was spectacular.

Our connection was powerful and romantic. Intimacy happened in a hurry. I felt like, *This is the woman I've been looking for.* Michele felt like, *This is the man I've been looking for.* The search was over. The heat was on.

There was a lot of heat on Michele due to the publication of *Black Macho.* I traveled around the country with her, listening to her publicize her book and supporting her against an army of black male intellectuals who took her to task. Not that she needed my support. Michele was—and is—perfectly capable of defending herself. But because we had fallen head-over-heels in love, I wanted to be at her side, and besides, I agreed with her critique of rampant sexism in the black community. To tell the truth about patriarchy in black America in 1979 took tremendous courage. Michele had tremendous courage.

She was under heavy pressure in this period. She was a pioneer, and pioneers often wander into alien territory. As her companion, I was not known. I hadn't published anything. I was merely her boyfriend. I was, however, attacked in much the way she was being attacked. I was accused of criticizing the black male community. The critique of my critique went something like: *Hey, Brother West, aren't the assaults from the white supremacists on black male-hood enough? Do we have to suffer assaults from you as well? Where's your manhood, Brother West? Where's your sense of solidarity with your brothers?*

My answer was that sexism, like racism, needs to be called out, and let the chips fall where they may. If anything, going through this ordeal—incurring the wrath of so many bright but, in my view, misdirected brothers—brought Michele and me closer. Soon we were living together. We had great times with Michele's best friend Jill Nelson and Jill's brother Stanley. Both Nelsons became significant figures in American culture—Jill as a writer, Stanley as a filmmaker. We also enjoyed frequent visits with the witty, insightful Jerry Watts.

Because Michele wanted to be close to the Yale campus where she was working on her Ph.D., she and I pooled our meager resources and shared a Greek-style red house in New Haven. I was so eager to spend every night with her that I commuted to New York—driving down every morning so I could teach at Union and driving back up to New Haven every evening. Michele helped me buy a beat-up third-hand Camaro. I was speeding down I-95, making that 90-mile drive twice a day.

I HAD BEEN PLANNING MY PH.D. thesis for many years. I finally decided the thing had to get done. It was an important work for me, not merely an academic exercise. I say important because it touched on the issues that concerned me most. Before I got to my final thesis, I had already thrown away two separate hundred-page drafts on T.H. Green and the Aristotelian foundations of Marxist ethics. The thesis that got completed, though, was *The Ethical Dimensions of Marxist Thought.*

Most people didn't think Karl Marx had any ethics. They said he was obsessed with the notion of power. But I had read the essay written by seventeen-year-old Karl Marx called "Jesus Christ, Liberator of the World." Karl's dad was a Jewish convert who had changed his name from Herschel Mordechai to Heinrich Marx. Heinrich raised his son as a Lutheran. And Karl fell in love with a powerful aspect of Christ—the identification with suffering on the deepest level. In my thesis, I tell the story of how religion shaped Marx's ethical sensibility before Marx became radically secular. Marxism and Christianity, I argue, are linked in ways that we cannot ignore. One does not cancel out the other. In fact, the rise of liberation theology in Latin America, where concern for the poor is linked to both a political and sacred agenda, is also linked to Marxism. No one, of course, has argued that Jesus wasn't in solidarity with the poor. Now the question becomes—how do you transform Jesus's love into social, political, and economic justice in the world today? I argue that Marx carries with him certain relics and remnants of the religious worldview he had embraced as a Lutheran, even as he calls into question the validity of a godhead and becomes an atheist.

My thesis was accepted and I became the first black person to earn a Ph.D. in philosophy from Princeton. My sister Cynthia accompanied me to graduation. I shall never forget the lovely party in the famous Tower Room of 1879 Hall sponsored by Professors David Lewis, Thomas Scanlon, Richard Rorty, and Raymond Geuss after my final oral exam. A decade later my thesis—advised by Sheldon—was published in book form. I'm gratified that it's still in print. It remains a record of what was going through my mind as the '70s spilled over to the '80s, a time when Ronald Reagan, our old nemesis from California, had ascended to the presidency. Reagan made it fashionable to be indifferent to the poor and gave permission to be greedy with little or no conscience.

DURING THIS TIME, MY OWN political activities accelerated. In addition to Sheldon Wolin and Raymond Geuss working on my thesis, two encounters had a tremendous impact on me. The first was my friendship with Stanley Aronowitz, the most enchanting intellectual interlocutor I had ever met. Stanley never stopped reading, never stopped analyzing the crisis of Marxist thought, never stopped pushing me into serious dialogue about the meaning of cultural politics. Both as an activist and thinker, Aronowitz energized my learning process. He and I helped found and taught at the Center for Workers' Education in New York.

The second empowering influence was Michael Harrington. In the early '80s, he formed the Democratic Socialists of America. It was the only multiracial organization whose progressive politics made me comfortable enough to actually join. I use the word "comfortable" cautiously. I had another take on Democratic Socialism, based on the work on Antonio Gramsci. I was a member of DSA, but a highly critical one. Yet Harrington's humanity and wonderful sense of intellectual generosity allowed competing points of view. I loved Michael and count it a blessing to have toiled in the fields of social change alongside him for many years. In addition,

I was fortunate to meet the renowned public intellectual Barbara Ehrenreich, for whom I have deep and abiding respect. After Michael's death in 1989, she and I became honorary chairpersons of Democratic Socialists of America (DSA.)

After the completion of my thesis, I got on a writing roll that has never stopped. I put together the lectures I had been delivering in Brooklyn at Reverend Daughtry's Pentecostal church, added to them and published my first and favorite book, *Prophesy Deliverance! An Afro-American Revolutionary Christianity.* A portion of the book was based on lectures that I delivered in San Jose, Costa Rica. Daughtry, by the way, began and led the National Black United Front. In the early days of Reagan's national rule, the United Front was one of the only organizations pitting progressive politics against the president's reactionary policies.

LOOKING BACK, I SEE HOW, at least to some extent, finally writing my thesis on Marx took me from the literary salon of the '70s to the political battlefield of the '80s. Of course, it was never that clearcut. I was politically involved in the '70s and I was still obsessed with literature in the '80s. The two have never been mutually exclusive. But there was definitely a shift. Hooking up with Michele, precisely at the time that her controversial book was published, drew me into a series of fascinating dialogues that were deeply political, not to mention racial. I relished those discussions, just as I relished my work toward social change alongside Michael Harrington and Stanley Aronowitz.

My thesis, no matter how imperfect, was my declaration of faith. Of course I came to faith, and remain in faith, as a prophetic Christian. In that regard, I must define myself as a non-Marxist socialist. Basic differences between Marxists and Christians can never be reconciled. I deal with fear and anxiety—with the sheer absurdity of the human condition—through the lens of the cross. Marxism has nothing to say about the existential meaning of suffering, death, or love. It is solely preoccupied with improving social conditions. But I know that my personal condition—then and now—needed the songs of James Brown and Marvin Gaye and the

Reverend James Cleveland, the King of Gospel, singin' 'bout "This Too Will Pass," the same James Cleveland who said, "I Don't Feel Noways Tired." I can't live along the slippery slope of life's abyss without the Jesus that I saw in the heart of my mom, my dad, my brother, and my sisters.

I didn't become a theologian for a single reason: I don't believe that religious dogmas and doctrines can be rendered logically consistent and theoretically coherent. The scandal of the cross shatters all theological efforts. I didn't become a full-blown philosopher because I saw so many philosophical truths outside of the philosophical canon, such as in the poetry of T.S. Eliot and the plays of Anton Chekhov. I became and remain a philosophically trained bluesman who looked to the good news of Jesus Christ. That's the news, as I wrote in a new introduction to *The Ethical Dimensions of Marxist Thought*, that "lures and links human struggles to the coming of the kingdom—hence the warding off of disempowering responses to despair, dread, disappointment and death."

I say bluesman because the bluesman, who comes out of the black Christian culture, is telling the story differently. He has good news, but *his* news puts a different kind of hurtin' on the gospel. His news says this: *If I sing my blues, I'll lose my blues—at least for those precious moments when I'm singing.* His news says that the story of our lives—our losses, our depression, our angst—can be simplified and funkafied in a form that gives visceral pleasure and subversive joy, both to the bluesman and his audience.

We all got the blues. We all wanna lose our blues. We all gotta look for ways to do just that. What were my ways?

"THINK"

I WAS ON THE VERGE OF MARRYING Michele Wallace when my brother Cliff called and said, "You better think, Corn." Cliff was quoting the Queen—Aretha had sung the daylights out of a song she'd co-written with Ted White called "Think."

"You better think," sang Aretha. "Let your mind go. Let yourself be free."

The song was about freedom of all kinds.

"I think you better hold on to your freedom," big bro argued. "You don't wanna rush into anything crazy."

"I'm crazy about Michele and she's crazy about me."

"I know she's a wonderful woman," Cliff said, "or you wouldn't be so involved. All your women are wonderful, Corn. But I'm just wondering if y'all really know each other well enough to tie the knot. Why not just give it a little time?"

Strange thing about me and Cliff: close as we are, we don't usually give each other advice about romantic relationships. We've both had a steep learning curve in this area. But we usually do what we do without consulting each other. So when my brother warned me about going too far too fast, I had to heed his words. I didn't marry Michele.

Meeting Michele was a blessing, and living with her in New Haven was a joy. But Cliff was right. The relationship wouldn't last. I'm challenged to tell you why. I'm challenged to understand the situation myself. It goes to the heart of many romantic involvements. I had grand hopes. I had dreams of long-lasting love. But I also had a calling that grew in intensity. The calling had me out there in the world, learning and teaching and dialoging with dozens of people whose minds nurtured my own. Women want and deserve inordinate attention. My attention was scattered, not by design but a force that I couldn't control.

OUTSIDE UNION THEOLOGICAL SEMINARY, New York City kept calling to me. Not only did I love going to shows, off-Broadway and on, not only did I frequent the dance clubs who played the jams that kept me moving, like Chic's "Good Times," I was always running up to the Apollo to catch the Isley Brothers, or Rufus with Chaka, or this new singer with the honeycomb voice named Luther Vandross.

The Apollo is where I caught DJ Hollywood, one of the founding architects of a musical/cultural form that would soon evolve into hip-hop. I got hooked from the get-go. I loved the technical innovation—using turntables as percussive instruments—and I loved the approach to storytelling: the voice, not sung, but spoken in a metric bark. It got to the people. It got to me. I saw how its freshness blossomed from a happy synthesis of unhappy socioeconomic facts. Music education was drastically cut in neighborhood schools. Poor kids couldn't get their hands on instruments. So self-invented artists—like Grandmaster Flash, Afrika Bambaataa, and Kool Herc—invented instruments of their own. Flash is the innovator whose Furious Five put out "The Message" about inner-city rage and black resistance, a theme echoing Marvin Gaye's *What's Going On*. He and his gifted brothers pulled radios and speakers out of discarded cars piled up in the junkyards of the South Bronx. They put together massive sound systems. They identified key sections to songs—the funkiest riffs, the baddest breakdowns, the parts where pure rhythm penetrated deepest—and ran them together in a manner that was itself wholly original. They created musical collages as brilliantly innovative as anything to emerge from elitist forms of avant-garde art. The early rappers were also startlingly fresh. I still have a bias toward Old School Hip-hop artists like my brothers KRS-One, Rakim, and Eric B. Their skill at rhyming, soon to grow more complex and technically dazzling, was evident from jump street. They rejected a white normative gaze. They understood that their gift of language—the poetic language of the streets where they were raised—was a special gift. They didn't have to unlearn and relearn another lexicon to express their artistic souls. They could be themselves. They could come at the world with their own equipment, their own stories, their own emotional and linguistic grammar. They were real.

My own reality was centered at Union and my ongoing dialogues with Jim Washington and Jim Forbes. These brothers helped me more than I can say. What a joy to be surrounded by friends who were not only intellectuals of astounding depth, but men who viewed theological and political systems with such critical acumen. On top of that, they were ministers who preached the gospel every Sunday! I loved them both more than words can express. I thank God that my own Christianity, challenged again and again by philosophies that rejected its tenets, was strengthened by my proximity to Wash and Jim who, in their very beings, exuded the love ethos of the Palestinian Jew we call Lord.

"HOW'S IT GOING, BRO?" Cliff was calling from California. It was October 1980.

"The Union gig is going great," I said. "I'm picking up a part-time teaching thing at Yale. Just trying to stay strong."

"You don't have to try to stay strong, Corn. You *are* strong."

"Had a date with a woman you need to meet. She's magnificent, man. Just magnificent."

"What's her name, Corn?"

"Ramona Santiago."

"Is that the Puerto Rican sister you told me that every man at Union has been trying to get next to? The one who heads up the personnel office?"

"The very same."

"She's quite a bit older than you, isn't she?"

"She's forty-one, Cliff."

"And you're twenty-seven."

"And she has a son," I said. "I hope to meet him soon."

"She's a beautiful person," I continued, "inside and out. Took her to see *A Chorus Line* on Broadway. We both had a ball."

"You see this as a serious situation?"

"She's a serious woman, Cliff, with a seriously wonderful outlook on life. I'm feeling this very strongly."

"Well, keep me posted, Corn."

"I always do. I always will."

Ramona lived in the Bronx. She was a believing Catholic. I was believing in her and she was believing in me. I started going to mass with her every Sunday. Wasn't that I was fixing to leave my Baptist stronghold and embrace the papacy. But I'm the kind of Negro who can worship in a lot of settings and still feel the presence of God. I was happy to accompany her to church. I was happy to be in Ramona's exquisite presence.

Ramona not only possessed extraordinary physical beauty but a sweetness that was out of this world. She spoke with a lilting Puerto Rican accent and had the kind of personality that put everyone at ease. She put me at ease. On the dance floor, she floated like a dream. We went to the clubs and danced the night away. We enjoyed a compatibility that was entirely free of stress. She spoke of fulfilling her ambition of becoming a first-grade teacher, and I supported her in that effort.

After our courtship continued for another six months, I called back Cliff.

"I think this is it," I said. "Ramona is amazing. I see spending the rest of my life with her."

"Sounds great, bro. As long as you're happy."

"Happier than I've ever been."

"You're going to propose?"

"I am."

"And you think she'll accept?"

"If I'm lucky."

I was lucky. And everyone at Union knew I was lucky. Everyone who knew Ramona knew I was lucky. This woman was an absolute blessing in my life. Her level of heart, soul, mind, and style put her in a category all her own. We were married by Jim Forbes in the small Union chapel on May 31, 1981. Brother Wash and Brother Cliff were my best men.

During our honeymoon—walking hand-in-hand across the historic plazas of Mexico City, marveling at the mighty revolutionary murals of Diego Rivera and the beautifully painful self-portraits of Frida Kahlo, exploring the charms of Acapulco, Taxco, and Guadalajara—I kept hearing the Ohio Players singing in my ear, "Heaven must be like this." That week in Mexico with Ramona was among the most glorious of my life.

Back in New York, we settled down in the Bronx. Ramona was devoted to the Bronx. She was also devoted to her son Nelson. Nelson and I were close. When he started facing some extreme challenges, my family in Sacramento—especially Cliff and Dad—volunteered to help. Nelson moved out there and actually lived in my parents' house until his life was straightened out.

Our life went on. My teaching reached a new level of intensity. At one point, I was conducting courses at Union, Yale, Haverford, and Williams. I was burning up the highways—New York to New Haven, the suburbs of Philly to the woods of western Massachusetts—racing from gig to gig. I welcomed the work, not only because I was finally learning to lecture in a free-form manner that both suited me and seemed authentic. I was seeing that my peculiar style, born in the black slices of Sacramento and the Shiloh Baptist Church, was working well with the students I was determined to reach. My classes were in demand. My life was in order. Or so I thought.

TRANE

AS A BOY, I LOVED THE MUSIC of my church and the music of my neighborhood. That meant gospel and rhythm-and-blues. Early on, I could feel how the genres related to one another. Underneath their infectious rhythms was the heartbeat of hope. The music was about getting up and getting on with the business before us. The songs moved us from fear to faith. Whether it was Andráe Crouch singing "The Blood Will Never Lose Its Power" or Curtis Mayfield singing "Keep on Pushing," a sense of relentless hope informed the body of African American popular music that came into my life at a very early age and remained as a daily provider of sane tranquility.

As a student of African American history, I had read about jazz. I had an understanding of its various periods and knowledge of its virtuosic innovators. I knew about its development from New Orleans to Chicago, down to the territorial bands of Oklahoma and Texas, and up to Fifty-second Street, where bebop blossomed. I heard jazz and appreciated jazz, but jazz never possessed my soul as strongly as gospel or R&B.

Until John Coltrane came along and blew off the top of my head.

I was an infant in the '50s when Coltrane was playing with Miles. I was kid in the '60s when he was breaking through one artistic barrier after another. When Trane died in July 1967, I was still in junior high. That year, though, I was busy listening to Aretha singing "Respect" and Martha and the Vandellas singing "Jimmy Mack." That was the year of Stevie Wonder's "I Was Made to Love Her."

Fifteen years later, though, I was approaching thirty. I had been married once and was now married again. I was convinced that, in Ramona, I had found the woman with whom I would live forever and a day. In my multitasking, multiteaching, peripatetic role as bluesman/teacher, I was gaining some traction. I'd thrown away my notes and found improvisation to be my most natural and effective style.

My lecturing style is often viewed as akin to preaching, yet I carefully distinguish between a passion to communicate that unsettles and unhouses, as opposed to a religious proclamation of good news. There is no doubt my rhetorical style is influenced by black preaching but the substance of what I have to say is thoroughly Socratic, prophetic, tragicomic, and democratic. I aspire to a level of intellectual and soulful presentation that sounds like the blues and jazz, if they could talk.

I WAS DIGGING DANCE MUSIC—in fact, digging it harder than ever in the pre-disco/disco/post-disco eras—when Earth, Wind & Fire said, "Sing a Song," Dazz Band said, "Let It Whip," and Evelyn "Champagne" King was talking about "Love Come Down."

And then here comes John Coltrane. Here comes Coltrane on the dozens of records he cut on the Prestige and Blue Note labels. Here comes Coltrane playing with Miles Davis on the "Kind of Blue" album. Here comes Coltrane when he jumps over to the Atlantic label to do *Coltrane Jazz* and *Giant Steps* and *My Favorite Things*. Here comes Coltrane when he switches to Impulse and releases *Live at the Village Vanguard* and *Africa Brass*. Here comes Coltrane with his partners, McCoy Tyner, Jimmy Garrison, and Elvin Jones. Here he comes doing a duet album with Duke Ellington, and then another with jazz vocalist Johnny Hartman, perhaps the most romantic album in the long and tortured history of human romance.

I had to catch up with these albums. And in the early '80s that's just what I did. For reasons I'm not sure I can isolate, at this point in my life John Coltrane pierced my heart. I heard his cry. His voice took root somewhere deep inside me, and I found myself listening to every Coltrane record, reading every article and book pertaining to Coltrane, studying the man's style and deriving from it a sense of strength that pushed me forward. He did not define his spirituality, as I did, in terms of Jesus Christ or Christian faith. But that didn't matter because his artistic muse—what he called "A Love Supreme"—had us walking down parallel paths. He led me to that same place as the preaching of my childhood minister, the Reverend Willie P. Cooke. His vocabulary was different, but his sonic attitude—now joyful, now mournful, now playful, now serious—was similar. You can't listen to Trane and not feel the tragic dimension of the stories he tells. "Alabama," for instance, the composition he wrote to memorialize the four young precious black girls killed in the September 1963 bombing of the Sixteenth Street Baptist Church in Birmingham, ranks alongside the speeches of Martin Luther King, Jr., whose poetic cadences had such a deep influence on this jazz musician. Like Shakespeare or Chekhov, Trane's work gave a narrative rhythm to our human tragicomic condition. Just as the playwrights turned that condition into drama, he turned it into sound.

Coltrane riffed in a setting of onrushing rhythm that seemed to reflect my own rhythms. One of the unforgettable moments of my life was meeting his beloved wife Alice, who invited me to speak at her concert in Newark, where she called me "a warrior of love" in the tradition of her husband. "I listen to the beautiful music of Trane," I said, "alongside my favorite string quartet—Beethoven's Opus 131."

Another inspiring moment came in Coltrane's stomping grounds, Philadelphia, when Steve Rowland approached me after I had lectured. Steve is not only one of the most outstanding Trane experts alive, but the coproducer, along with Larry Abrams, of the best thing ever done on the jazz giant, a radio series called "Tell Me How Long Trane's Been Gone."

"Brother West," Steve said "you remind me more of Trane than anyone I've ever met."

"You've got to be kidding," I replied. "That's the highest compliment I could ever be paid."

Meanwhile, I was moving fast. I had to move fast. I had to hold down these three teaching jobs to feed the wolf that turned up at the door every month. Hilda was down there in Atlanta with Cliff, and they had their needs. Ramona had gone back to school to get her teaching degree. I needed to stay on it.

WILLIAMS COLLEGE WAS A WONDERFUL intellectual experience. God put me in the right place at the right time because it was at Williams where I met and befriended two of the giants of the humanities: the august E.H. Gombrich, author of the classic *The Story of Art*, and the distinguished historian Geoffrey Barraclough. I was also part of a high-powered seminar on the philosophy of Jacques Derrida led by Brother Mark Taylor. The highlight of my time at Williams was meeting my dear brother Professor David L. Smith and his lovely wife Vivian.

But even in this stratospheric atmosphere, I was a black man in America. Dig this:

One day, driving to Williams from New York, I was somewhere around Albany when the police stopped me. Figured I was speeding. I figured wrong.

"Get out the car, boy."

Here we go.

Policeman looked over my driver's license, looked me in the face, and then nodded his head.

"Yup," he said. "You're the guy."

"What guy?"

"Nigger we been looking for."

"For doing what?"

"Selling cocaine."

"I don't sell cocaine."

"What do you do?"

"Teach philosophy and religion at Williams."

"And I'm The Flying Nun."

"I'm a professor," I reiterated.

"You've been snorting up your own merchandise. We got you down as a major dealer."

"Impossible."

"That's what they all say."

We went down to the station where the officer was convinced he'd made a major arrest.

"You can call your lawyer," he said.

"Don't need to. Just call my dean at Williams. Here's his number. He'll set you straight."

The dean was outraged. He read them the riot act, and they immediately let me go, even if they did forget to apologize.

When arrested, threatened, or persecuted, I give myself permission to be full of righteous indignation and moral outrage but I try to never allow righteous indignation to degenerate into bitter revenge, or let moral outrage become hateful anger. My blues sensibility or tragic-comic disposition leads me to juxtapose the sheer absurdity of the situation with the utmost seriousness of the injustice. So I retain a painful smile on my face even as I respond to the undeniable hurt with intense ethical energy.

I LIKE MOVING IN FIVE different directions at the same time. It seems to suit my style, or maybe it just *is* my style. In any event, it's how I'm still living my life. Back in these early teaching years, shuttling back and forth between a quartet of colleges, the notion of settling down with one gig never really entered my mind until I got a call from Vanderbilt University in Nashville, Tennessee. They offered me a professorship with tenure. To this wandering Negro, tenure was a big deal. Tenure meant no more multitasking overtime hustling. Tenure meant security for life.

"What do you think, baby?" I asked Ramona.

"I couldn't leave the Bronx, Corn," she said. "I've never lived anywhere but the Bronx."

"Nashville is nice, baby. Nice countryside, nice people."

"Don't know anyone there."

"We'll make new friends."

"My friends are in the Bronx, Corn. My life is in the Bronx. If you wanna go, I understand. But this is home, honey."

I turned down the offer with major reservations. I turned it down because I wasn't willing to sacrifice my marriage. I have to thank Ramona for influencing me to turn it down. In that regard, she saved my life. Had I gone, I would never have been happy. I didn't quite know it then, but I needed the stimulation of the East Coast and all its cultural fervor. Outside of that environment, I might well have withered away.

When I met Ramona, she hadn't finished college. Her graduation, on my thirtieth birthday, was cause for celebration. She adored children, and her lifelong dream of teaching first grade was coming true. A New York City school in Washington Heights, where the students were primarily Dominican, hired her. I'd drive over there every afternoon to pick her up, and she positively glowed with the love of her work.

Ramona's career had taken a happy turn. My career was moving along at a good pace. Things should have been good between us. And for a while they were. Underneath, though, there was an undercurrent of discord. Our lives were very separate. There was her Bronx, her school, her students. Then there were my universities, my intellectual pursuits, my work. I remember once when my mother came to New York. I was giving a public lecture and Mom was getting dressed to attend.

"Aren't you coming along?" Mom asked Ramona.

"Oh, no, Mama West," my wife said. "I don't go to those sort of things."

"Well, you should, honey. You'll be proud of the way your husband speaks in public."

"I am proud, but I'm not sure I'd understand what he was talking about," Ramona said.

"Sure you would," Mom reassured her.

Ramona conceded, got dressed, and joined Mom. Later my mother reported my wife's reaction.

"It was strange, son," said Mom, "but she said that she didn't recognize you. She didn't recognize the man up there who was standing before the audience and delivering a lecture. She said that was a Cornel she never knew."

Paternal grandfather Reverend Clifton L. West, Sr.

Paternal grandmother Lovie West O'Gwynn

Maternal grandparents Nick "Big Daddy" and T'Rose Bias

President: Cornel West

SPRING STUDENT GOVERNMENT

CHAMBER ORCHESTRA

(L to R) Cornel West, the immortal Jesse Owens, and Clifton West, June 1967

Margaret McBride and Cornel West, John F. Kennedy High School Junior Prom, 1969

Top left: The Loving Brothers West: Cornel and Clifton [© Arnold Turner/WireImage/Getty Images]

Top right: Grandson Kalen

Middle: The West Family: (Standing) Cheryl, Clifton III, Cornel, and Cynthia; (Sitting) Clifton Jr. and Irene

Bottom left: Daughter Zeytun and son Clifton West

Bottom right: Daughter Zeytun

All additional photographs courtesy of Cornel West collection

West in dialogue [Union Theological Seminary Records at The Burke Library (Columbia University Libraries) at Union Theological Seminary, New York City]

The Grand Foursome at Union Theological Seminary: (L to R) Cornel West; James Cone; James Forbes, Jr.; and James Washington [Laima Druskis/Union Theological Seminary Records at The Burke Library (Columbia University Libraries) at Union Theological Seminary, New York City]

Top: "Black Intellectuals in the Age of Crack," November 1992—(L to R) bell hooks; Henry Louis "Skip" Gates, Jr.; Cornel West; Glenn Loury; Eugene Rivers; Margaret Burnham; and moderator Kwame Anthony Appiah [© M. Stewart]

Right: Atlanta 1993 [© Robin Nelson/Black Star]

Bottom: (L to R) Cornel West and Reverend Osagyefo Uhuru Sekou getting arrested protesting an unjust war in Iraq, 2004 [Courtesy of Cornel West collection]

The angelic artist Alice Coltrane, wife of John

The Matrix: the inimitable Roscoe Lee Browne and the renowned Laurence Fishburne

The great Smokey Robinson

The genius Michael Eric Dyson and the soulful Sam Moore of Sam and Dave
[© Isaac Singleton, Spotlight Productions, Inc./The Smiley Group, Inc.]

All additional photographs courtesy of Cornel West collection

Top: Teaching "Intro to African American Studies" at Princeton, 2008 [Courtesy of Brian Wilson/ Princeton University]

Middle left: The Power of Paideia: Freshmen Seminar "The Tragic, the Comic, and the Political," Princeton University [Courtesy of Denise Applewhite/Princeton University]

Middle right: Spelman College commencement, 2009 [Courtesy of Spelman College Office of Communications]

Bottom: The Cornel West Wall on Martin Luther King Boulevard, Trenton, NJ by Luv One, 2009 [Courtesy of Luv One]

My beloved mother Irene B. West
[Courtesy of Marcellus Brooks]

Irene B. West Elementary School, Sacramento, CA
[Courtesy of Jim Summaria]

My dear mentor, Harvard Professor
Martin Kilson, Jr. [Courtesy of
Cornel West collection]

Cornel West Academy of Excellence led by
Antoine Medley, Raleigh, NC, 2009 [Courtesy
of Antoine Medley]

My dearest brother Tavis Smiley and the legendary Reverend Dr. Herbert Daughtry,
Sr. [Courtesy of the Reverend Dr. Herbert Daughtry, Sr.]

MAKE UP TO BREAK UP

WHEN YALE OFFERED ME A FULL-TIME tenured position in 1983, I accepted. I'd be the first black person tenured by their Divinity School. I was twenty-nine. Meanwhile, though, Ramona refused to move to New Haven. Understandably, she didn't want to leave the Bronx. Also understandably, I couldn't pass up this offer. For a while I tried to keep the thing with Ramona alive. I continued tearing up the roads between New Haven and New York, running back and forth from home to gig and gig to home. More and more, though, it looked like it wasn't going to work.

Yale had its distractions and its pleasures. Among the biggest blessings was my friendship with Farah Jasmine Griffin, then working on her Ph.D. Later she would write *If You Can't Be Free, Be a Mystery: In Search of Billie Holiday*, a beautifully thoughtful meditation on Lady Day. Farah and I developed an inextricable and endless love for one another that continues to this day. What an intellect! What a woman of spirit, style, and positive purpose! Our relationship had a power that was almost too strong to be contained. In every way imaginable, Farah enriched my life.

Yale was an intellectual feast. I thrived on the intense discussions and numerous lectures, especially the monthly gathering of the Yale Legal Worship led by Brother Owen Fiss. I also initiated a series of public debates in the huge Common Room. The topic was Christian theology. In regard to race, gender, and empire, I defended my version of prophetic Christian thought and witness. My highly sophisticated and learned colleagues Paul Homer and

Timothy Jackson offered their more conservative-leaning views of the gospel. We had fun.

Unintentionally, I also made history in New Haven. I became the first Yale professor to be arrested on Yale property. It came as a result of my participation in the 10-week strike of the university's clerical workers, the vast majority of whom were inadequately paid women. When they struck to form a union, I took up their cause and marched on their picket line. I was the only black faculty member to do so. In fact, the black studies department was against the strike. That's because the administration was giving them money, including funds for research on Frederick Douglass, and they didn't want to rock the boat. The thing got ugly.

A brother from black studies approached me and said, "Look here, West, you're hurting all of us by going public on this issue."

I said, "My dear brother, let me ask you a simple question. How long have you been studying Frederick Douglass?"

"Twelve years."

"Well, after twelve years of studying Frederick Douglass, what side of this issue do you think he'd take—the administration's or the clerks'?"

"That's not the point, Brother West."

"That *is* the point," I insisted. "How you gonna be documenting the work of Frederick Douglass on one hand and supporting injustice on the other?"

He didn't have an answer.

Meanwhile, I went back to the picket lines, was arrested and hauled off to jail—with close comrades like Brother Joseph Summer. The judge, sympathetic with the Yale administration, jacked up the bail well beyond the normal amount and, because I was broke, I had to cool my heels behind bars. Were it not for David Montgomery, the great social and labor historian, I would have had to stay there another week. David graciously bailed me out.

Yale was unhappy with my expression of solidarity with its female workers and, to this day, I believe it had much to do with the cancellation of my sabbatical, which had been promised to me in the spring. Spring semester was when I was due at the University of Paris who had invited me over as a guest professor.

"Looks like this university is determined to jack you up one way or the other," a friend said to me. "I guess you're going to have to cancel your appointment at the University of Paris."

"That's what Yale would like me to do, but that's exactly what I have no intention of doing."

"What will you do, Corn?"

"I'll do both."

"Both?"

"On Monday morning and afternoon, I'll teach my two classes at Yale. Then fly to Paris where I'll teach a class on Thursday and another on Friday. Fly back to New Haven over the weekend and be fresh to kick up the cycle again Monday morning."

"How long do you think you can keep that up?"

"All semester long."

Believe it or not, it worked out. Determination trumped exhaustion. The travel was grueling, but I saw that if you don't mind sitting on jet airplanes, you can cover a mess of territory. From what I could tell, the students in both New Haven and Paris were happy to see me. I fought off my jet lag and found myself, the bluesman in perpetual motion, teaching in two countries at once.

Praise the Lord.

"WHAT'S HAPPENING, CORN?"

It was Cliff calling from California. Years earlier, Cliff started working for IBM. He became a computer wiz in addition to the most beloved coach in the Sacramento area. He coached 'em all, younger kids and older kids—in baseball, football, and cross-country running. He was a motivator and educator, never using intimidation or fear. His wisdom and loving nature led him to techniques that turned him into a legend among his peers and students. At the same time, big brother shared one of the big challenges I faced: female relationships. His first marriage, to the wonderful Phyllis, had ended.

"Cliff," I told him, "looks like Ramona and I are spending most of our time to make up to break up."

"That's how it goes sometimes, Corn."

"Seems like that's how it's going *all* the time with me. I'm in New Haven, Ramona's in New York. Would love for her to take one of these trips with me to Paris—I'm in Paris every other week—but it's tough to get her out of the Bronx."

"She's devoted to her kids, man. There's never been a more beautiful teacher. I can see where she's coming from."

"I'll go back to the city for a weekend," I explain, "and we're cool. Then the distance seems to do us in."

"I've been virtually in the same city for my whole life, bro, and I still have those problems."

"What do you think it is?" I asked.

"We started young," Cliff said. "We loved the opposite sex way 'fore we even understood the word 'opposite.' We gravitated toward them, they gravitated toward us, and the spark of new romance was something that lit up our little hearts. I'm not sure much has changed since then."

"But the thought of having what Mom and Dad have, man, that's always been my ideal. One woman, one home, a love that keeps the family straight, a family that overcomes all obstacles . . . "

"That's the ideal. But the real is something else."

"You got that right. This marriage really is something else."

"Hang in there, Corn."

"I will. Long as I can."

WITH HIS LYRICAL LISP and rough-hewn baritone, James Cleveland sings a song called "The Lord's Expecting Me." His voice was filled with determined hope. He also ministers to us in "Jesus Is the Best Thing That Ever Happened to Me," a sacred version of Gladys Knight's secular hit. These are the songs, with their tremendous spiritual hope and deep-rooted gratitude, that got me straight. These are the songs I put on when it looked like the bottom had fallen out. The music got me up when I was down, the music kept me on the high road. Meanwhile, the road led to the restaurant at the Holiday Inn in New Haven.

It was 1986, and my marriage to Ramona had eroded. We were no longer living together and it was just a question of time before we'd file for divorce. I was teaching an evening seminar on Hegel at Yale. Afterwards, I'd go out to eat. On this particular night, I spotted a Holiday Inn and figured they'd have decent hamburgers. Walked in the restaurant, sat in a booth in the back, took out my copy of Hegel's *The Phenomenology of Mind* and began to take notes when I suddenly looked up and saw, without question, the most beautiful woman I had ever seen in my life. I put down my pen.

She handed me a menu. All I could was say, "Hello." She nodded sweetly. Other than serving me a burger, she showed no interest in me.

I was too smitten to even make small talk. The check was $10. I left her a $12 tip—all the money I had in my pocket. I returned the next night to seek her out. She wasn't there, but another waitress—turned out to be her first cousin, name was Tutu—told me that the woman I was looking for was Elleni and that last night, going home from work, Elleni had been in a car accident. I expressed my concern, and asked whether I could visit her. Tutu was good enough to give me Elleni's address.

I found a florist, bought a dozen roses and turned up at Elleni's apartment. I gently knocked on the door. An older woman appeared. This was Elleni's mother. Later I would learn her name was Harigewain Mola.

"I am here to see Elleni," I said, "and wish her a speedy recovery."

She smiled but obviously did not understand. She spoke no English. Then Elleni came to the door. She wore a large neck brace that in no way diminished her astounding beauty.

"Oh," she said, "you're the big tipper from yesterday."

"I heard about your accident. I've come to see how you're doing and offer you these flowers."

"Thank you. I hurt my neck, but I'll be fine."

"I'd love to have your phone number."

"For what reason?"

"So I might call."

"In my culture we don't give out our phone numbers so quickly."

I understood. There's something superficial about the overnight pseudo-intimacy of American courting. But I was American, and I had come courting, and I was determined.

"Can I come back soon and see how you're doing?"

"Well, give me a few days. I need my rest."

After a few days, I was back.

PART III

RACE MATTERS

ELLENI

ELLENI WAS BORN IN ETHIOPIA and came to the United States at age seventeen. Her mother, Harigewain Mola, was born into royalty. She was a descendant of one of the noble families of the troubled country. That family was headed by Bulo, leader of the Oromo people, who married the sister of Menelik II, the nineteenth-century creator of modern Ethiopia. In 1935, Elleni's mom married Gebre Amlak, who came from another of the country's great families. Three days later, Italy invaded Ethiopia.

Some four decades after that, Emperor Haile Selassie was deposed and a revolution, communist in name and militaristic in form, swept the country. It was among the most vicious revolutions in the history of communism. Some estimate that over 20 percent of all young people were killed. If your offspring was murdered, and you wished to reclaim his body, you were forced to stand in line and pay for the bullets that killed him. One out of every three members of the landed class was murdered. The inhumanity was beyond brutal.

Elleni's father died when she was young. When the revolution came, her brother-in-law was killed by the new government. Elleni and her mom were forced to go underground. With the aid of anti-communist United States evangelical Christians, they managed to flee from Africa to America. When she arrived, she found herself under the protection of an older Ethiopian man in New Haven who helped her adjust to the new land. Unlike Elleni, he was not an aristocrat. Understandably, he was struck by her beauty and fell hopelessly in love. He became obsessed with her, even when she made it clear that she had no romantic interest in him.

Given these events, you'd think Elleni had to be living in some deep post-traumatic state. She wasn't. She had just received her degree from Southern Connecticut State University. She had deep wisdom, not of the academic or intellectual variety, but wisdom of the heart. She was lovely. She was pleasant. She was willingly, even joyfully self-sacrificing. Elleni entered my life as one of those angelic figures whose soul glows with sunshine. Yet she was in trouble.

On our first date, I heard myself saying things that sounded crazy even to me. Yet I said them.

"Elleni, marry me and become the First Lady of Black America."

"You're truly out of your mind. You don't know me."

"I know I want to marry you."

"You're not serious."

"I am," I said. "I've never met anyone like you. And I never will."

"I have many entanglements and many problems. You will not want to be burdened by me."

"You can never be a burden. Only a blessing. There's no problem that we can't overcome."

"I have a problem that won't go away."

That's when Elleni told me about the older Ethiopian man. For some years she had been with him. Then, no longer able to tolerate his possessiveness and insane jealousy, she finally broke it off. That had happened only months before we met. His reaction was frightening. He told her that if he ever saw her with another man, he'd kill him and her.

"He meant it," she said. "He's not stable."

"I understand," I said, "but you can't allow him to dictate what you can and cannot do. If you want to date, well, that's your decision, not his."

"I'm having this date with you, but it must be the last."

It wasn't. I persevered. I persuaded Elleni that we couldn't be fenced in by fear. Our lives had to be lived the way we saw fit.

She wasn't interested in my teaching and lectures, which was fine with me. I loved taking her to movies. Going out to dinner. Dancing. We became romantically involved. And then one night, driving home, I glanced out the window to see another car speeding at us. I caught a glimpse of the man's wild eyes as he tried to crash into the side of my car. I was barely able to swerve out of the way. Then it was on. He ran two red lights trying to run into us. Elleni was crying, "He has a gun!" I managed to lose him, but decided I wasn't going to be unarmed again, not with him on the loose. I got a serious BB gun for symbolic protection and I intensified my prayer life. This guy was not to be taken lightly.

Things got funkier. Elleni went from waiting tables at the Holiday Inn to working at a hot dog stand in West Haven. The guy wouldn't go away. He'd come by her gig and threaten her. He said that if she didn't break it off with me he'd kill us both.

"Don't worry about it, baby," I said. "That's just talk."

"I wish it were, Cornel," she replied. "But I know this man. He's truly crazy. I can't see you anymore."

"I can't see myself *not* seeing you. This guy is not scaring me off."

But he did scare Elleni off. She was so frightened for her life that she decided to leave New Haven.

"I can't take the pressure any more," she said. "I can't live this way. Please help me escape before it's too late."

At this point, there was no arguing with Elleni. The crazy man was in pursuit, and she saw no way out. One of her girlfriends and I went to her place in the middle of the night, snuck her out, drove to the station and put her on a train to New York.

"Thank you, Cornel," she said. "I really appreciate everything you've done for us. But this is it for us."

But it wasn't.

IT WAS THE MIDDLE OF THE NIGHT when she called from New York.

"He knows I'm here," she said.

"How could have he found you?" I asked.

"I don't know, but he called me on this number and said he was coming here to find me."

"It's a big city," I said. "It would be like finding a needle in a haystack."

"He'll find me," she said. "I know he will. I can't stay here. I have to go somewhere even further way."

"Wherever you go, Elleni, I'll come see you. I need to be with you."

"You need to forget me. Please forget me."

PROPHETIC FRAGMENTS

IN 1988, MANY OF MY LECTURES, essays, and articles were collected in a volume I called *Prophetic Fragments: Illuminations of the Crisis in American Religion & Culture*. It was dedicated to my parents and carried a foreword by my brother Cliff. The quote at the front of the book came from scripture, John 6:12:

> *He said unto his disciples,*
> *Gather up the fragments that remain,*
> *That nothing be lost.*

I had been writing in journals and speaking in public for years now. To some degree, I felt as though I'd been offering fragments of my thoughts and, rather than lose them, I needed to reread them, in some instances rewrite them and, put together, see if they did depict the cultural and spiritual crisis I was seeing all around me. As I wrote, the aim was "to examine and explore, delineate and demystify, counter and contest the widespread accommodation of American religion to the political and cultural status quo. This accommodation is suffocating much of the best in American religion; it promotes and encourages an existential emptiness and political irrelevance. This accommodation is, at bottom, idolatrous—it worships the gods created by American society and kneels before the altars created by American culture." I go on to say that, "[l]ike so much of American culture, exorbitant personalistic and individualistic preoccupations in American religion yield momentary stimulation rather than spiritual sustenance, sentimental self-flagellation rather than sacrificial self-denial."

At this moment in time, during the Ronald Reagan '80s, I was trying to figure out who I was and what I had to say. "To be a contemporary religious intellectual—and person," I wrote, "is to be caught in this creative tension on the boundary between past and present, tradition and modern—yet always mounted in the barricades on this battlefield on which life is lived and history is made."

Thus I offered the book as fragments. A jazzman would call them riffs, pieces of prophetic insight and even prophetic poetry that could explain what was troubling my soul. I wrote, "These fragments—which feebly reflect the Christian faith that shores me up against the ruins in our world—are linked together by my response to one basic question: How does a present-day Christian think about and act on enhancing the plight of the poor, the predicament of the powerless, and the quality of life for all in a prophetic manner?"

I wrote about my friend Michael Harrington, whom I called "the socialist evangelist of our time and the bearer of the mantles of Eugene Debs and Norman Thomas." I wrote about what I called "Winter in Afro-America" in which "the impact of mass culture, especially through radio and television, has diminished the influence of the family and church. Among large numbers of black youth, it is black music that serves as the central influence regarding values and sensibilities. Since little of this music is spiritually inspiring, black people have fewer and fewer spiritual resources to serve them in periods of crisis. With the invasion of drugs in the black community, a new subculture among black youth has emerged, which thrives on criminal behavior and survives on hopelessness. The black rap music of Grandmaster Flash and the Furious Five's 'The Message' and 'New York' makes this point quite clear. For the first time in Afro-American history, large numbers of black young people believe that nobody—neither God, mom, nor neighbor—*cares*. This spiritual crisis cannot go unheeded, for there can be no economic empowerment or political struggle without spiritual resources."

I wrote about contemporary Afro-American social thought and the brilliant bell hooks. "Mindful of the degree to which both white feminists and black male activists are captives of liberalism, hooks promotes cultural transformation in present-day patriarchy in American society and in the black community, and links them to structural changes in the U.S. economy. Like Alice Walker and Audre Lorde in literature, hooks is one of the few black thinkers grappling with the complex relation to race, class, and gender oppression."

I wrote about deep and original thinkers like Orlando Patterson, and serious scholars and leftist activists like Manning Marable. I wrote about "subversive joy and revolutionary patience in black Christianity," how "the gospel in Afro-America lauds Calvinistic calls to transform the world yet shuns puritanical repression . . . and how life is viewed as both a carnival to enjoy and a battlefield on which to fight." I restated my faith that "Afro-American Christianity promotes a gospel which empowers black people to survive and struggle in a God-forsaken world."

I wrote about the troubled state of Black-Jewish relations, a theme that would engage me for years to come.

I wrote about the tragic death of Marvin Gaye, shot by his father in 1984. He was, I explained, "first and foremost, a Christian artist, imbued with a deep spiritual sensitivity anchored in a Christ-centered ethic of love."

I wrote at length about the various genres of Afro-American popular music, drawing analogies from Charlie Parker's bebop to George Clinton's technofunk. I discuss rap, the art form that had captivated me from its beginnings. I had first published a piece on rap as the American correspondent for *Le Monde Diplomatique* in 1982. I argued that "black rap music indeed Africanizes Afro-American popular music—accenting syncopated polyrhythms, kinetic orality, and sensual energy in a refined form of raw expressiveness—while its virtuosity lies not in technical facility but rather street-talk quickness and linguistic versatility. In short, black rap music recuperates and revises elements of black rhetorical style—some from our preaching—and black rhythmic drumming. It combines the two major organic artistic traditions in black America—black rhetoric and black music."

I wrote about many of the major world figures of modern theology in an attempt to understand and explain what the best minds, past and present, have to teach us. I bemoaned the fact that "theologians and preachers are reluctant to engage in what Gramsci calls a 'self-inventory'—a critical self-examination of their own middle-class status, academic setting, or social privilege. Yet a more self-critical viewpoint is imperative if the Body of Christ is to function in a more Christian manner."

In the late '80s, then, as a man in my mid-thirties, what was my own self-inventory? What did my critical self-examination look like?

I was surely a product of the black lower-middle class with working-class origins. I was surely supported by the academy. And I surely enjoyed social privileges not afforded the average guy. I also struggled with the position that my class, job, and social status gave me. As a middle-class black brother, I was well aware of the materialistic drive that characterized that group. I wouldn't call myself materialistic, but, after two failed marriages, I had a financial weight hanging over my head. In that sense, I was bonded with millions of other middle-class men who found themselves in similar shape. The academy was my source of income, but the academy often clashed with my own sense of integrity. At Yale, for instance, I vehemently fought their opposition to the clerical union. I also fought against Yale's support of South African business interests. I made my views clear and, as a result, was viewed by the administration as an outsider. Social privilege was of little interest to me; I didn't care about hanging out at fancy parties with fancy people. I cared about articulating, with as much effectiveness as possible, my conviction that this crazy world of ours requires close scrutiny and vigorous Socratic questioning. I was looking to challenge and be challenged, looking to teach and be taught, looking to be a good student, an honest thinker, and a decent human being. I was trying to balance the personal with the professional.

After my fight with Yale, I returned to Union Theological Seminary—back with Brother Wash and the others. But after a few months, I received a call from the Sarah Vaughan of contemporary world literature—Toni Morrison. This is the greatest compliment I could pay anyone. To me, Sarah Vaughan is the height of artistic genius in twentieth-century culture. Any time Sarah appeared in

New York, I was there in the front row. Between sets I was there in her dressing room, lighting her cigarettes with gentle reverence.

"Are you sure you're not hurting your throat, Miss Vaughan?"

"I'm fine, honey. Thank you."

Now I had to thank Toni Morrison for suggesting my next move.

"Would you seriously consider coming with me to form an intellectual neighborhood in Princeton?" Toni asked.

I was really planning on staying at Union, but when Sarah Vaughan, the Divine One, sings, you listen. I thought of Toni as a kind of divine vehicle beckoning me to pursue my calling at Princeton. Princeton had been my Ph.D. stomping grounds. Princeton had embraced me early on. Princeton had a super-bad faculty and Princeton was just down the Jersey Turnpike from New York City, where I could hear all the jazz, lectures, Broadway plays, and Stephen Sondheim musicals.

"I'll be there," I said.

PRINCETON WAS AN ACTION-PACKED SCHOOL. After eleven years of teaching, this was also my first full-time position in the secular academy. The idea that I would be heading up a program, especially one devoted to a subject matter so close to my heart, gave me hope that I could make some significant difference. I was to be the director of African American Studies. My dear brother President Harold Shapiro, Professor Daniel Rodgers, and especially my dear sister Vice Provost Ruth Simmons made it possible.

I'll never forget the warm welcome given me by my good friend Michael Walzer at the Institute for Advanced Study at Princeton. He regularly asked me to lunch and to spirited seminars with outstanding figures like Clifford Geertz and Albert Hirschman. Walzer also invited me to serve on the board and write for *Dissent*, the famous democratic socialist journal founded by the renowned New York intellectual Irving Howe. Walzer was the nemesis of Edward Said. Yet both remained my good friends.

In a personal sense, my intense professional activity at Princeton also became a distraction from the distress I felt from Elleni's situation. She was in Tampa, and the idea of us being together, a long-held dream of mine, seemed to be on permanent hold.

There was much to do at Princeton. Naturally I had to attend to the curriculum, the faculty, and a wealth of administrative issues. I was much aided by the marvelous manager of the African American program, Dr. Gayle Pemberton. The lovely Hattie Black and the supportive Comfort Sparks made my job a joy. I was determined that my first act would be to honor two of the men who led the way in Afro-American studies: Harold Cruse and St. Clair Drake.

Cruse was a courageous thinker, writer, and teacher who, along with Amiri Baraka—then known as LeRoi Jones—had founded the Black Arts Repertory Theater in Harlem. His masterwork, *The Crisis of the Negro Intellectual*, published in the '60s, had a profound influence on generations to follow, though my favorite of his is *Rebellion or Revolution*. He began teaching at the University of Michigan and was a principal architect of their Afro-American and African Studies Department. The man was far ahead of the curve. In fact, he helped design the curve. Most astoundingly, he held a high position at the University of Michigan until he retired in the '80s—yet he had never graduated from college. He didn't have to. His intellectual creativity excelled the vast majority of those holding degrees. No doubt about it, I wanted to honor Harold Cruse.

When I first met St. Clair Drake through my high school partner Glenn Jordan after my first year at Harvard, the man impressed me mightily. Early on, he had set up Stanford's African American Studies. In doing so, he faced powerful forces that argued against his approach, but by virtue of his commitment, scholarship, and pure tenacity, he prevailed. I respected Professor Drake and wanted to bring him to Princeton, where we could applaud him for his grand achievements.

Finally, with the considerable prestige of Princeton behind me, I had the wherewithal to publicly recognize black thinkers who had triumphed in academia on their own terms against heavy odds.

You can imagine, then, how excited I was when St. Clair Drake was on his way from California to accept this honor from Princeton. I drove up to Newark Airport to pick him up in my shiny new, pitch-black 1988 Cadillac Sedan DeVille. (By the way, I'm glad to report that twenty years later I'm still driving that car. I still consider it the coldest ride on the road. Dad had bought his first Cadillac in 1962. Seeing how happy it made him, I always wanted a Cadillac of my own.)

I was at the gate when Dr. Drake's plane landed. Next thing I know, they're carrying out a man on a stretcher. It was St. Clair Drake. He had a stroke during the flight, and suddenly I found myself following an ambulance to the hospital. The stroke was severe, and for four days and nights I stayed by his side. I slept at the foot of his bed, hoping that my presence might offer him some comfort. Through an act of friendship that I'll explain in a minute, I had the majestic Kathleen Battle come and sing to him at his bedside.

His recovery was only partial—he died some two years later—and we had no choice but to give him his award in the hospital room.

This turn of events deeply touched my heart. I was reaching back to a man who had reached out to me when I was a college kid looking for direction. He was what I wanted to be—a broadly engaged thinker whose sense of the academy rejected traditional restrictions and offered a vision that was generous and expansive. His stroke brought home the fact that it was up to my generation to ensure that his legacy lives on.

I have tried. I have not always succeeded, but I have never lost sight of the trail blazed by brave pioneers like St. Clair Drake and Harold Cruse.

IT WAS ALSO MY PRIVILEGE to bring Professor Edward Said to Princeton, where he had studied as an undergraduate. Back when I was teaching at Union, Edward had told me that he had been diagnosed with leukemia. Even though he was an impassioned secularist and nonbeliever, he didn't object when three hard-core black Christians—James Washington, James Forbes, and myself—prayed for him in his apartment. His teary eyes revealed how deeply our love had touched him. He would live an amazingly productive life for the next sixteen years.

When Said, a prominent Palestinian intellectual and critic of Israeli policy, came to lecture at Princeton in the late '80s, it was a period when I had befriended Omar Pound, the only child of the legendary poet Ezra Pound. Omar, a fine teacher of writing and free of his father's vicious anti-Semitism, also helped me sponsor Arno J. Mayer, an iconoclastic historian whose recent book on the Holocaust had stirred controversy. Both lectures proceeded in the face of threats against all of us. At one point while Edward was speaking, someone cut off the lights and we wondered whether this was our moment of truth. Fortunately, the lights went back on and Professor Said was able to speak his truth at our beloved alma mater.

IT WAS NOT ONLY PROGRESSIVE INTELLECTUALS like Edward Said whom I encouraged to come to Princeton, but conservative figures as well. The most prominent of these was Rush Limbaugh.

I was in my office as director of Afro-American Studies when late one afternoon the phone rang.

"Professor West, this is Rush Limbaugh. I just want you to know that I have contacted virtually every Ivy League university in this country, requesting a debate with whomever they choose. It probably won't surprise you to learn that I have been rejected at every turn. So it is with small hope that I make one final request. Would you, Professor, agree to a public debate?"

"Dear Brother Rush, my brother Clifton and our friend Bob back in Sacramento have been talking about you. I'd be delighted to host a serious and substantive debate with you."

Rush seemed flabbergasted and quite interested. When scheduling conflicts prevented the debate, I was disappointed. But I also have to point out that for the next twenty-plus years, with all the attacks and assaults on leftist intellectuals, Brother Rush has never said a bad word about me. In fact, the only time he ever mentioned me on his show was—believe it or not—when he agreed with me.

"THE WAY YOU DO THE THINGS YOU DO"

KATHLEEN BATTLE SANG THE FIRST LINE: "You got a smile so bright . . ."

I sang the second: "You know you could have been a candle . . . "
Carly Simon sang the next line: "I'm holding you so tight . . . "
Kathleen: "You know you could have been a handle . . . "
Corn: "The way you swept me off my feet . . . "
Carly: "You know you could have been a broom . . . "
Kathleen: "The way you smell so sweet . . . "
Corn: "You know you could have been some perfume."
Carly: "Well, you could have been anything that you wanted to . . . "
Kathleen: "And I can tell . . . "
All: "The way you do the things you do."

It was the summer of 1988, and we were all gathered around the grand piano at Carly Simon's home on Martha's Vineyard. The air was sweet and the songs were sweeter. It was a thrill to know that Kathleen, the magnificent coloratura soprano, and Carly Simon, the wonderful pop vocalist, knew the song that Smokey Robinson had written for the Temptations as well as I did. I relished the moment. By then, Kathleen and I had fallen in love.

We had met in the spring. Kathleen had given a magnificent recital at Carnegie Hall, and I was blessed to be in the audience. I was riveted, not only by the sheer beauty of her voice, but the majestic beauty of her person. As best I recall, she sang Handel and Mozart. My head swam with melody, my spirit excited by the emotional power and delicacy of her interpretations. I was transported. I saw her standing there—a statuesque woman of rare delicacy and un-questioned dignity, a brown angel.

Mutual friends introduced us after the recital. That evening we had a late dinner. We had instant rapport. She had grown up in the black church; her roots were gospel. In fact, she would later invite me to speak at the African Methodist Episcopal Church in Portsmouth, Ohio, the sanctuary where she had sung as a child and where her family still worshipped. That was a singular thrill.

We had worlds in common—not only our passion for classical music, but rhythm-and-blues and Broadway as well. Kathleen had an easy laugh and beautiful outlook on life. She was bright, curi-ous, and sophisticated in a way I never would be. Because she was constantly traveling the world, she had firsthand familiarity with political and social issues of countries from all over the globe. Her facility with foreign languages was amazing and her understand-ing of foreign cultures deep and compassionate.

I also loved her self-confidence. I saw in Kathleen a free black woman who maintained her sense of strong identity no matter the circumstance. She is unquestionably a diva in the best sense of that term, but I never saw any arrogance in her bearing, only a self-assuredness that had been earned over an illustrious career and was expressed with grace and charm.

Our initial dinner led to a second, and then a third. I then began traveling with her as she performed in Ann Arbor, Pitts-burgh, Boston, Washington, D.C., and other cities. Every second or third night, I was treated to still another Kathleen Battle recital. When they called me "Mr. Battle," I smiled. Couldn't have cared less. I was there to carry her bags, and happy to do so. Honored to do so. To others, she was a radiant star. To me, she was a sugar-sweet down-home sister. We brought out the best in each other. One night she was singing in *The Barber of Seville*. The next night Luciano Pavarotti would cook us a gourmet meal.

At the end of her American tour, she was off to Europe for the rest of the summer. "I'll see you after the Salzburg Festival, Cornel," she said.

But I wanted to see Kathleen and I wanted to see Salzburg, so as a surprise I showed up for her fortieth birthday in Austria. Her performance was sublime and our time in the mansion of Herbert von Karajan was beyond this world.

Back home, I invited her to Princeton, where she heard me lecture and sat in on several classes. I introduced Kathleen to Toni Morrison and suggested that they collaborate. They did, and the magnificent result is *Honey and Rue*, lyrics by Toni, music by André Previn. It's an original song cycle connected to the African American experience. It was released on record and debuted at Carnegie Hall.

In New York, Roberta Flack invited us to her apartment at the Dakota, where we stood around the grand piano and sang Supremes songs. Kathleen also took me to Carnegie Hall to see what would be Maestro Herbert von Karajan's last performance. By then he had become my friend and invited me to stand in the wings to watch him conduct Bruckner's Seventh Symphony. By the time he put down the baton, he was so depleted that he couldn't walk. I carried him off the stage.

Kathleen and I built up memories to last a lifetime. She introduced me to the opera legend Jessye Norman, whom I then introduced to Toni Morrison. I shall never forget Jessye's first words to Toni: "Ms. Morrison, all my life I've wanted to be you and like you."

"And all my life, Jessye," Toni replied, "I've wanted to be you and like you."

Kathleen also introduced me to two fabulous maestros: the inimitable James Levine—her mentor from Cincinnati, Ohio— and the famous conductor Christoph von Dohnányi. Dohnányi and I spoke late into the night about the life and death of his godfather, the uncompromising German theologian and martyr Dietrich Bonhoeffer. When Bonhoeffer, who had once joined a plot to kill Hitler, came to study at Union Theological Seminary, he regularly attended services at the historic Abyssinian Baptist Church in Harlem. The German spiritual radical testified that it was the rich black church worship that enabled him to feel the full joy of Jesus.

No doubt, Kathleen and I had a powerful and abiding love for one another. We longed to be together all the time. But we also couldn't deny the reality of our different lives and different obligations. We were on different paths moving in different directions. It became increasingly difficult for me to get away. Same for Kathleen. The pull of our professions was strong. And that pull, of course, wasn't fueled by a sense of mere obligation—it was pulled by passion. Kathleen had to sing. I had to teach. We had to go our separate ways. And yet we remained connected—and still do—by mutual respect and powerful love.

AS THE '80s SPILLED INTO THE '90s, I began a series of dialogues with the wonderful bell hooks who, I said, "writes with a deep sense of urgency about the existential and psycho-cultural dimensions of African American life—especially those spiritual and intimate issues of love, hurt, pain, envy, and desire usually probed by artists." The result of our in-depth conversations was a book we co-authored, named *Breakin' Bread*, a title that refers to friends chatting over a good meal as well as the delicious song by Fred Wesley—called "Breakin' Bread," of course—that has to do with a critical recovery and revision of one's past. We lectured together all over the country on this book. We had worked together at Yale and had danced together in clubs like Brick 'n' Wood in New Haven in the early '80s.

bell and I spoke about a wide expanse of subjects. Thinking about my new position at Princeton, I said, "Afro-American studies was never meant to be solely for Afro-Americans. It was meant to try to redefine what it means to be human, what it means to be modern, what it means to be American, because people of African descent in this country are profoundly human, profoundly modern, profoundly American."

When bell asked what the essence was of my recently published book, *The American Evasion of Philosophy: A Genealogy of Pragmatism,* I answered that it was "an interpretation of the emergency, the sustenance, and the decline of American civilization from the vantage point of an African American. It means that we have to have a cosmopolitan orientation, even though it is rooted in the fundamental concern with the plight and predicaments of African Americans."

I went on to argue "that there are fundamental themes, like experimentation and improvisation, that can be found in the works of Ralph Waldo Emerson, for example, that are thoroughly continuous with the great art form that Afro-Americans have given the modern world, which is jazz. And therefore to talk about America is to talk about improvisation and experimentation, and therefore to talk about Emerson and Louis Armstrong in the same breath."

I told the story of the cultural and political significance of the major native philosophic tradition in America best represented by Charles Sanders Peirce, William James, John Dewey, Sidney Hook, C. Wright Mills, W.E.B. Du Bois, Reinhold Niebuhr, Lionel Trilling, W.V. Quine, Richard Rorty, and Roberto Unger. My own prophetic pragmatism was the culminating point of the story.

bell and I talked about suffering. I'd once told Bill Moyers that I saw the vocation of the intellectual as an endless quest for truth in which we allow suffering to speak. In that light, I spoke of jazz and blues encompassing "a profound sense of the tragic-comic linked to human agency, so that it does not wallow in a cynicism or a paralyzing pessimism, but it also is realistic enough to project a sense of hope. It's a matter of responding in an improvisational, undogmatic, creative way to these instances in such a way that people still survive and thrive."

These were public talks that had us determined to offer ourselves, in bell's words, "as living examples of the will on the part of both black men and women to talk with one another, to process, and engage in rigorous intellectual and political dialogue."

"At a time when there are so many storms raging and winds blowing through black male and female relations, it is important to at least take a moment and look, see, examine, question, and scrutinize a particular black male intellectual and a particular black female intellectual who are grappling together, struggling together, rooted in a very rich black tradition but also critical of that tradition such that the best of the tradition can remain alive."

That was me and bell, talking about everything and everyone from Spike Lee to Eddie Murphy to the songs of Babyface, processing what was happening in our popular culture—and why—as well as trying to understand the profundity of the works of our literary heavy-hitters like Richard Wright, James Baldwin, and Ralph Ellison. When bell pointed to the grandmother's sermon on the necessity of love in Toni Morrison's *Beloved*, I called it "one of the great moments in modern literature. You don't find that kind of sermon in Wright or Baldwin or Ellison. There's a depth for black humanity which is both affirmed and enacted that, I think, speaks very deeply to these spiritual issues. And I think this relates precisely to the controversy in the relations between black men and women."

"Cornel," asked bell, "what does it mean for a progressive black male on the Left to ally himself with the critique of patriarchy and sexism, to be supportive of the feminist movement?"

"We have to recognize that there cannot be relationships unless there is commitment, unless there is loyalty, unless there is love, patience, persistence. Now, the degree to which these values are eroding is the degree to which there cannot be healthy relationships. And if there are no relationships then there is only the joining of people for the purpose of bodily stimulation.

"And if we live in a society in which these very values are eroding, then it's no accident that we are going to see fewer and fewer qualitative relationships between black men and women.

"At the same time—and this is one reason why I think many black men and women are at each other's throats—there exists a tremendous sense of inadequacy and rage in black men, just as exists a tremendous sense of inadequacy and rage in black women."

A little later in our dialogue, bell said, "I think we also have to break away from the bourgeois tradition of romantic love, which isn't necessarily about creating conditions for what you call critical confirmation. And I think this produces a lot of the tensions between heterosexual black men and black women, and between gays. We must think of not just romantic love, but of love in general as being about people mutually meeting each other's needs and giving and receiving critical feedback."

"That's true," I agreed. "We actually see some of the best of this in the traditions of contemporary Africa that has a more de-romanticized, or less romanticized, conception of relationship, talking more about partnership. I know this from my loving Ethiopian wife."

It is dangerous to make broad generalizations about the rich diversity of African culture. But it is safe to say that less romantic conceptions of love do prevail there.

During the winter of 1990, in the courthouse in Rockville, Maryland just north of D.C.—a community known as the Reno of the East—for the third time in my life I asked a woman for her hand in marriage. I was overjoyed when she accepted. I was thirty-seven.

AFRICAN DREAMS

*To the love of my life, my precious wife
Elleni Gebre Amlakheir
of a great family and civilization of faith
and harbinger of hope to come*

THIS WAS THE DEDICATION IN THE BOOK I wrote called *Keeping Faith: Philosophy and Race in America*, published in 1993 and recently re-issued as a Routledge Classics. The experience of recommitting myself to the courtship of Elleni was a long process but one that I could never abandon. We had broken up before I began seeing Kathleen, but when that relationship proved impossible on a long-range basis, I realized that I couldn't forget Elleni. I had loved her once. I had, in fact, never stopped loving her. I had to see her. I started flying down to Tampa, where she was working as a waitress and was still in hiding from her obsessed suitor. I flew to Florida every two weeks. I begged her to relocate somewhere closer to me. She agreed to Rockville, a reasonable drive from Princeton. We were back together at last. Soon I was able to convince her to leave Maryland, and marry and live with me in New Jersey.

Heaven. This was the marriage. This was the woman. This was the soulmate I had been seeking. This was the spouse with whom I would share my life. This was domestic stability, romantic excitement, and spiritual fulfillment. This was right.

As an Eastern Orthodox Ethiopian, Elleni wanted us to travel to her motherland and be married in church. I was all for it. By the late '80s, the Ethiopian People's Revolutionary Democratic Front had mostly collapsed. The country had been ravaged by economic catastrophe and political corruption, not to mention deadly retribution to all those who opposed the Communist regime. There was reason to be hopeful, and it seemed that we would be welcome in Addis Ababa, former home of my wife and her mother. The plan was to hold the ceremony in the grand Coptic cathedral known as Haile Selassie Church. Two thousand were to attend. Naturally I was bringing over my family. The plans were coming along beautifully until I was told, a mere ten days before our wedding day, that it couldn't happen.

"You'll have to convert to Ethiopian Orthodoxy."

The speaker was the highest official of the church who, ironically, had a Ph.D. in theology from Princeton. He was a learned man whom we thought would marry us.

I had some background on his religion. I understood how Eastern Orthodoxy broke down along regional lines. You've got Greek Orthodoxy, Egyptian Orthodoxy, Armenian Orthodoxy, and, along with many others, that deep, deep Russian Orthodoxy. Among these divisions, though, Ethiopian Orthodoxy is the most ancient. It goes back to the caves. It isn't about theological texts— it's about how the priest filters the spirit. The holy men live exemplary lives. In other words, they don't give answers in books. They show you how to live by the way *they* live, by their fleshified response to suffering.

I have great respect for the tradition, but I had to tell the man, "No way I'm converting from *my* tradition. I *love* my tradition. I *am* my tradition."

"Then you'll have to cancel the wedding."

"Can't cancel now," I said. "Plane tickets have been bought. I got my family flying in from California. Then there's all the work that's been done by my wife's brother, Sirak, one of the loveliest men to ever walk the earth. He's been organizing wedding plans, along with the rest of his family and prominent citizens in Addis Ababa, for months. Ain't no stopping us now, my good brother."

"I will not permit a marriage in our sacred cathedral when one of the parties is not of our faith."

"We're going to have to talk this out," I said. "No way in the world I'm going to disappoint Elleni's dear mother, Harigewain Mola. After all, she's a relative of Menelik II, the founder of your nation." And my dear Brother Sirak, Elleni's brother, had already paid for all the wedding events.

"That's part of the problem, Professor West. The Emperor's throne is in that very sanctuary where your ceremony will take place. The throne cannot and will not be desecrated by a marriage that is not sanctioned by the church. I strongly suggest that you formally convert."

"I already said that's out of the question," I said.

"I don't see why. You're a sophisticated scholar. You must understand that Christianity in America means nothing. It's shallow. It's little more than a commercial on television, a superficial non-theology espoused by preachers looking for fame and wealth. You become an Ethiopian Orthodox, Professor West, and you'll have the most glorious wedding in the history of modern Ethiopia."

"I'm afraid, my good brother, that you have a misunderstanding. I'm very serious about being a black Baptist. Fact is, I'm as serious about being a black Baptist as you are about being an Ethiopian Orthodox."

"But surely you see that in America, Professor West, Christianity is just another consumer choice. I saw it in the seminary. I saw black seminarians switch back and forth from one denomination to another like children trading candy. It meant nothing. It was a whimsical and thoughtless process."

"Yes," I said, "there's more denominational mobility in America because we have more choice than, say, you have in Ethiopia. And in many parts of the country religion doesn't cut as deeply as I would like. No argument there. I could critique American Christianity all day long—and I have. But your description of the folks you encountered in seminary does not fit this Negro at all. This Negro is a believing Baptist. And this Negro, with or without your help, will marry Elleni Gebre Amlak in that grand church in Addis Ababa."

My man backed down a bit. "I won't do it, but if you can find a priest who will, then I'll drop my objections."

So I went on a hunt to find the righteous priest to do the job. It was something like locating a Philip Berrigan, the left-wing Roman Catholic renegade. In Ethiopia, though, such rugged individualists within the church do not have the public profile that they do in the U.S. No matter. I found such a priest, and the wedding was on.

THE WEDDING WAS SOMETHING TO BEHOLD. Blessings, blessings, blessings. Blessing surrounded me. My brother Cliff, my best man. My precious mom. My precious dad. Elleni's magnificent mother. And in the center of it all, my radiant bride. The grand Coptic cathedral, which had been closed tight during that most brutal of communist regimes, was recently reopened. It was a time of celebration and gladness. The wedding itself was organized by a committee of leading Ethiopian citizens. The throne of Haile Selassie was brought out. Crowns were placed on our heads. I was given an honorary Amharic name: Ficre Selassie, "Spirit of Love."

The blessed event, though, was not without tension. Within Elleni's family, there were a group of rebellious cousins who violently opposed our union. We were never clear about the reasons behind their opposition, only that they considered my marriage to Elleni an outrage. Then came alarming reports: the rebels were set on assassinating the newlyweds. I had to send Mom and Dad home early. Cliff stayed by our side. Elleni and I slept with guns by our pillows, a militia guarding the house. Then we had to go underground. It was a serious situation. Our lives were on the line, even as our lives turned impossibly and extravagantly beautiful. Catastrophe shadowed joy, fear fought with faith. Finally, the threats subsided. We came back to the United States, determined to spend at least two months a year in Ethiopia. Despite everything, Africa had become my second home.

What I saw in Ethiopia was a people who have never been colonized by Europeans with the exception of Eritrea. They're free of the mind manipulations engineered by white supremacists. They've never been fooled into believing that they're less than human. The result is a feeling of self-assurance. They understand the value of their deep culture and unique civilization. Their history is one of epic struggle—against every conceivable kind of negative power and corrosive force, from soil erosion to corrupt tyrants. Yet their humanity persists, strong, steady, clear of the self-doubting notion implanted by cultures that considered themselves superior.

Ethiopia nourished me. Ethiopia changed me. It gave me a new and compelling point of view of what it means to be both African and American. I crossed back and forth between two cultures, and in doing so found myself immersed deeper in both.

I particularly enjoyed trying to reform the humanities curriculum at Addis Ababa University after the collapse of communism. In my deliberations and my lectures I suggested large doses of Plato, Dewey, Chekhov, Du Bois, and Morrison.

A year after our wedding, Elleni and I were in Addis Ababa for another ceremony, one in which Elleni's mother transferred her house to us. Another amazing ritual, this one lasted five hours. Elleni's family told stories about their own struggles—and the struggles of their nation—that had split them apart and brought them together. The narratives were riveting, epic tales of an ancient line of patriarchs and matriarchs who had fallen and risen, only to fall and rise again. We laughed uproariously, we wept openly, we exposed our hearts and, at the end, we kissed the feet of Harigewain Mola, Elleni's brave and steadfast mother.

In the preface to *Keeping Faith,* written two days after this ritual, I reflected upon my divisiveness at this juncture of my life. I was bequeathed a home in Ethiopia. I had an excellent job at Princeton University. Where did I really want to live?

I wrote, "After nine generations of family roots in America, I feel an urge to leave. This urge rests on neither a romantic attachment to Africa nor a paternalistic commitment to uplift Ethiopians. Yet Africa does have a special appeal to me that Asia or Antarctica lack. And my project of prophetic criticism does commit me to promote the wise expansion of democratic practices in Ethiopia—as elsewhere. My thoughts of making Ethiopia my 'home' are not based on brutal experiences of being black in America, or the relative paucity of enjoyable relations with Americans of all hues and colors. But, in all honesty, the extent to which race still so fundamentally matters in nearly every sphere of American life is—in the long run—depressing and debilitating. And my good fortune to have such fine friends across the racial divide is certainly not sufficient reason to be naïvely optimistic about America.

"To put my cards on the table, the decline and decay in American life *appears,* at the moment, to be irreversible. Yet it may not be. This slight possibility—the historic chance that a window of opportunity can be opened by our prophetic thought or action—is, in part, what keeping faith is all about."

I went on to say that "I do not harbor vulgar anti-American feelings—I'm too much of a radical democrat to overlook how difficult it is to hammer out democratic practices over time and space." I tried to express the agony of my ambivalence: "Loving family and friends, the pleasures of American popular music and humor, the opportunities to pursue the life of the mind and the chance to help make America more democratic and free are major impediments to leaving the country. Yet . . . the idea that the deferred dream of black freedom may, out of pessimism, dry up like a raisin in the sun or, out of nihilism, simply explode is too much to entertain. The only options are to stay 'at home' in exile in America and fight what may be a losing battle, or go to my 'house' as an exile in Ethiopia and fight on a different front the same battle—a battle that holds up the bloodstained banner of the best of Euro-American and New World African modernities. I am sure that Ethiopia and Old World African modernity have much to teach me. Maybe I am simply too busy fighting in America to shift terrain as I approach forty."

In fact, I didn't shift terrains. I remained in America. Several significant events—sudden shifts that I could have never anticipated—reshaped my life.

RACE MATTERS

I AM MORE A NATURAL READER than natural writer. If I were told I could never read another book again, I'm not sure I could survive. I read a minimum of three hours a day, regardless of my schedule. If I were told I could never write again, I have no doubt that I'd be fine. That isn't to say that my writing isn't born out of passion. It is. But my writing requires a concerted effort and forced discipline. Conversely, I read as easily as I breathe.

After stalling in the '70s, by the late '80s I had a found a good writing groove. I felt that I had something to say. Lectures, talks, and other forms of teaching had become a strong outlet, but my desire to reach more people moved me to write in what I hoped might be a popular vein. At the same time, I had low expectations for the commercial prospects of my books. They were, after all, the books of an Ivy League professor. The books began appearing at regular intervals and brought me some attention, but mostly in academia. In 1993, I published *Keeping Faith: Philosophy and Race in America,* and two other volumes, *Beyond Eurocentrism and Multiculturalism: Volume One: Prophetic Thought in Postmodern Times; Volume Two: Prophetic Reflections: Notes on Race and Power in America.* These volumes would go on to win the American Book Award that year.

Nothing, however, prepared me for the success of a relatively short volume of connected essays published on the issue that never ceased tugging at my heart and hammering inside my head. The idea for the book came from my dear sister Deborah Chasman of Beacon Press. She brought together essays of mine lying around my office at Princeton. In 1993, *Race Matters* would bring me to the attention of the general public—and, for that matter, the president of the United States—in a manner I had never before experienced.

It was the right book at the right time. In response to the brutal police beating of Rodney King, L.A. had exploded in rebellion. At the request of my dear brother Mark Ridley-Thomas, a highly respected black civic leader, I immediately flew out and engaged in marathon radio dialogue with prominent Korean intellectuals and politicians. It reminded me of my dialogues in Boston with my dear brother Reverend Raymond Kim and my dear sister Professor Ivy George on black-Asian relations.

In the early '90s, America's rawest nerve—race—had been exposed again. I was asked to speak everywhere. *Race Matters* appeared on bestseller lists. It was used in classrooms around the world. President Clinton read it and gave it to his daughter and wife to read. Then he invited me to the White House. Bill and Chelsea engaged me in spirited conversation. Hillary, on the other hand, simply said, "I can't understand why blacks don't take advantage of all these opportunities they have." I said to myself, *Man, I'm not sure my dear sister has read* Race Matters. Rather than confront the first lady, though, I explained that the opportunities she was referencing were earmarked for the black upper-middle class. My book was about the working poor and abjectly poor, people who simply do not have an abundance of high-quality educational opportunities. Since that first encounter, I came to respect Hillary, but not enough to support her in her historic 2008 race for the Democratic Party presidential nomination.

The evening when I first met the Clintons ended with Bill inviting me to the Oval Office after his wife and daughter had retired. He was eager to engage in serious intellectual conversation about culture and politics. The brother was absolutely brilliant and I was having a ball. When I looked at my watch, though, I saw it was far into the middle of the night. We had been at it for hours. I realized I had an early morning flight back to New Jersey to teach at Princeton and needed just a little nod of sleep. But he was as fresh as ever. I remember thinking to myself—*Does this brother have a job?*—when I realized—*He's the president of the United States!* I did leave, but only after another hour of conversation.

Race Matters, the book that got me invited to the White House, has a simple thesis: black people count and black suffering matters in how we think and act in the world. Black folk in the United States are different from all other modern folk because of the horrific violence that has been leveled against them. That violence is both psychological as well as physical. To control and exploit blacks, white supremacists have taught blacks an insidious and corrosive form of self-hatred. No other black people have had to endure the terrorism of Jim Crow after the nightmare of slavery.

I discuss nihilism in black America and how both liberal structuralists and conservative behaviorists ignore the core issue—the nihilistic threat to blacks' very existence. The liberal doesn't want to talk about culture because it takes attention away from government programs. The conservative focuses on values, ignores political-economic realities, and denies victimization. How, then, do we cope with depression, low self-worth, social despair? I discuss the cultural buffers that black forbears created against nihilism, how they valued service, and built churches that reached out to comfort and care for the community. I discuss the consumer-crazed, market-driven, hyper-materialistic, oversexed, overstimulated society that defines American culture and fuels nihilism, especially among poor blacks. I discuss how the defenses against suicide—the loss of mind, of hope, of spiritual health—have fallen. I point out that suicides among blacks have risen. In short, unregulated capitalism was literally killing the souls, minds, and bodies of some black folk.

In *Race Matters*, I point out what I call the pitfalls of racial reasons. I show how, during the Clarence Thomas–Anita Hill hearings, blacks got trapped by "racial reasoning." No black leader was willing to say in public that a black Supreme Court nominee was unqualified. This notion of black authenticity led to a black mentality of closing ranks that led to a subordination of black women in the interest of the black community within the racist nation.

I try to break down the reasons for the crisis in black leadership. I say that black leaders lack real righteous indignation and humility that arise from inner security. I point to three kinds of black leaders—the race-effacing managerial types who thrive on political savvy; the race-identifying types who stay on black turf and become power brokers with non-blacks; and the race-transcending prophetic leaders, like Jesse Jackson in 1988, who demonstrate genuine vision and courage.

There's a section I call "Demystifying the New Black Conservatism" and a discussion that attempts to throw light on where we must go "Beyond Affirmative Action." I revisit the subject of black-Jewish relations, calling for more compassion and understanding on everyone's part. A disproportionate amount of attention is given to black sexuality. I put it plainly—that Americans are obsessed with sex and fearful of black sexuality. I point to that most baffling of paradoxes—behind closed doors, kinky and funky sex associated with blacks is often seen as intriguing by whites, but in public that's something that can never be discussed. Any way you look at it, you can't talk about race without introducing the red-hot topic of sex. I argue for the demythologizing of black sexuality and extend special empathy for black women who are subject to racism from white men and scorn from black men, as well as black lesbians and gay men, whom the black community so coldly ostracizes.

The fact is this: fear of black sexuality often drives white racism and is, alongside the attempt to control black labor and bodies, at the very core of racist viewpoints.

There is a long look at Malcolm X and the meaning of black rage. I state what may be obvious to blacks but news for whites: Malcolm X was the prophet of black rage primarily because of his indisputable love for black people. I describe how Malcolm X crystallized the interlinking of black self-affirmation, desire for freedom, and rage against American society, and the disturbing likelihood of early black death. I examine the relationship between Malcolm X's idea of psychic conversion as an implicit critique of the double-consciousness idea expressed by W.E.B. Du Bois—an idea that says, in essence, we're looking at ourselves through the eyes of others who devalue us. Malcolm X believed we can escape the double consciousness through psychic conversion, but never tells us how. I discuss at length the problems of black nationalism and black separatism, recognizing that the basic aim of black Muslim theology was to oppose white supremacy. In doing so, though, white people are still the main reference point. I go on to look at Malcolm X's indifference, or at least lack of attention, to what is unique about black religion and black music. That's because he looked away from the hybrid nature of those phenomena. Black music and black religion, influenced so deeply by African, European, and even Amerindian elements, are new phenomena in the modern world. Malcolm X wasn't comfortable with that mix.

And in that sense, Malcolm X wasn't comfortable being what I term a jazzman—until the last months of his short life. By that, I mean someone who can deal with the world as an improviser, maintaining a fluid and flexible outlook while realizing that the either/or, absolutist, and supremacist mindsets lead to spiritual dead-ends. At the same time, I express deep and abiding respect for Brother Malcolm who was, after all, one of the most profound of all truth-tellers in the face of white racism. His courage was contagious and his inspiration lives on. In *Race Matters*, I am his student who, following his example, must question the teacher, no matter how revered the teacher might be.

Race Matters is filled with such questions. In trying to spark a provocative public dialogue about race, I put everything I had into this small book. If I shed some light on these dark issues, I was gratified. If a small but serious audience of readers responded with questions of their own, I felt satisfied. When, in fact, the audience turned out to be massive, I was surprised and thrilled. The publication of *Race Matters* changed up my game. As far as my life went, I was still making it up as I went along. But living in the spotlight proved tricky.

It was far easier enjoying my dear sister Toni Morrison's time in the spotlight. In December 1993, Elleni and I traveled with her to Stockholm, where she received the Nobel Prize for Literature. It was a glorious event. We were joined by Nelson Mandela, who had just won the Nobel Peace Prize in Oslo, and Wole Soyinka, who was the first African to receive the Nobel Prize for Literature back in 1986. We partied all night. My dear brother Skip Gates, the acclaimed black intellectual; Errol McDonald, the renowned editor; Ford Morrison, the superb architect and Toni's oldest son and I performed a Delfonics medley in the middle of a Swedish club. We killed with "La La Means I Love You."

THE DREAM TEAM

PROFESSORS HENRY LOUIS "SKIP" GATES, JR. and Kwame Anthony
Appiah had been soliciting me to leave Princeton for Harvard.
Other universities with other offers had contacted me, but this
was a different deal. These brothers were not only dear friends,
but among the most distinguished scholars in the country. On a
personal level, I had great love for them. Beyond that, Skip had
a vision for putting together what he said would be an African
American Studies Department without precedent. He was open to
all sorts of new paradigms of programs and professors. He laid out
his plan with unbridled enthusiasm and irresistible energy. Skip
was burning to get this thing done and have me join him. Making
matters even sweeter was the fact that Harvard offered me a joint
appointment between African American Studies and the Divinity
School. Because my heart was in both camps, I found this especially attractive. Harvard President Neil Rudenstine—my dear and
courageous brother—made it clear that I had the full support of
the administration.

Leaving Princeton wasn't easy. I loved the institution and
many of the beautiful people who taught and studied there. I was
blessed, for example, to work with one of America's finest playwrights and directors, my dear sister Emily Mann. She inspired me
to work with the visionary Melanie Joseph, founder of the Found-
ry Theatre in New York. My Princeton connections were deep.

But on another level my Harvard connections were even deeper. Harvard, after all, was where my serious formal education had
begun. My undergraduate years had shaped me. Harvard was where

175

I found my voice as a student and began building my chops as a scholar. Those tumultuous '70s, surrounded by spirits as inspiring as Martin Kilson and Preston Williams, were absolutely essential to everything I'd become. No doubt about it, Harvard was home. I accepted the position and signed up with the dream team.

AFTER OUR MANY ADVENTURES IN NEW HAVEN, Tampa, Rockville, and Addis Ababa, Elleni and I yearned for a home. We found a magnificent house in Newton, Massachusetts that had been owned by the president of Brandeis University. We bought it, filled it with fine furniture, invited our friends and colleagues over for a housewarming, and thanked God for our blessed life. We were living large. Life was good.

Then, just as quickly, life turned frighteningly dangerous. Ever since the publication of *Race Matters*, my public profile had risen. I had appeared on many national TV shows. My arrival at Harvard was treated as major news in and around Boston, an area where bold progressivism and raw racism live side by side. My classes were so oversubscribed that we had to move to an off-campus auditorium to accommodate the students. In many ways, I felt deep appreciation and boundless love. In other ways, I felt out-and-out hatred. The manifestation of that hatred was a series of threats to my life. I'd get postcards and letters, phone calls at the office or at home.

"People are looking for you," Skip told me one day on campus.

"What people?"

"Who knows, man. Crazy people. Haters. We've gotten reports from security. They want us to take your name off your office door and remove it from the faculty directory. That way you won't be so easy to find."

"If they want to find me," I said, "they'll find me."

"I understand, brother," said Skip, "but there's no reason to make it easy for them."

I agreed and had my name taken off the door and directory.

Later that semester, I was home in Newton, taking a shower in our upstairs bathroom, when I heard a blood-curdling scream.

Grabbed a towel, ran downstairs to see Elleni pointing and yelling at a man running down the driveway.

My wife was hysterical. Through her tears I learned that a man wearing a mask had broken into the kitchen and put a gun with a silencer to her head. He wanted to know where I was. When she screamed, he ran off. We reported it to the police, but the police said there was little they could do without a detailed description.

Two weeks later, I was driving in from Cambridge when I spotted two guys sitting in a car in my driveway. One was holding a shotgun. Fortunately, Elleni wasn't home. I wheeled around and sped right over to the Newton Police Station. The officers were nice folk, but they were Geritol brothers—old and tired and uninterested in my case. They said I better contact the FBI.

The FBI let me know that my name was on the list of all sorts of hate groups. They had their eye on many of them, but of course they had nothing close to twenty-four-hour surveillance. Tension mounted when I made a trip to the University of Utah to give a lecture. When I arrived, the local newspaper reported that I had been killed. Even the Harvard *Crimson* picked up the story. Maybe I'm wrong, but I didn't detect much regret in their reporting. Mom had been called about the false reports and was frantic until I let her know that I was fine. When I got home to Newton, Elleni was a nervous wreck. What to do?

Elleni wasn't about to stay at our house, not after what had happened. I understood her anxiety and felt obligated to protect her, emotionally and physically, from what was becoming an insane situation. Someone suggested that we move into the Four Seasons Hotel on Boylston Street in downtown Boston where security was tight. We did just that, leaving our big house in Newton to live in a fancy hotel condo. Naturally there was little not to love about living at the Four Seasons—the height of luxury and convenience—but the irony of this condition never quite left me. My success at broadcasting the need for a candid national conversation about race had resulted in my seeking shelter in the most privileged of sanctuaries. No matter. Elleni could enjoy some peace of mind, and that was most important to me.

During this crazy time, I did Pat Buchanan's radio show. We battled it out, and afterward, in a friendly gesture, he invited me to lunch. I noticed he had no security.

"Brother Pat," I said, "you mean to tell me with your right-wing anti-Semitic antics, you get no threats?"

"None, Professor," he said. "Not one."

"I'm surprised," I said.

"Why is that?"

"Well," I said, "I have no reputation of being anti anything, and I'm getting cards, letters, and calls from crazy folk practically every day. They showed up at my house and threatened my wife. I would have thought that you guys on the far Right, with that xenophobic overflow in your language and your vehement anti-immigrant stance, would be subjected to all sorts of threats."

"It's your image that turns you into such a target," said Buchanan.

A little while later, a friend of mine also brought up the subject of my appearance. He argued that my looks only brought more attention to me, and in that sense could be construed as provocative. He was referring to the fact that I had stopped cutting my hair and had decided, on a daily basis, to wear a three-piece black suit, white dress shirt with gold cuff links, black tie, black scarf, black socks, and black shoes every day of my life. I had also refused to wear an overcoat or even carry an umbrella, regardless of the weather.

"You got the bushy Afro," said my friend, "you got the formal attire with the gold watch chain coming out of the vest pocket. What's the point? Why draw so much attention to yourself?"

My answer was simple: "As a free black man, I look the way I want to look and dress the way I want to dress."

"When's the last time you shaved?"

"Like my fellow bluesman Robert Johnson who is said to have bragged he never shaved, I, too, have never shaved in my life and it's not a brag. I have never shaved in my life. Not once. I'm too busy to shave. If I had to get up every morning and shave my face, I'd give it all up and be homeless."

"Seriously, what is the real meaning of your appearance?"

"The meaning's deep and operates on lots of levels at once," I told him. "First of all, I like the three-piece black suit and tie because I think it looks cool. It makes me feel cool and ready to face the world. Ready to teach, talk, read, listen, and alertly engage in the business set before me. My outfit gets me going and keeps me steady. It also reminds me of the dignity displayed by the regal bands of Duke Ellington and Count Basie, and also vocal groups like the Dramatics and Blue Magic. Naturally the look also refers to the ministers I loved so dearly in my lifetime, especially my beloved grandfather the Reverend Clifton L. West, and Shiloh Baptist's beautiful pastor Willie P. Cooke, and the greatest of all living Christian preachers, Gardner C. Taylor."

"But candidly, Corn, you also look something like an undertaker," said my friend.

I laughed and agreed. "There's something to that, dear brother," I said. "Because the all-black outfit does have some visual reference to the fact that I live on the edge of the abyss. We all do. Like Chekhov's mournful heroine Masha in his masterpiece, the play *The Three Sisters*, I believe we all struggle to persevere in the face of life's ever-present deep disappointments. We live in a creative tension with catastrophe. Catastrophe is our constant neighbor. He lives next door, and he may be moving in at any moment. My outfit reminds me of that truth. We're born to die, and the bluesman, who dances around the edges of disaster, must also be a righteous funeral director, directing his life in a way that never denies the certainty of a calamitous ending. I am a sad soul with a joyful disposition."

To be a philosopher is both the most serious of vocations and the most playful of dispositions. Serious because the love of wisdom puts everything at stake in one's thinking and living. Playful because even in one's deepest moments one still might be wrong and therefore prone to a humbling laughter at oneself. There is a sense in which philosophy is the love of wisdom in the consciousness of folly.

The blues philosopher is the teller of the tales and the singer of the songs that keep alive the best of our historical legacies. Such inheritances sustain our courage to think critically about the past and act compassionately in the present and offer an alternative future. In this way, the bluesman descends from both the griot tradition and the prophetic tradition.

No true philosopher can avoid the subject of death. The subject had really never left my mind since those death shudders washed over me as a child. The examination of what my brother Cliff calls "the other side of time" has been a constant part of my thinking. To a large degree, though, that consideration has been an abstraction, a notion to consider from afar.

Then one day the abstract became real. On May 26, 1994, my dad died.

WHAT MATTER OF MAN?

I HEAR THE CRY OF JOHN COLTRANE. I hear the heartbreaking moan of Billie Holiday and the anguished scream of James Brown. I feel the pain in Marvin Gaye's soul when he cries, "Father, Father." I am fortified by the faith of Dorothy Love Coates when she sings, "That's Enough." I see the tear in the voice of James Cleveland when he pleads, "Lord, Help Me to Hold Out."

I needed help to hold out. I needed help to get through. I had been asked to give the eulogy at my father's funeral, and I didn't see how I could manage it. I was too torn up inside, too overwhelmed with grief and loss, too devastated, too down.

Back in 1959 when we were kids, Dad had suffered a near-fatal ulcer attack. Half his stomach had to be removed. But he bounced back like the fighter that he was, and we'd never heard another word about his health after that. In fact, he was the picture of health, filled with positive energy and a robust vitality. Only a few months before his passing, Dad and my sister Cynthia had come to hear me deliver a public lecture in Oakland. I cherished the moment when I proudly introduced them to the audience, pointing out how essential family had been to every aspect of my formation. Then in late April, Mom had called to say that Dad wasn't feeling well and had agreed to see a doctor. That's when we knew it was serious. Dad's attitude about illness was simply to tough it out. I had daily reports about the tests they were giving him. His pain continued but the doctors were unable to say what was wrong. He went in for a battery of new studies at one hospital where, again, no specific disease was identified. That's when he went to Kaiser. Cliff was there. Cliff was witness to what happened.

"On Tuesday, May 25, we took Dad to Kaiser," Cliff remembered, "where they put him to sleep for a long probing procedure. When they brought him back to the room, he was still asleep. I was by his side when the doctor came in to say that Dad had pancreatic cancer, a fatal form of the disease. I stayed with him till midnight. Before I left, I prayed, 'Dear God, don't let this good man suffer.' The next morning at five o'clock, the hospital called to say that Dad had passed. I couldn't believe it. Mom couldn't believe it. We rushed over there and ran into his room. Mom, usually the most composed of women, pounded on Dad's chest, crying, 'You're still alive. I know you're alive.' He wasn't. The doctor said he had died of a pulmonary embolism.

"I felt something wasn't right. I didn't understand what had happened. Dad's sudden passing only hours after he was diagnosed with the fatal disease was never explained to my satisfaction. He was only sixty-five."

My father's death changed everything. It had me looking at the world through a whole different center. It made me acutely aware of an obvious fact that had never been an active part of my emotional reality: the things we prize most highly and the people we love most deeply can be lost in an instant. My presumption— which is to say, the presumption of a child—was that Dad would always be there. I'd call him like I'd always called him. It could be a Monday morning or Saturday night.

"Dad," I'd say, "just checking in. Just calling to say how much I miss you and Mom."

Then that voice would come on the line, the voice I'd heard my entire life, the voice of comfort and reassurance, the voice of calmness and unquestioned integrity. My dad's voice would say, "Son, we miss you too. Mom and I were just talking about how proud you make us. We were just saying how much we love you."

"I love you too, Dad."

And that would be it. A conversation no longer than a minute, but a conversation strong enough to get me through another few days, until the next conversation, and the one after that. In my little-boy way, I never doubted that these conversations would go on forever. Dad would outlive me. Dad would outlive everyone. Dad would defy death because . . . well, Dad was Dad.

Mr. Cool.

Mr. I'm-There-for-My-Kids.

Mr. Lean-on-Me.

But now Dad was gone, and I didn't see how I could express the terrible grief and pain assaulting me. I didn't know what to say.

Somehow, though, I got up before the assembled group of friends and family at church and managed to speak my heart. I spoke about how I took Dad's ever-constant presence for granted. I said that I felt most human and vulnerable standing before the deceased body of this wonderful man whom I love so completely.

"This is when we find out what we are about on the deepest level. We have no choice but to live with this loss, to absorb this terrible blow and see if the wound it inflicts upon our soul can move us to love with even greater purpose and energy." I spoke about the despair I felt at never being able to see, hear, or embrace my father again. And then I said, "Because he was strong, I know he wants us to carry on with strength. He believed in strength, not manly, macho strength, but strength of the spirit that resists shutting down in the face of disaster. In the aftermath of Dad's passing, I could easily shut down. I could give in to the melancholia that wants to envelop me. I could be paralyzed. I could break down. But Dad's spirit was—and is and forever will be—an active spirit, one that says, 'Go on. Move on. Do what needs to be done. Care for those who require care. Spread love wherever you walk. Spread love whenever you talk.'"

More than a decade later my brother Cliff expressed our love for Dad in a song he wrote. We recorded it on a CD called *Never Forget: A Journey of Revelations*. The selection is "What a Matter of," and, in tribute to Dad, I mixed my spoken-word message into the melody written by Cliff and the soaring vocal sung by Lenny Williams.

"We are who we are because somebody loved us," I said. "To be is to be loved."

As Lenny sang, "Every once in a while in the heart of a child, something makes you say . . . what a matter of man."

"My blessed father," I continued. "Strong man. Tender man. Sweet man. Full of compassion. Always there when you needed him."

"The measure of a man is such," sang Lenny, "that he gives a lot but he don't need much . . . through it all, you've been right there."

The miracle of my brother's song, sung from the purest part of Lenny's soul, brought Dad's spirit to life. That spirit lives with me to this day. He is gone, but he is not gone. When I think I need to be more patient with someone in my life, I think of Dad and patience arrives. When I think I need to be more understanding of someone, I think of my dad and somehow understanding comes my way. When love seems in short supply, I invoke my father's sweet spirit and love shows up at my door.

I bless the name of Clifton L. West, Jr. and thank God that I am blessed to be his son.

WHAT HAPPENED TO THE SQUEEGEE FOLK?

THE MID-'90S WERE A SUPER ACTIVE time for me. I was writing, teaching, and lecturing at a furious pace. Someone clocked it and said that, of all the lecturers in the country, Dr. Maya Angelou and I were leading the pack. Sister Maya was well ahead of me, with something like over 200 lectures a year. I was clocking well over a hundred—beyond my teaching duties at Harvard—and feeling good that my no-notes jazz-riff style seemed to be maturing into what friends were calling an art form. For me, these lectures were not simply money-making gigs, but occasions to make the world my classroom and all people my congregation.

I have an uncontrollable passion to communicate. I find great joy in life and seeing others smile and feel good about themselves, but that does not exempt anyone from thoughtful critique or intense scrutiny. For me, reexamination and rejuvenation go hand in hand. So critique and praise are inseparable.

I have kept this lecture pace for over three decades. And if I die on the road, I shall do so with a smile on my face.

Back in the '90s, I was especially involved in the relationships between blacks and Jews, the groups I called "the most unique and fascinating people of modern times." That these once close allies had experienced such bitter estrangement in recent years hurt my heart. If I could do something to foster a respectful dialogue between Jews and blacks, I was down.

I was especially grateful that such a dialogue emerged between Michael Lerner and me. Michael is a man I love, someone who has taught me a great deal. He comes out of the '60s Free Speech

Movement and Students for a Democratic Society at Berkeley, where he received a Ph.D. in philosophy. He also has a Ph.D. in psychology. He also became an ordained rabbi. As a progressive intellectual, he has courage and vision. We'd encountered each other back in the '80s when Michael invited me to write for *Tikkun*, a Jewish left-wing magazine that invited non-Jewish contributors like Christopher Lasch and Harvey Cox.

On an intellectual and spiritual level, I always felt a bond with Michael, despite the differences between us. I remember the day we were arguing out on the street in front of the National Black Summit. Michael was picketing the NAACP event because the Honorable Louis Farrakhan had been invited to the conference. The *New York Times* snapped a photograph of us barking at each other. It was also caught on film and shown on CNN. Michael was saying that such an alleged anti-Semite like the minister should have been excluded. I was defending my dear brother by arguing that, first of all, Farrakhan's remarks had been twisted out of context, and that, even more significantly, his deep love and service for his people more than justified his presence. He bravely stood up against white supremacy at a time in our history when to do so required courage and character. I pointed to Winston Churchill, that much-lauded figure in world history, and said his stand against Hitler has us forgiving him for having been pro-Mussolini, pro-Imperialist, and a subscriber to the notion that blacks are subhuman. If we can forgive Churchill's disagreeable views, why can't we also forgive the disagreeable views of Farrakhan while celebrating his contribution to the cause of black freedom?

In any event, Michael had his arguments and I had mine. We saw that, despite our differences, our dialogue was rich. We defined ourselves in radically different ways. Michael's a progressive Zionist, a nationalist. I'm not a nationalist on any level, not for any political entity, religion, or race. Dr. King, one of my heroes, was an American nationalist and a patriot. In that regard, I disagree with him. I am not first and foremost a patriot. America is not great because it is a nation chosen by God. It is great because people chose to fight for justice to make America more free and democratic. God does not wink at America and close divine eyes to other nations. My position is that all countries are subservient to the cross—which is to say, subservient to Jesus Christ's mandate that we are to serve the least among us.

Michael and I co-authored *Jews & Blacks: Let the Healing Begin* and also took our show on the road, giving joint appearances across the country for over a year. I loved the black Christian–white Jewish connection because of my view of Christianity as an extension of prophetic Judaism. I see the Old Testament/New Testament narratives as part of a continuum. In prophetic Judaism, as in Amos and Isaiah, justice is already universal. As a Jewish brother, Jesus is confirming this concept. Hillel, a contemporary of Jesus, is already on board the love train. But now Jesus is going even further—he's riding this train into enemy territory. He's telling us to actually *love* our enemies, a radical notion for which he's labeled insane.

Some said Michael and I were insane to take our discussion public. We didn't care. We thought it was a potent idea and we pursued it with passion. We encouraged audience participation and, for the most part, were able to provoke spirited interchanges. As you might imagine, we couldn't avoid a couple of speed bumps.

Michael and I were in Oakland at Marcus Books when the members of the Nation of Islam turned up at the event. The vibe was tense. At first, the discussion went reasonably well. Then Michael said the words.

"Louis Farrakhan is a dog."

Farrakhan's supporters responded in kind, yelling, "You're a dog!"

It went downhill from there. I had to protect Michael from the brothers. I got them to back off and I got Michael to let me say, "Rabbi, I'm not sure you want to go around calling someone's spiritual leader and my dear brother a dog." He tried to interrupt, but I wouldn't let him.

"You start calling the minister a dog, these brothers start calling you a dog, and soon we're looking at clenched fists and pointed pistols. Soon we've wiped out civility and excited pure rage. All because of the use of a three-letter word. The challenge here is to disagree with a degree of respect."

My words did only limited good. The word "dog" continued to be thrown around, but at least everyone got to vent. No punches were thrown.

Later on the tour, we were at Howard University in D.C. The subject of my friend Minister Farrakhan came up again. The very mention of the man's name triggered Michael, who turned on the questioner.

"If you had read more books about the history of anti-Semitism," Michael told the man challenging him, "you wouldn't ask such an inane question."

"That's the kind of arrogance that trumps any kind of conversation," I said to Michael. "Many black people associate that kind of arrogance with Jewish brothers and sisters who claim to be concerned about them. That's the stereotype. We're on tour trying to shatter the stereotype that, ironically, you're reinforcing here. So I want to stop and just let everyone know that you, my dear brother Rabbi Lerner, are one of the chief critiques of that stereotype. But like all of us, sometimes we fall into the muddy waters that we're trying to avoid. I do it. Now the rabbi has done it. But it can all be undone with a little understanding and compassion on everyone's part."

Michael gave me a smile, backed off, and let it go.

The tour went on. For all the goodwill that it engendered, though, my relationship with the good rabbi was tested when I had to cancel my keynote address at Michael's annual conference. Mom had suffered a heart attack and the family rushed to her side. She'd be in the hospital for six weeks and would eventually recover. Today she's in remarkably good health. But after the initial prognosis, her condition was critical. I cancelled everything and flew to Sacramento. Michael was sympathetic, but also eager that I attend. When I made it clear that nothing could keep me from being with Mom, Michael then insisted that I give my speech on a videotape and send it to Washington.

"Sorry, Michael," I said, "I can't even think about anything except being a loving presence for my mother."

My refusal put a strain on my friendship with Michael. No matter, I love the good rabbi and always will. I forgive but never forget such moments. The other thing I'll never forget is the introduction Michael gave me to the most brilliant and compassionate literary agent in the world, my dear sister Gloria Loomis.

THE SAME YEAR—1995—THAT Rabbi Lerner and I began our Black/Jewish dialogue, I was viciously attacked by Brother Leon Wieseltier, a prominent Jewish intellectual, in the pages of *The New Republic*, a neo-liberal journal with a distinguished history in American letters. Wieseltier called my books "almost completely worthless." It was nonetheless shocking to learn that, in a lengthy and mean-spirited critique, a respected member of the intelligentsia set out to destroy my reputation. Of course I knew about the hand-to-hand combat that characterizes much of the behavior among prominent critics. You try and destroy me . . . well, I'll come back and destroy you. Such vitriolic exchanges go on forever. Intellectual mud wrestling attracts a crowd, at least among a small circle of readers. There is, of course, a different way to understand the phenomenon. The rabbinical tradition of challenging text is a noble one. A vigorous back-and-forth on a high and respectful level is often illuminating. Socratic questioning—and challenging—is at the very heart of my being. But Wieseltier had no interest in questioning or challenging. He was intent on demonstrating that my life's work was a farce and that I was a fraud. He was, in fact, not only dishonoring the tradition of honest exchange but corrupting it with ruthless character assassination.

One of the reasons I am so deeply grateful to my family tradition is because, in the church of my elders, encouragement is the key. A little girl gets up to sing and the congregation, even before hearing the first note, shouts out, "Go on! Sing, baby, sing!" A young boy gets up to preach and the congregation is right there with him, assuaging his trepidation with shouts of praise. That's how I was raised.

You grow up, of course, and find yourself crossing from one culture to another. That's a beautiful thing. I bring my culture into your life, you bring yours into mine. We learn and share. Yet the hypercompetitive culture of warring critics never set well with me.

I couldn't play the game and even today find myself uncomfortable in a setting where the aim is to destroy rather than learn. It is disheartening but also true that, of all my colleagues, only two professors defended me against Wieseltier's ugly assault in print: my dear brothers Henry Louis Gates, Jr. and Richard Rorty. From the hundreds of other academicians who had told me how much they respected my scholarship—a deafening silence.

Another such moment came years later when I was asked by the Graduate Center of the City University of New York to speak at Sidney Hook Reconsidered: A Centennial Celebration. Hook was one of the grand intellectual figures of our time and perhaps the most prominent student of John Dewey. I had studied Hook as a young man. I had lectured and written about him on several occasions. I knew his work intimately. In fact, I had written a well-received book on American pragmatism with an entire chapter devoted to Hook. The man had had a profound influence on me. I was honored to be part of this celebration and excited to attend the conference. That's when the stuff hit the fan.

Three neo-conservative New York Jewish intellectuals said that if I spoke, they'd boycott—and they did. Art critic Hilton Kramer, essayist Irving Kristol, and historian Gertrude Himmelfarb were no-shows, all because of me! A fourth, historian John Patrick Diggins, who is not Jewish, also said he was withdrawing. He even said this to the *New York Times* in a page-one article: "In order to comment on Sidney Hook, one would have to read at least twenty of his books. Cornel West is such a celebrity intellectual, I don't think he'll have time for it." Well, the truth is that I had read *all* of Hook's books—and more than once. When the *Times* contacted me to comment, all I could say was that "I have learned much from the art criticism of Kramer, the fine historiography of Himmelfarb, the intellectual history of Diggins and some of the essays of Kristol. I just see through their nonsense."

Diggins, good man that he is, changed his mind and decided to attend. In introducing me, though, he said that he understood the point of those invitees who had refused to attend because of me. What point? That, as an author of highly regarded works on pragmatism, I was still unqualified? Undeterred, I ventured forth and gave my lecture. Afterwards, Hook's son came up to thank me for my insights. That was gratifying. So was the positive response of those in the lecture hall. Even more satisfying was that, at Princeton, I was warmly welcomed by Gertrude Himmelfarb's niece, my dear sister Professor Martha Himmelfarb, chairman of the Department of Religion, as a colleague and fellow scholar, a gesture that meant a great deal to me. And of course I wouldn't be the person I am without the support of many loving Jewish brothers in the academy like Hilary Putnam, Israel Scheffler, Paul Benacerraf, Robert Nozick, Sheldon Wolin, and Stanley Cavell, just to name a few. Unfortunately, though, that initial Hook conference is remembered more for the controversy surrounding it than the contributions of those who attended.

ANOTHER SIGNIFICANT RELATIONSHIP WAS STRAINED when I refused to support Bill Clinton for his second term. Back in 1992, I traveled the country speaking for him. I liked the man, and saw him as open-minded to new and progressive ideas. Naturally I was gratified when Clinton invited me to the White House and spoke highly of my books. But my outrage at his welfare bill—and the unconscionable crime bill—kept me from supporting him. In my view, Clinton was using the poor as a political football to win the 1996 election against Bob Dole. This bill, deeply damaging to the disenfranchised, was the president's way of stealing thunder from the Republican Right. This was a bill so heartless that even Ronald Reagan would have refused to sign it. Reagan had concerns about job training; he also had concerns about what would happen to impoverished children after the time limits for support ran out. Clinton ignored these concerns. He ignored what would happen if the supportive networks for those in need were abandoned.

I was also sickened when I saw that at the signing ceremony Clinton had a black woman standing right next to him. He needed the symbol of the "Welfare Queen" to approve his action. Without that symbol, the president couldn't justify signing a major piece of legislation that denied the most vulnerable members of our society: poor children. The historical subtext, of course, is that black women were the only females forced to work the fields during 244 years of slavery. When slavery was over, they were moved into white households to help raise white children. Yet they symbolize lazy people in America?

Clinton's approach to the nation's poor echoed Rudolph Giuliani's approach to New York City's poor. Giuliani proudly pointed to the deodorized and sanitized Times Square. No more homeless, no more funk, no more guys running up to your car to clean your windshield for change. But what happened to the squeegee folk?

For all Giuliani cared, they could have been dumped into the Hudson River. They could have been deported to Jersey City and Newark, falling into lives of crime and committing felonies left and right. But that didn't matter as long as our bourgeois tourism trade prospered. As long as the visitors from Sydney or Tokyo feel safe in the city, who cares about the squeegee folk?

The squeegee folk, the impoverished folks in the ghetto, people without means or hope—those who, as Ray Charles said, "Ain't got nothing yet"—these were the human souls that Clinton's welfare bill coldly and cruelly neglected.

The cultural equivalent of the elimination of the squeegee folk was the eradication of the arts program in inner-city schools. It was Carol Proctor who introduced me to my dear sister Natalie Lieberman, a compassionate and generous New Yorker, who founded the Learning Through Art Program to speak to this void. When I was asked to serve on the board of the Guggenheim Museum, I agreed with the stipulation that their foundation contribute to Mrs. Lieberman's program. Ironically, it was during this period when poor people were under fierce assault that the Guggenheim gave its first exhibition of African art. I was honored to support the show and write the introduction to the catalogue. And I was also delighted to provide the Black Radical Congress—the major leftist black organization in this period to defend poor people—with $10,000 as the seed money for its founding.

Meanwhile, Clinton, despite his concrete neglect of poor people, was reelected. I spoke at the inauguration for his second term and was invited back to the White House to discuss a range of issues. The president joked about my non-support and was good-natured about the fact that I had been highly critical of what I considered his abandonment of the poor. We could still talk to each other, still learn from each other, still remain friends. But none of that diminished my conviction that, on one of the most critical issues of our time, Bill Clinton blew it—and blew it bad.

LOSS

IN THIS MEMOIR, I MUST mark the loss of my dear, dear friend James Melvin Washington. I must declare my love for this man and everything that he represents. I must publicly mourn my precious brother. In another era and in a far different context, W.H. Auden mourned the death of the Irish poet W.B. Yeats with these lines:

> *In the deserts of the heart*
> *Let the healing fountains start,*
> *In the prison of his days*
> *Teach the free man how to praise.*

Jim Washington taught us all how to praise. Perhaps his most enduring legacy is his monumental *Conversations with God: Two Centuries of Prayers by African Americans.* Jim left us with our people's most beautiful praise. In the introduction to the book, he writes, "African-American prayers, a literary genre and a religious social practice, assume that God is just and loving, and that the human dilemma is that we cannot always experience and see God's justice and love. We pray for faith to trust God's ultimate disclosure. Thus prayer as act and utterance teaches the believer to exercise what Adrienne Rich calls 'revolutionary patience.' But the literary history of African-American prayers suggests that, besides anticipating God's ultimate self-disclosure in the history of the oppressed, we are the trustees of a spiritual legacy paid for with the blood, sweat, tears, and dreams of a noble, even if not triumphant, people. The culture, grammar, and promise of the African-American prayer tradition are in our hands. Only time will tell whether or not their faith in us was worth the price they paid."

He includes this prayer from 1902 by Katherine Davis Chapman Tillman:

Oh, God, when days were dark indeed
When we were fast in Slavery's chain
Thou then our parents' prayers did heed
And helped us freedom to obtain

And this "Pagan Prayer" by Countee Cullen, written in 1925:

Not for myself I make this prayer
But for this race of mine
That stretches forth from shadowed places
Dark hands for bread and wine.
For me, my heart is pagan made,
My feet are never still
But give them hearts to keep them warm
In homes high on a hill...
Our Father, God; our Brother, Christ
Or are we bastard kin,
That to our plaints your ears are closed,
Your doors barred from within?
Our Father, God; our Brother, Christ,
Retrieve my race again;
So shall you compass this black sheep,
This pagan heart. Amen.

There is Dr. King's "A Pastoral Prayer" from 1956 in which he says, "We thank thee, O God, for the spiritual nature of man. We are in nature but we live above nature. Help us never to let anybody or any condition pull us so low as to cause us to hate. Give us strength to love our enemies and to do good to those who spitefully use us and persecute us."

Jim's book of prayers, a gift both from his people and to his people, became a bestseller and a permanent part of the African American library. It's a living tribute to his faith. When he died of a stroke in 1997, he had just turned forty-nine. His other books—*A Testament of Hope: The Essential Writings and Speeches of Martin Luther King, Jr., I Have a Dream: Writings and Speeches That Changed the World* and *Frustrated Fellowship: The Black Baptist Quest for Social Power*—all carry the strength of spirit and the purposefulness of scholarship.

Jim asked the deepest questions we can ask: Why evil? Why oppression? Why the absurdity of human existence? He didn't offer easy answers. Jim was never glib. He let the weight of those questions sit on the shoulders of those who asked them. He knew the questions wouldn't go away; not then, not now, not ever. What he did do, though, was to live his life with a spiritual vigor—a kindness, a gentleness, a radiant love—that had you looking for the source of his strength.

If you looked closely, you saw Jesus Christ in Jim's eyes. If you listened closely, you heard Jesus Christ in Jim's voice. James Melvin Washington argued for the reality of God by not arguing at all. He proved the existence of the Prince of Peace through the exquisite peace that you felt in his very presence. Such peace lives forever.

Shortly after his passing, it was a blessing to be able to dedicate my book *Restoring Hope* to Jim. It was a collection of conversations held at the historic Schomburg Center in Harlem headed by my dear brother Howard Dodson. I also co-edited, with Quinton Hosford Dixie, a group of essays in honor of Brother Wash, *The Courage to Hope.*

Faith, hope, and love—the Christian virtues—were what Brother Wash was all about.

JUST TO KEEP YOU SATISFIED

LIKE JOHN COLTRANE AND JOHN KEATS, Marvin Gaye understood the tragicomic condition of human existence. Marvin was adored by women, yet his relationships with women were troubled. In typical autobiographical mode, he wrote the music to the film *Trouble Man*. Maintaining that same sense of candid self-revelation, in 1973 he recorded a song entitled "Just to Keep You Satisfied" and placed it at the end of *Let's Get It On*, his erotic follow-up to *What's Going On*

"Just to Keep You Satisfied" is not a typical love song. It is essentially free-form storytelling. There is no verse, chorus, or bridge. There's only the tormented tale of Marvin's marriage to his first wife, Anna Gordy Gaye. It is, in fact, an indication that the marriage has failed and anticipates another Marvin masterpiece that will come five years later, *Here, My Dear*, the complete delineation of that complex relationship and its bittersweet conclusion.

I cite Marvin because there are times when singers and songs say things about our lives that we can't. Back in high school, it was common for the folk to put on a love song—say, Smokey's "Ooh Baby Baby" and tell his honey, "Darling, this is how I feel about you." In short, the song says it better. In that spirit, Marvin's "Just to Keep You Satisfied" brings to mind my complex relationship with Elleni and its unfortunate demise. The lyrics are by no means a literal description of our situation, but the spirit—the pathos, the regret, the sense of defeat—are all emotions to which I relate.

You were my wife, my life, my hopes and dreams
For you to understand what this means
I shall explain...
My one desire was to love you
And think of you with pride
And keep you satisfied...
Farewell, my darling, maybe we'll meet down the line
It's too late for you and me, much too late for you and I...
We tried, God knows we tried...

Marvin's anguish is palpable. There is in his voice the terrible recognition that the dream of domestic tranquility has ended in what can only be called failure. Listening to the song I keep hearing those words of Samuel Beckett: "Try again. Fail again. Fail better."

"WHY DO YOU THINK IT'S FAILING?" Cliff asked me, referring to my marriage to Elleni. "It began so beautifully."

"She's still beautiful," I said. "She'll always be beautiful. Beautiful heart. Beautiful soul. Beautiful mind. She's also grown beautifully as an aware human being in the years that I've known her. She's taken up the AIDS cause in Africa and assuming a leadership position that's truly impressive. Man, she's just an impressive woman."

"I know, Corn," said Cliff. "We all love her. Mom loves her like a daughter."

"Mom also saw what was happening. Last time Mom was here, she was talking to Elleni about my work. She asked Elleni whether she'd watched me on C-SPAN the week before. 'Oh no,' Elleni said. 'I don't always watch Corn when he's on TV.'"

In talking to Cliff, I realized that my initial reaction to Elleni's disinterest in my work was happiness. I was happy that she was not emotionally invested in my career. That meant she loved *me*, rather than the public person I'd become. I found that gratifying and reassuring. But then here comes the pull between the personal and professional. Here comes the pull between the passion, as Marvin put it, "to keep you satisfied," and the passion to satisfy those unrelenting demands of the bluesman's mission to keep singing his blues whenever and wherever he can.

"Here's the problem," said Cliff. "You love her too much to stay. You love her so much you gotta leave. The more successful you become, the less she sees herself as being part of you. It's not that she's jealous of your success. She loves your success. But paradoxically, the better you do, the worse she feels. That's been the pattern with all your women. The truth, bro, is that everything comes second to your calling. You have so much multifaceted love and energy that the affirmation you bring your partner is off the scale. That's your genuine gift. But sooner or later, the calling will have its due. Your sweet is so sweet that it only makes it that much more painful for the partner when the calling comes a-calling."

Years later, my dear brother Tavis Smiley put it like this: "When you talk to students, or even to strangers, you make them feel good about themselves. You listen to their points of view, and even if you disagree, you give them the courtesy of considering whatever they say. They go away from those encounters feeling like, *'Good Lord, Cornel West has listened to me and validated that I've got something to say!'* Those encounters are beautiful, and they're empowering for the people who interact with you. But, in character, they are diametrically opposed to the long-term relationships you've had with women. Those women could never quite figure out where they fit into your life. How does a mate deal with someone like you? In order to do so, they have to be unbelievably confident about their own place in the world—and their place in *your* world. Without that confidence, they can't help but feel less-than. It deepens their insecurities. And when you sense that feeling coming over them, to protect them—in fact, to save them—you leave. You see that, in order to grow—for you to grow *and* for them to grow—you need to get out of the way."

Analyses of my relationships with women could go on endlessly. My brother Cliff has his point of view. Close friends like Tavis have theirs. My own perspective is that, whatever the reasons, I was unsuccessful in maintaining marriages three different times. Each began with dedication and hope. Each ended with the recognition that it simply wasn't working. Each began in love and ended in love.

The basic problem with my love relationships with women is that my standards are so high—and they apply equally to both of us. I seek full-blast mutual intensity, fully-fledged mutual acceptance, full-blown mutual flourishing, and fully felt peace and joy with each other. This requires a level of physical attraction, personal adoration, and moral admiration that is hard to find. And it assumes a depth of trust and openness for a genuine soul-sharing with a mutual respect for a calling to each other and to others. Does such a woman exist for me? Only God knows and I eagerly await this divine unfolding. Like Heathcliff and Catherine's relationship in Emily Bronte's remarkable novel Wuthering Heights or Franz Shubert's tempestuous piano Sonata No. 21 in B flat (D.960), I will not let life or death stand in the way of this sublime and funky love that I crave!

The words of Brother Marvin bear repeating. He said it better than I ever could:

> *And when we stopped the hands of time*
> *You set my soul on fire*
> *My one desire was to love you*
> *And think of you with pride*
> *And keep you satisfied*
> *Oh baby, we could not bear the mental strain*

Elleni Gebre Amlak set my soul on fire. I'll always think of her with pride. It pains me to this day that I somehow couldn't stay with her. She is a magnificent woman. But the mental strain broke down our bond, and the result, in spite of the deep love, was a divorce that left me with a broken heart and a busted bank account.

THE BLUESMAN, BROKE OR NOT, keeps on keeping on. When it comes to money, by now you know that this particular bluesman has always been funny. I've had folk come up to me and say, "Brother West, I'll never forget the time you reached into your pocket and gave me $300 cause I couldn't pay the rent." And the funny thing is, I was behind on my own rent. If I have it and somebody else needs it, it's theirs. Beyond the money woes, though, there was work to do, songs to sing, books to write, struggles to wage.

As the '90s neared a close, I had the unadulterated joy of collaborating with my dear sister Sylvia Ann Hewlett. For five long years, she and I collaborated on a seminal text called *The War Against Parents,* a defense of the ultimate non-market activity—parenting—in a market-driven culture. Nothing, we argued, is more crucial than loving, caring, and nurturing our precious children in the face of materialism, hedonism, and narcissism. I worked with her National Parenting Association in local branches across the nation. Her family is family, and I love them dearly.

I have always believed that I am who I am because somebody loved me. The love saturation that I received from my parents has been the wind at my back throughout my life. My decision to highlight the delicate and difficult challenge of parenting is my tribute to the supreme parenting that I received. There is a sense in which so much hurt in the world is attributable to unsupported, frustrated, or neglectful parenting. The decline of concern and decay of care for children is a fundamental feature in contemporary society. If we do not address it with personal care and public policy the future looks grim.

In 1998, the same year of *The War Against Parents,* I was blessed to publish with the grand philosopher Roberto Mangabeira Unger *The Future of American Progressivism,* a book based on our course taught at Harvard Law over a number of years. Unger, of Brazilian origin, is a passionate lover of truth and justice, and one of the world's unrivaled public intellectuals. Around this time, I was surprised by a request to offer my opinion in the field of pop culture. The request came from Warren Beatty. He called me early one morning from Hollywood to say that he had just finished a film called *Bulworth* and wasn't sure whether to release it.

"I'd be grateful if you could take a look at it, professor," he said.

"I wish I could, but my time is tight and I don't see how I could get out there."

"I'll come to you, and I'll bring the film."

"When?"

"I'll fly out on a private jet this morning, buy out a movie theater in Copley Square, and we can watch it there tonight."

That's exactly what happened. The other invited guests were Norman Mailer and his wife. When the film was over, Warren turned to me and asked the $64,000 question, "Should I release it?"

I didn't hesitate. "Absolutely," I said. "It's a fascinating critique of capitalism and market-driven politics. I think it's provocative and needs to be seen."

Warren was relieved. Afterwards, he, the Mailers, and I talked our heads off till three in the morning in the bar of the Four Seasons Hotel, dissecting everything from German philosophy to South Bronx hip-hop.

In a similar vein, my dear brother Will Smith, whom I met at the Million Man March, called me to meet in Boston just prior to the premier of his film *Ali*. We could not stop talking. It could have been hours. It could have been days. We dialogued along with his beautiful wife Jada and his gracious mother-in-law the pivotal role of Muhammad Ali in the turbulent '60s. I am no way surprised that Will is the biggest box office star of our time given his talent and determination.

A few years later, I had encounters with several major hip-hop figures. The first was with Sean Combs, AKA P. Diddy. Serious criminal charges had been leveled against the brother, and he was at one of the low points of his life. His attorney, my dear friend Johnnie Cochran, Jr., called.

"Corn, Sean is in deep trouble. Could you possibly come to the courthouse and lend some moral support? Having a man of integrity like you, sitting right there next to him, is going to mean a lot to everyone."

"I'll be there," I said.

I spent a number of days in the courthouse with Sean and his lovely mother.

"It's going to all right, brother," I told him. And it was. I was elated when Sean was acquitted.

I was also flattered when I was asked to help out Jay-Z. American Express was looking to put him in a major commercial, but they were being extremely cautious. That's why they requested Geoffrey Canada, the founder of the historic Harlem Children's Zone, and I meet with him. Next thing I knew I was kicking it at Jay-Z's townhouse with the man himself. The three of us had a beautiful three-hour conversation. Not only did American Express give him the gig, but I wound up with a star guest at my seminar. And he wasn't the only one. Jay-Z joined Toni Morrison and Phylicia Rashad in a discussion of the "Black Intellectual Tradition," where he said that he was aspiring to be Plato to Biggie's Socrates.

Another fascinating moment for me came when the Rosa Parks Foundation sued my dear brothers, OutKast, for defaming the name of Ms. Parks in the hip-hop duo's popular song. The chorus said, "Ah-ha, hush that fuss. Everybody move to the back of the bus." Jesse Jackson and Al Sharpton, among others, supported the foundation. Knowing the political sensitivity and poetic creativity of OutKast, I was convinced that they had been misunderstood. In no way were they demeaning Rosa Parks. My feeling was that OutKast was the victim of a certain intolerance when it came to hip-hop and rap. I went so far as to write a brief on their behalf. Happily, the suit was settled in a just manner.

O'HARE AIRPORT, AFTERNOON FLIGHT to Houston. I was on my way to Texas to deliver the keynote address to a formal affair for black professionals. The minute I stepped on the plane I spotted Snoop Dogg and, just like that, announced publicly, "Lyrical genius on the plane!"

Snoop and I embraced.

"Snoop," I said, "it's a blessing to meet you. Your flow is a species of historical memory for me. The way you rap reflects the struggle of a great people. And there are several other things I love about you. First, I love your love for the Dramatics."

"You got that right," he said. "I was raised listening to them. And you know, there is a slight difference between folk who love the Dramatics and those who love the Temptations."

"Yeah, it's Stax versus Motown. We love both of them, but the Dramatics are a little funkier."

"I'll go with you on that."

"I also want to offer congratulations to you and your son, Snoop. I just read how your coaching helped him win the state championship. But the main thing I want to tell you, man, is that I feel in your lyrical flow the spirit of Curtis Mayfield. In fact, my own calling is to keep alive the spirit and legacy of Martin Luther King, Jr., John Coltrane and Curtis."

Snoop's eyes lit up with astonishment. He called over one of his guys.

"Tell Brother West," Snoop said, "the name of the one old-school cat who I never stop talking about, the one who moves me the most."

"Curtis Mayfield," his guy responded. "Man, you've been locked into Curtis ever since I've known you."

At that moment, we couldn't do anything but give each other another big hug.

"Are you performing in Houston?" I asked Snoop.

"Yes, tomorrow night. And I'd love to have you as my guest."

"I'd love to be there, but I take a plane out early tomorrow morning. But, say, why don't you be my guest at my lecture tonight?"

"I'm kinda jammed up, but I could swing by for fifteen minutes or so."

That evening the top brass and black elite of Houston packed the hotel ballroom—men in tuxes, women in evening gowns. Lo and behold, just as I was walking up to the podium to speak, here comes Brother Snoop and his posse, dressed in classic hip-hop style. I acknowledged his presence and proceeded to lecture on the rich tradition of struggle for freedom in black history. After fifteen minutes, I saw that Snoop still hadn't left. After twenty-five minutes, the brother was still sitting there. And then, amazingly enough, when I had completed my talk, some seventy minutes after I had begun, there was Snoop, deeply engrossed. I then invited him to the stage.

"I'm going to take the wise words of Professor West," he said, "and not just walk with them, but run with them. Run, run, run."

PART IV

THE MATRIX

THE MOST PASSIONATE LOVE

JAMES BALDWIN SAID IT BEST in *No Name in the Street*. I used Brother Baldwin's quote at the start of a book, *Democracy Matters*, that I'd begun writing after my marriage with Elleni had dissolved:

"To be an Afro-American . . . is to be in the situation, intolerably exaggerated, of all those who have ever found themselves part of a civilization which they could in no wise honorably defend—which they were compelled, indeed, endlessly to attack and condemn— and who yet spoke out of the most passionate love, hoping to make the kingdom new, to make it honorable and worthy of life."

Writing *Democracy Matters*—superbly edited by Sister Emily Loose—brought me more joy than any other book I've done. I could literally feel the fire emanating from my pen to paper—since I've never owned or used a computer. We had reached the low point of the age of Reagan—the second Bush years—and I was full of righteous indignation. Most of the intellectuals, media, and politicians were duped by the "magic" of unregulated markets, militarism in the Middle East, and fewer liberties at home owing to the threat of terrorism. My blues sensibility of deep democracy led me to say we were on the brink of catastrophe—on the national and global fronts. Sadly, I was right.

Democracy Matters lays bare my project more clearly than any other book I've written. And my grand attempt to weave the rich legacies of Melville and Emerson through the genius of Morrison and Baldwin in the deep democratic American grain still make me smile. Despite predictable neoconservative and neoliberal attempts to trivialize the book, it sold over 100,000 copies (reaching No. 5

on the *New York Times* bestseller list) and continues to influence many. The underlying thesis of the book is that the legacy of Martin Luther King, Jr. is the culmination of not only the democratic tradition in the USA but also the humanist tradition of Socrates and Jesus—Athens and Jerusalem. Needless to say, King is a Christian bluesman of the highest order! Like him, I try to be a prisoner of hope, a fanatic of fairness, and an extremist of love.

As the twentieth century, the bloodiest in human history, came to an end, I saw our market-driven, hypermaterialistic, consumption-craving culture in sorry shape. Right-wing demagogues were galvanizing their power and spreading their venom on the airwaves with ever-growing influence. For all its serious imperfections, the Clinton Era would soon look good next to the Bush Ice Age. Fear would freeze out hope. Fear would dominate American politics during the illegitimate regime of Bush the Younger. Small-minded bigotry, insensitivity to the poor, self-delusional arrogance in foreign policy, misguided overreaction to terrorist threats, a horrific war based on blatant lies, strategic miscalculations, and a frightfully xenophobic world view being perpetuated by an administration whose heartless neglect of its very own people in the face of natural disaster . . . the early years of the twenty-first century would challenge whatever hope we could muster. It seemed as if the dangerous dogmas of free-market fundamentalism, adventurous militarism, and myopic authoritarianism were strangling our fragile democracy at home. And abroad, I called for forging democratic identities in the Middle East. I highlighted progressive Jewish voices, such as Albert Einstein and Ahad Ha'am, and prophetic Islamic figures, like Mahmoud Mohamed Taha, who is the Muslim Gandhi.

I am in no way a mystic, since I cherish my unique individuality. Yet I do have a profound appreciation of mystery that transcends reason and fact. I acknowledge the human inadequacy of fully comprehending the unpredictable ways of life and the world. A nihilist would view time as loss, but I would also view time as a gift—not only a taking but also a giving. My kind of negative capability fuses humility with a courage to endure the unknowable and the inexplicable with grace and dignity. Therefore, when I encounter overwhelming darkness, I still believe I can discern some light, even if it is at the end of the tunnel.

Even during the pervasive gloom of our nation's political Ice Age, my understanding of negative capability enabled me to keep track of both an overwhelming mean-spiritedness and social destructiveness as well as noble and ultimately righteous struggles for justice.

Meanwhile, the bluesman's job never changes: you keep singing the blues. From that point of view, the world really doesn't get worse or better. It isn't a question of optimism or pessimism. The blues are simply the blues. The blues are how humans, blessed to be conversant with the deepest parts of their soul, tell their story. It's a comedy, it's a tragedy, it's a farce, it's a sitcom; it's an epic, it's a sonnet, it's the straight-ahead twelve-bar blues.

I had the Oh-Lord-these-legal-bills-are-killing-me-blues.

I have nothing against lawyers until lawyers work their way into divorce procedures that result in increased acrimony. The bigger the arguments, the bigger the legal bills. The legal bills I had to pay during my divorce from Elleni were astronomical. Even worse, the settlement left me flat on my backside. I walked out with practically nothing except my trusty '88 Cadillac. I'm still driving that baby today. But hundreds of thousands of dollars worth of a house and furnishings—all gone. Not to mention an alimony worthy of the salary of a rock star, not a professor.

Should I have fought the legal battle with more aggression? Do I have a right to complain about being left broke when, at the end of the day, it was my decision to walk away from possessions that might have otherwise been mine? When it comes to women, I am not a fighter. When it comes to women, it is difficult—in fact, impossible—for me not to ultimately succumb to their material demands. I wish it were otherwise.

In 1999, I met a stunningly brilliant and beautiful woman named Aytul, a Kurdish journalist who came to Harvard as a Neiman fellow. We had a love relationship that resulted in the birth of our beloved daughter, the precious Dilan Zeytun West, who was born on November 11, 2000. She is a blessing to all who know her, a child of extraordinary grace and intelligence. Good God almighty, I love that girl! Breathtaking.

Dilan means "song" in Kurdish. Zeytun means "olive" in Kurdish, Arabic, and Persian. When we named her Dilan, we realized it would be difficult for Aytul to live in Turkey, where Kurdish culture is suspect. Until recently, it was forbidden to simply pronounce a Kurdish name in Turkey. Things are changing now and hopes are high. For her part, Aytul is devoted to her people and for years has been working on the definitive contemporary history of the Kurds. She and Zeytun, the name most commonly used by my daughter, settled in Bonn, Germany. The distance is difficult, but not impossible. I call daily and fly over every six weeks. Zeytun, who speaks Turkish, English, and German fluently, is a remarkable spirit and, along with my gifted son Cliff, are two of the reasons my life is worth living.

Yet in both cases, I've found myself in situations where the fundamental clash between my deep commitment to be a loving father and my deep calling as an intellectual bluesman could not be resolved. The result was pain—pain for my children, pain for their mothers, pain for me. Despite this soul-wrenching pain, Cliff and Zeytun are my heart.

In talking about the sad ending of happy relationships, I quoted Eddie Kendricks, one of the two lead singers from the Temptations' classic '60s lineup. The other, of course, was the inimitable David Ruffin. Just as Eddie's "Tell Her Love Has Felt the Need" was a song he sang after leaving the Temps, Ruffin's "Walk Away from Love" was also recorded when David had left the group. The song starts:

It's not that I don't love you, you know how much I do
And it's not that I've found someone to take the place of you
It's just a fear that builds within me, every time you touch my hand
And a dread that shakes my body, that even I don't understand
So I'm leaving, this time I'm playing it smart,
I'm going to walk away from love, before love breaks my heart
Oh, you're clinging to me tighter than you ever had before, I don't
understand it
But I know it's going to take everything I've got to keep walking out
the door
But those arms you got around me, will let me go someday
And I'd rather leave you holding on, than pushing me away . . .

Because I've never been an advocate of psychotherapy as a path to self-understanding, I'm sure I have limitations in this area. I've avoided such therapy because I worry about how it might exacerbate narcissistic tendencies. I have friends who argue just the opposite— that psychotherapy, done with sensitivity and an eye to serve others, may be the very thing to break the bond of self-preoccupation. I'm not certain. I'm not sure I know myself well enough to share my whole self with others. This, in part, might explain my volatile relationships with women. One might argue that because I don't know myself, the more time I spend with a woman, the more various parts of myself emerge—parts that are, in fact, foreign to me. In short, my whole self surfaces, and it is precisely my whole self that strikes me as a stranger. To maintain a long-term and long-lasting bond with a woman may require the kind of soul-sharing or self-sharing that's beyond my capability. I hope not.

Certain people are attracted to certain facets of us. At an early point, a particular facet might dominate. Later, a less appealing facet might raise its head and take over for a minute, an hour, or a day. We're all multidimensional. These dimensions appear and disappear, rise and fall, please and displease, placate and irritate. How do we discuss such facets of ourselves? How do we negotiate them with our partners who have conflicting facets of their own? Or, as Brother Al Green put it, how can you mend a broken heart? How can you stop the rain from falling?

With Aytul, the rain fell on our relationship. She and the precious Zeytun settled down in Germany. It broke my heart to see them so far off. But every time I make the trip to see my blessed daughter, there was sunshine in her eyes, in her smile, in the way she showered love on her mom and dad. Back in America, I was juggling two separate legal actions. Elleni's lawyers argued that she was entitled to big alimony as well as every last material object in my life. Meanwhile, Aytul's lawyers were demanding that I pay her huge child support as if I had no other legal obligations to Elleni. Both sums of money resulted in a major negative cash flow.

How blue can a brother get? Let's see.

MESSIN' WITH
THE WRONG BROTHER

THE COLLEGE PROFESSOR AS BLUESMAN isn't a concept easily embraced by the college president. The academic intellectual as bluesman is another notion that doesn't go down easy with the powers that be. How about the teacher making a hip-hop record? Few university administrations would applaud such a move. As a rule, university administrations like their teachers contained. They're comfortable with strict definitions and tight boundaries when it comes to faculty members and their public posture.

I've always seen it another way. I believe in specialized studies. I believe in dedicating oneself to a focused field of scholarship. I've done my fair share of scholarly writing. *The American Evasion of Philosophy: A Genealogy of Pragmatism*, a book I wrote in 1989, was such a work. *Keeping Faith*, from 1993, was another. But that's never been enough for me. If I'm to address what's wrong with the world in which I live, if I'm going to sing the blues that stirs the deepest part of my soul, I need to follow the bluesman's lead. I have to get out there. I have to sing in front of groups of people—at schools and churches, in prisons and on the streets, on TV, on records, on iTunes and iPods—because the blues message is universal—universally true and universally healing.

The blues message is real, the blues message is pain, and the pain is real as rain. When the blues led to rhythm-and-blues and rhythm-and-blues to hip-hop, I was not put off by the changes. I saw them all as branches of the same tree. That tree has roots deep in the soil of history. I liked the idea of hanging out on those branches. Together with Mike Dailey, Derek Allen, and my brother

Cliff, I wrote a hip-hop/spoken word record that, in many ways, was a teaching device. The songs were serious. They addressed our past, our future, and our present condition. The beats were as strong as the message. I loved being in the studio and working with the grooves. I saw the operation as part of the radical democratic impulse and tragicomic truth-telling that comes directly out of the blues root.

I see my role as an educator, as someone who feels both a Socratic and prophetic calling, to implement what Nietzsche called a singing paideia. I am always compelled to remember that paideia represents an unfathomable education in which self-examination and service to others produces a mature, compassionate person willing to speak, live, and sacrifice for truth.

I see hip-hop as part of a movement linked to a danceable education, teaching that can both delight and instruct. I know that I am not a rapper like KRS-One, who has been lecturing in my classes for years. I am surely not a singer any more than I am a preacher. But, in some small way, if I can help bring the social consciousness of a Curtis Mayfield or a Nina Simone to hip-hop, if I can reach one young person with a message embedded in a sound that stirs his or her soul, then I have not labored in vain. My point of reference as an educator is tied to a mighty mission: unsettling minds and motivating hearts to be forces for good.

Hip-hop is a young game. Some might ask, "Why is this old fool turning out hip-hop CDs?" My answer is that the generation of the Dramatics and the O'Jays can—and must—offer their insights to the ongoing culture. I believe it's a continuum, not a conflict or a contradiction, but, in the language of rap, a continuous flow between one generation and another. The '60s and '70s of Sly Stone and Stevie Wonder are more pertinent and compelling than ever. Hook them up with what's happening today and you have a fusion, a kind of hybrid, that looks backward and forward at the same time. It's a beautiful thing.

I say all this to introduce a monumental conflict that I had with Harvard President Lawrence Summers just after my first hip-hop record, *Sketches of My Culture*, came out in 2001. Skip Gates, my dear friend and department head, told me that Summers, newly installed in his job, wanted to see me. Before our encounter, though, I knew several things about Summers, a distinguished academic who had served as chief economist of the World Bank as well as Clinton's Secretary of the Treasury.

After assuming his post as Harvard president, he had met with all department heads except Skip. He made a point of ignoring the Afro-American Studies Department. He had also been saying that he wasn't sold on affirmative action. What's more, I had heard of a sarcastic memo at the World Bank where Summers reportedly suggested shipping polluted materials to sub-Saharan Africa. The reasoning was that the region already suffered from overpopulation and was under-polluted.

Then there was the matter of his administration directing me to cut down my course on Afro-American studies from 700 to 400 undergraduates. When I was told Harvard did not have a room for this large a group, I refused to reject any student. My position was that if a student wanted to take this lecture class, he or she could darn well take it. I found a prophetic priest whose close-to-campus church housed a basement big enough to include everyone. The class went on and, for me and I hope for the students as well, it was a joyful and deep experience.

Before my meeting with Summers, Skip called me to his office. "Corn," he said, "I want to show you this letter I just wrote Summers. It's about you."

"Why are you writing Summers about me, Skip?"

"Well, it seems that you're under scrutiny."

"For what?"

"I'm not sure, but I'm not giving Summers any breathing room. I laid it out as plainly as possible."

Skip's three-page, single-spaced letter was a spirited defense of me, listing my sixteen books, my eight co-edited books, and detailing my faculty advisory roles. But why, I wondered, was a defense necessary?

At that point I was one of Harvard's very few University Professors. In fact, William Julius Wilson and I were the first black University Professors in Harvard history. That meant that I was attached to no program or department. I could teach whatever I wanted. It also gave me the option of reducing my teaching load whenever I cared to. I hadn't cared to. In fact, my passion for teaching had me adding rather than eliminating courses. When it came to student involvement, I was known for long office hours and easy accessibility. Given all this—and the fact that I had been granted tenure—I couldn't understand why Summers was suddenly putting me under review.

No matter, I walked into the president's office, ready to meet the man for the first time and hear what he had to say. From the get-go, the meeting was strange and strained. Summers seemed super-uptight. To break the ice, he told me that I was just the man to help him undermine Professor Harvey Mansfield. In describing his desire to upset Mansfield, Summers used a language that he presumed I'd find familiar.

"Help me f___ him up," he said.

As a vehement critic of affirmative action and someone who openly criticized the growing number of black men and women at Harvard, Brother Mansfield held views diametrically opposite to mine. We had, in fact, engaged in a heated public debate attended by more than a thousand students and faculty members. At the same time, though, I had high respect for Mansfield. He was a respected scholar and world-renowned intellectual. He was a friend. There was no way in the world I would ever participate in any activity that would impute his reputation or challenge his integrity. I told Summers that, despite the intensity and even intellectual ferocity that marked my debates with Mansfield, neither he nor I had ever once used a disparaging word to describe one another. There had never been name-calling or cursing. I considered Mansfield my brother. In fact, I had recently seen him at the faculty club, where I congratulated him on his superb translation of Alexis de Tocqueville's classic, *Democracy in America*, that he had translated together with his wife, Delba Winthrop.

Summers was taken aback. I guess he thought that bashing a faculty member—one that he was sure I loathed—would be a good way to kick off our talk. For my part, I was astounded that the president of Harvard would stoop to such tactics.

"Professor West," he said, "let me get to the purpose of this meeting."

"Please do."

"While you were working for Bill Bradley's presidential campaign, you cancelled your classes for three straight weeks."

I could tell that Summers was getting warmed up, and rather than respond to the charges one by one, I decided to stay silent and let him present his case in full.

"I also don't understand why in the world you would then go on to support another presidential candidate who didn't have even a remote chance of winning," he added. "No one respects him."

Here he could have been referring to Ralph Nader or Al Sharpton, both whom I love and respect. I presumed Sharpton was the man he disapproved of so vehemently. In any event, I didn't ask and allowed him to go on. His list of complaints and reprimands was long.

"Professor West," he said accusingly, "I'm afraid there's evidence that you've been contributing to grade inflation.

"Professor West," he added, "you need to write an important book on a philosophical tradition to establish your authority and insure your place as a scholar.

"Professor West, you need to write works that are not reviewed, as your books have been reviewed, in periodicals like the *New York Review of Books,* but rather in academic journals.

"Professor West, you have to cease making rap albums that are an embarrassment to Harvard."

I took a deep breath before replying. I began by saying, "Professor Summers, when you say 'an embarrassment to Harvard,' which Harvard are you talking about?"

"The Harvard I have been hired to lead," he said.

"But your Harvard, Professor Summers, is not my Harvard. And I'm as much Harvard as you are. Look, we all know that Harvard has a white supremacist legacy, a male supremacist legacy, an anti-Semitic legacy, a homophobic legacy. And we also know that Harvard has a legacy that's critical of those legacies. That's the Harvard I relate to."

"None of those Harvards have anything to do with rap albums," said Summers.

"First of all, it wasn't a rap album. It can loosely be described as hip-hop."

"Still, an embarrassment," repeated Summers.

"For me it's an honor to be associated with hip-hop. Isn't our mission to relate to the young, make them curious, challenge their minds, and excite their imaginations? My album contains many musical forms but is essentially tied to the struggle for freedom. I couldn't be prouder of it."

"I cannot tolerate teachers missing classes like you have," he said, moving on to his next complaint.

"And I cannot tolerate the disrespect you show me by attacking me without a shred of evidence. The straight-up fact is that, in twenty-six years, I've missed one class—and that's when I went to Africa to give a keynote lecture at a Harvard-sponsored AIDS conference in Morocco. And as far as your direction for me to write an important philosophical treatise, I did that some twelve years ago. My scholarship was deemed distinguished enough by Union, Yale, and Princeton to award me tenure. As far as your complaint about the *New York Review of Books*, a quick search will show that no book of mine has ever once received a major review in that magazine. Which brings me to a major question about my books, Professor Summers. Have you read any of them? Have you listened to my CDs?"

"That's beside the point."

"I'm afraid that *is* the point. You're making unsubstantiated accusations against someone whom you know nothing about. If you really wanted to learn about my relationship with students, your research would show you that I've given no less than fifty lectures to student groups in my seven years here. I have a reputation for extending my office hours up to six hours to make sure every student is heard. Student meetings are absolutely vital to my mission as an educator."

"Then you'll appreciate what I'm about to say, Professor West. I want to have bi-monthly meetings with you."

"For what purpose?"

"To review the grades you give your students and stay abreast of your publications."

"Professor Summers, I am glad to meet with you whenever you like. You're the president of Harvard and, as such, you're surely entitled to meet a faculty member whenever you like. But if you think that I'm going to trot in here every two weeks to be monitored like a miscreant graduate student, I'm afraid, my brother, that you've messed with the wrong brother."

With that, I got up and left.

FOR DAYS AFTERWARDS, I THOUGHT about the meeting. I was asked about it by friends, family, and faculty. I had a heart-to-heart with my closest friend, my blood brother Cliff.

"Sitting in there, listening to this man go off on me," I told Cliff, "do you know what I was thinking about?"

"You were probably thinking about the way Dad's bosses treated him. Dad was the most talented and popular man in his department, but every time he'd be up for a promotion, the managers would come down on him like he wasn't worthy and needed to prove himself all over again."

"That's *exactly* what I was thinking about, my brother. Dad went through some stuff. He put up with some arrogance that I can't personally stomach."

"It's the way you're being disrespected, Corn, that gets to me. Given how hard you've worked and all you've achieved, being dishonored is a serious sign that's something really wrong with the way this new president is thinking."

"And the way it came out of the blue. I don't have to tell you, Cliff, that there's no real precedent for this in my adult life. I've never been attacked by any college where I've taught. Never been insulted. Never been abused. And so when this motherhucker jumps up and starts telling me what I should start writing and how I should stop hip-hopping, man, I think he's lost his cotton-pickin' mind."

"I feel you, Corn. What you going to do now?"

"I still got that other thing I need to focus on."

"You got that right, Corn. I'm praying about that other thing. That other thing's a lot more important than any messed-up Harvard president."

The other thing Cliff was talking about was cancer. Cancer was trying to eat its way through my body.

WOMB TO TOMB

THERE ARE MANY FORMS OF CANCER. There's the kind that gets
you from the inside and the kind that gets you from the outside.
When my inside cancer came on, the new millennium had started
and the George W. Bush days were about to begin. The cancer I
saw outside in the world was the one eating at the body politic.
That cancer was fueled by greed, and indifference to the poor and
disinherited. As it spread, it would corrode the nation's spirit and
weaken our economic immune system. It would darn near destroy
that system. It was a fast-moving cancer, an aggressive cancer
fueled by the toxins of unrestrained market-driven greed and a
misguided foreign policy based on imperialistic notions of entitlement and superiority. At the end of this period, the cancer would
leave the country wobbling, its culture in a state of deadly decay.

My internal cancer was unknown to me until I found myself
at a bar mitzvah in New Jersey. I was accompanied by my dear sister Leslie Kotkin, with whom I had begun a long-term companion-
ship. I originally met Leslie in her professional capacity as a skilled
dental hygienist. I immediately saw her as a warm and generous
Jewish sister of extraordinary sensitivity. I fell for her quickly, and
within a short period of time we were a couple.

After the bar mitzvah, Leslie and I attended the reception
when I ran into a friend. He started telling me about the alarming
results of his recent PSA exam, the test used to check out the possibility of prostate cancer.

"What were your last PSA results?" he asked me.

"Man," I said frankly, "I've never had that test."

"Well, Brother West," he said, "you may be a scholar when it comes to books, but I'll tell you this—you won't get high marks for taking advantage of modern medicine. You need to have that test."

Of course he was right. This was October 2001. Other things, though, were weighing heavily on my mind, namely legal procedures—the ongoing divorce lawsuit with Elleni and the child support demands being made by Aytul. The combination of both demands exceeded my resources. As I danced between courthouses, I let a couple of months go by before seeing a doctor.

When the PSA results came back, the doctor sat me down and said, "Professor West, this isn't good. You're off the chart. You're in trouble. If you were white, you'd have an 80 percent chance of surviving. As a black man, your chances are 20 percent. It's last-stage prostate cancer. This means the cancer is aggressive and spreading fast."

Naturally I was shook. But I was also not completely terrified. After all, the death shudder had come over me as a kid and never entirely gone away. It wasn't as if I hadn't been considering my own mortality for most of my life. Now, of course, it wasn't an abstract notion. Death was staring me in the face. I was told I had only a two-out-of-ten chance to survive.

My first thought? Deep and overwhelming gratitude for being allowed to sit at the banquet of life for nearly fifty years, bombarded by the indescribable love of family and friends that sustained me on each step of my journey.

"Well," I told Leslie, "if this thing gets me before they get it, I can't complain. I've had an abundance of blessings. I have no regrets. At the same time, let's see what the surgeons at this Boston hospital have to say."

"I think we might want to go to New York and see the surgeons at Sloan-Kettering," said Leslie, who was up on these things. "Sloan-Kettering is the best."

With that statement, Leslie may have well saved my life. Leslie also mentioned my condition to Skip Gates, who was extremely helpful. "Corn," said Skip, "you got to see Jerome Groopman. Jerome's the man." Groopman is famous for several books, including *Second Opinions* and *The Anatomy of Hope*. Brother Groopman, who worked out of Mass General in Boston, was quick to say, "Go see Peter Scardino. He's head of surgery at Sloan-Kettering. He knows more about prostate surgery than anyone."

So we ran down to New York and hooked up with Brother Scardino, a great guy. Scardino made a point I couldn't ignore. He felt that his method gave me a better chance for ongoing sexual functionality. There was no arguing with that.

Just before the surgery the nurse took my blood pressure. It was 120/79. She was surprised it was so normal. Prior to a four- or five-hour surgery, one's blood pressure usually elevates to high levels. She asked me how I felt.

I said, "I've reached an acceptance of my fate and especially an embrace of death, if God so wills it."

On the operating table, I was thinking once more of all the unbelievable blessings that I'd been given throughout my life. I didn't know whether I was going to die or not. I had to wait and see. But I refused to let death come in like a thief in the night and steal the joy and love I had already given and received. I was so grateful that God had allowed me to pursue my spiritual vocation of promoting unarmed truth and unconditional love.

Deep and mature spirituality is rooted in a wrestling with catastrophe. This is why Walter Benjamin is my secular soul-mate in twentieth-century philosophy. This is why the Garden of Gethsemane is so important. Even though God came into the world in human flesh to love, serve, and die, even God had to choose. Jesus said, "Let this cup pass from me." He still had to choose to have His will conform to the will of God. For me, death could come, because I had made my choice. Our unimagined victories in the face of catastrophic conditions like life-threatening illness are majestic evidence of God's love.

Armed with Groopman's hopeful mindset and Scardino's super surgical skills, they cut out the cancer and, some eight years later, I seem to have beaten the odds. Scardino was also right about the functionality. Thank you, Jesus.

The irony is that in my life, shot through with terrifying death shudders, I felt no terror in the face of the cancerous threat of death. In fact, I felt a profound sense of gratitude in having been alive, in being alive, and remaining alive after the surgery. And I have not felt a death shudder since that day.

Post-surgery was rough but made easier because Mom and Cliff flew in. Along with Leslie, they cared for me during recovery. Without those three incredible people—my mother, my brother, and my beautiful companion—I would not have made it. But make it I did. Dr. David Lodge continues to keep me healthy.

MEANWHILE, MY INTENTION WAS TO KEEP the whole Summers affair private. It was enough for the public to know that I was leaving Harvard for Princeton. I had deep connections to both schools. But the media got hold of the story and suddenly I was in the news. The media liked the story—they saw it as a heavyweight fight between a well-known African American prof and a brash new Harvard honcho. They gave it a Black-versus-Jewish subtext, making the conflict even sexier. The *Boston Globe* ran a story followed by the *New York Times*, which put it on page one. The *Times* never bothered to interview me. Instead they talked about Summers's equivocation on affirmative action. The subject of affirmative action, though, never even surfaced during my conversation with Summers. After the *Times*, things got crazier. I was getting calls from media the world over.

The attacks were vicious. Conservative columnist Brother George Will wrote that I got my post at Harvard only because of "racial entitlement." Summers's accusations were echoed by others. Without checking the facts, writers and TV pundits stated the charges as if they were facts—that I skipped classes all the time; that I refused to write new books; that the few books I had written were published eons ago and were mediocre at best; and that I was mau-mauing the Harvard president to boost my salary. One writer referred to me as the Eminem on the Charles, referring to the rapper and the river that runs by Cambridge. Enough was enough. How long do outrageous claims go unanswered? After months of silence, I decided to answer assertively. I appeared on Tavis Smiley's show, as well as *The O'Reilly Factor*. I also granted the

New York Times an interview. I told the simple truth about what had transpired in Summers's office.

Meanwhile, large numbers of students and certain faculty members—especially Professors David Carrasco and Randy Matory—were vocal in their support of me. A search was made that showed I had more academic references in academic professional journals than all other black scholars in the country with the exception of my Harvard colleague, friend, and fellow University Professor William Wilson. It was pointed out that I had more academic references than fourteen of the other seventeen Harvard University Professors, and, ironically, I had twice as many as Summers himself. In the beginning, the press seemed interested in beating up on me, but when the facts were made clear and the truth came out, the media became more critical of Summers. Seeing that he may have messed up, Summers called me for another meeting.

I was back in his office. He began with sincere questions about my health. I told him that I appreciated his concern, and that I was hopeful all would be well. I was surprised and moved to learn that he had once fought cancer, survived, and showed distinctive courage in the battle. All was cordial.

"I want to thank you for not playing the race card during this entire unfortunate episode," Summers said.

"In America," I said, "the whole deck is full of race cards. In this instance, though, other issues were at stake."

"I want to apologize to you, Professor West," he added.

"I accept your apology, Professor Summers, but I do want you to know that your accusations against me somehow authorized an army of right-wing and even neo-liberal writers to vent a flood of pent-up hostility in my direction. They have tried to destroy me."

"I want to apologize to you again, Professor West."

"I appreciate that, and again, I accept your apology."

That should have been that. But it wasn't. The next day, the *New York Times* went front-page with a story about our meeting, indicating that Summers had *not* apologized and, in fact, hadn't budged an inch from his original position. I immediately picked up the phone and called the president's office.

"Professor Summers," I said, "I'm sure you've seen the *Times*. Am I crazy, or did you or did you not apologize to me at least twice?"

"I did, Professor West," he assured me. "The reporter just got it wrong."

A little later, a contact of mine called and said, "Corn, I talked to the *Times* reporter. The reporter says that during the interview with Summers, Summers adamantly insisted that he never apologized to you—and never would. I'm afraid Summers is giving you the run-around."

The press wanted to know my version and this time I didn't hold back. I was ready with an analogy: "Larry Summers," I said, "is the Ariel Sharon of American higher education. The man's arrogant, he's an ineffective leader, and when it comes to these sorts of delicate situations, he's a bull in the China shop."

That led to counter-accusations that I was being anti-Semitic. I had heard those charges when I backed Minister Farrakhan's Million Man March and when I, along with my friend Rabbi Lerner, went to jail in opposition to Sharon's oppressive Palestinian policies. In any event, I wrote off Summers as a man I could never trust. That was a sad conclusion, but sadder still was the big picture that was finally coming into focus.

After this controversy had raged on for months, I was amazed at how few faculty members and journalists were actually interested in getting to the truth. When rumors started flying, why didn't the faculty members simply call me to ask what had really happened? Why didn't the journalists covering the story come to the source rather than repeat the false innuendos? My conclusion was that the academy was more spineless than ever, and the press was more intoxicated with sensationalizing than substantiating. I was also amazed how few observers got the bigger point. This was, in essence, a debate about the place and purpose of the university in the American empire. Here I was, a professor who had been tenured at Yale, Princeton, and Harvard, a scholar with more publications than 95 percent of his colleagues. Suddenly this professor was being bullied by a university president. This professor was being told how to live his intellectual life. Don't do hip-hop.

Don't write for mainstream journals. Restrict your audience to academics. Watch whom you campaign for. And submit to my scrutiny. Submit to my technocratic vision of higher education.

From my perspective, Professor Summers can express any views he likes on every subject from affirmative action to Israeli-Palestinian relations. And what better place to debate those issues than a free and open university, rather than one run by an administrator dealing in threats and blatant disrespect? The issue was academic freedom. Yet only an article in *Vanity Fair* by Brother Sam Tananhaus about the controversy addressed that issue. Most of the others were mere gossip.

The even larger question goes to the nature of academic engagement. I see it as a split between the technocratic and the democratic view of intellectual life. I want to move away from narrow elitism and address the larger culture. I want to reach youth culture. Without sacrificing scholarly excellence, I want to bridge the gap between what's happening in the ivory towers and what's happening in the 'hoods. Young folk of all of colors and classes need to know that we're concerned and involved in their lives. They need to feel that we're listening to them, not just with our ears but our hearts. They deserve our attention. Our attention is an extension of our love, and without loving compassion, no real dialogue can be established.

The fact that Summers, as the first Jewish president of Harvard—a school with an anti-Semitic and racist legacy—did not feel the need to deal with me and the Afro-American department with respect and sensitivity was a major disappointment. Given the dynamic between blacks and Jews, especially in the world of intellectuals, Summers could have shown real leadership. You lead with respect, not scorn. You treat others honorably, not suspiciously. In the place of haughtiness, you offer curiosity, understanding, and a genuine desire to learn. That the dialogue broke down between me and Professor Summers saddened me deeply. I wish we could have worked it out. But we didn't, and it was time for me to move on. How else could I respond to such deep disrespect? Nothing that Summers could say would eradicate the way he had dishonored me. And of course I never—not for a single instant—even considered acquiescing to the insulting monitoring program that he had demanded. The cool thing was to simply quit. But where would I go?

I'd first met my dear sister Shirley Tilghman, president of Princeton, at the inauguration of my dear sister Ruth Simmons at Brown University. That was the day Professor Simmons became the first black president of an Ivy League school.

"Cornel," Shirley said to me, "our door is always open to you."

When I left Harvard, Shirley was good to her word.

"Come on home," she said.

Her comment reminded me of when I originally came to Princeton to teach at the urging of Toni Morrison. The second time around, when Toni discovered that I was living in a house with no furniture, she graciously gave me a couch and two chairs.

In my discussions with Shirley, I saw that her visionary approach to higher education in many ways mirrored my own. I admired and adored her and, with gratitude, accepted the position—University Professor. The bluesman moves on.

DEATH, TAXES, AND LOVE

WHEN I WAS A YOUNG MAN, I heard an older brother say, "There are only three things in this world, son, that you gotta do—pay taxes, die, and stay black."

The words stuck but the meaning took time to hit home.

After the legal, professional, and financial challenges facing me, the words hit home. And they hit hard. The tax issues were entangled with the love issues. Ever since I found myself sleeping in Central Park as a result of giving everything to my first wife, Hilda, I hadn't gotten back on an even keel. Because I was the one who left the marriage—and in Aytul's case, the relationship—it was especially important to me that my spouse not feel as though I was being anything less than generous. Unfortunately, that put me in a vulnerable position, particularly when lawyers were introduced into the equation.

On top of that, for years I had a bad case of the IRS blues. I got behind and could never catch up. I could give you lots of reasons why but, on the most fundamental level, I can't excuse myself for creating a monetary mess. No matter how hard I tried, every year I found myself deeper in debt.

Someone once said, referencing James Brown, that "Cornel West is the Ivy League soul brother and the hardest working man in academia." Naturally I loved the analogy, but I can hardly prove the statement. The distinguished cultural critic, Greg Tate, once wrote to me that my soulful, intellectual work was an extension of James Brown's funk and Du Bois's intellectual calling. Other profs teach lots of courses, give lots of lectures, write lots of books, and do lots of political and societal work. I can say, though, that my work ethic is as much a part of my being as my Christian faith. Hard work was instilled in me from the gate. That drive has been a blessing. At some point in my life, the drive was accelerated when it became married to a mission. The mission was connected to a passion that has grown stronger every year.

When I arrived at Harvard as a teenager, I went through the experience of being born again. The Christian connotation is not inappropriate. Academically, intellectually, and spiritually, I was willing to die to emerge a more courageous, loving, and decent human being. Old assumptions were challenged. I was introduced to new ways of thinking—ancient ways of thinking, modern ways of thinking, non-Western ways of thinking—that resulted in the reconstitution of my psyche. After Harvard, I'd never be the same again.

At the same time—praise God!—I found that the new me and the old me could sit side by side in the church of my grandfather. I had developed intense scrutiny, only to learn that precepts of my childhood faith measured up to the test—and then some. The lesson taught by my elders—the same lesson, in fact, that their elders taught them—was that love is the core of it all. The rest is just sounding brass and tinkling cymbal. To come from a people who were denigrated, enslaved, and despised, and still place love in the center of life is to be part of a miracle. To love myself without hating others—even and especially those who may harbor hatred for me—is another expression of that miracle.

My conclusion became my calling: that justice is what love looks like in public, just as deep democracy is what justice looks like in practice. When you love people, you hate the fact that they're being treated unjustly. Justice is not simply an abstract concept to regulate institutions, but also a fire in the bones to promote the well-being of all.

Given my passion for love and its many healing forms, I have to ask myself these questions: why have I so often found myself in financial and romantic disrepair? Part of me wants to avoid the question and, instead, point to the successes that these women enjoyed after our relationship ended. I want to tell you that El-leni has become an international spokeswoman for the effort to conquer AIDS. The woman I met in a Howard Johnson restaurant so many years ago has emerged into a political leader who speaks in public before tens of thousands of people the world over. She is the head of the AIDS project at Harvard and often meets with the highest-ranking United Nations officials involved in solving the cri-sis. Stanford University has recognized her extraordinary work.

Hilda has had a number of careers, each more successful than the last. Today, she runs her own high-tech electronics firm and has become a businesswoman of ingenuity and integrity. Ramona is per-haps the most-loved schoolteacher in all of New York City, a shining light and positive influence in the lives of her many students.

Mary Johnson and Michele Wallace continue to make their mark in the highest of intellectual circles. And of course the di-vine Kathleen Battle continues to grace the stages of concert halls and opera houses in the great cities of world culture. Aytul contin-ues her work as an outstanding journalist and author. And Leslie continues to thrive in heart and mind.

Thus I build my case as a blessed man, a man who has known, lived with, and loved these beautiful women. But I also realize that my inability to stay with a woman cannot be counted as char-acter strength. I look, for example, at the character of my own fa-ther and his unmatched example as a family man of stability and remarkable integrity. The mature love between Mom and Dad set a standard I could never ever approximate, let alone achieve.

Only a few months ago, some fifteen years after Dad had passed, an extraordinary thing happened to me. After a lecture in Memphis, several hundred people lined up just to say hello. One of them, though, stopped me cold.

"You don't know me, Brother West," he said, "but I knew your mama Irene, your sisters Cheryl and Cynthia, your brother Cliff, and your daddy. I was in Shiloh with Reverend Cooke. I even knew your man Deacon Hinton. I knew 'em all."

"Lord, have mercy!" I said. "What's your name?"

"I'm Nate Walker. And I've stood in line not only to tell you that you gave a good word today, Brother West, but also to tell you something about your daddy you never knew. You see, I worked with the man at McClellan Air Force base. Yes sir, I worked beside Cliff West for many years. He was the leader of the black caucus on the base, where everyone knew that racism was intense. We just didn't get promoted. Discrimination was rampant.

"Well, one day your father was asked by his superiors to write a report about which jobs could be eliminated among the black employees. Cliff took the assignment seriously. A week later, he read the report to both us and the white power establishment. There was only one recommendation: that Cliff's own job be eliminated. We were shocked. Couldn't believe it. Rather than doing us in, he offered himself up as a sacrificial lamb.

"In the end, though, the white folk wouldn't fire him. You see, he was their bridge builder between us and them. They also knew that we'd go crazy if anything happened to big Cliff. So nothing did happen. He told us not to tell anyone, especially your mama. Miss Irene wouldn't be happy knowing that her husband, with all them mouths to feed, had put his neck on the chopping block like that. But believe you me, when your daddy walked through that base, every last one of us bowed down to him.

"So when I hear you talking on television that you ain't half the man your daddy was, much as I respect you, Brother West, I couldn't agree more."

Amen.

TEACHABLE MOMENTS

SOME ENTERTAINERS ARE ALSO BLESSED to be profound teachers. I think of the genius of Bob Dylan. Dylan came to mind not long ago when I was at the airport on my way to Germany for Zeytun's birthday. I was at the gate talking to Mom on the cell when I noticed a brother patiently waiting to approach me. When I hung up, he came over and, with a sweet sincerity, said, "Professor West, my name is Winston, and I've only wanted to meet two people in my life. Frederick Douglass and you. I'll never meet Frederick, but thank God today I can meet you."

"Well, thank you, my dear brother," I said. "That's a mighty compliment."

"I don't want to take up too much of your time, professor," Winston went on to say, "but I do have to tell you this: I've played drums for Bob Dylan for years. We travel the world together, and sometimes your name comes up. Both Bob and I love and respect you. Once, when I mentioned you to Bob, he said something I'll never forget. 'Cornel West,' said Dylan, 'is a man who lives his life out loud.'"

"Lord, have mercy!" I said. "I've never heard that formulation before. Tell Brother Dylan that I love him as well, and that even though he doesn't know me personally, he sure-enough knows my heart."

Dylan's heart rests in his vocation. He is a white bluesman par excellence. His voice is born out of that vocation, informed by a vision rooted in reaching and teaching as many people as possible.

Reaching and teaching is my greatest joy as well, especially lighting a fire in the minds of young people. Every year at Princeton

I insist on teaching freshmen. I want to be part of their academic lives, knowing that connecting with them at an early juncture might move their stories in a positive direction.

In my freshman seminar on "The Tragic, The Comic, and The Political," we read works such as Plato's *Republic*, Sophocles's *Antigone*, Dante's *Inferno*, Shakespeare's *Hamlet*, essays by Kant and Hume, fiction by Dostoyevsky, Kafka, and Nathanael West, and plays by Ibsen, Chekhov, Hansberry, Lorca, Williams, O'Neill, Soyinka, and Beckett. The course focuses on the never-ending activity of paideia—deep education—and the problem of evil. Freshmen begin with a sense of trepidation in the face of this formidable parade of great texts.

How does my freshman seminar in humanities differ from those of my colleagues? My lens as a bluesman is to begin with the catastrophic, the horrendous, the calamitous and monstrous in life. So Plato's discussion of death that inaugurates the *Republic*, Hamlet's discussion of Yorick with the grave diggers in Shakespeare's classic play, or Gregor's transformation into a huge, foul vermin in Kafka's *The Metamorphosis* initiates us into the traumatic coping with "humando"—with burial, death, and the worms waiting for us in the soil. In this way, the tragicomic sensibilities of a bluesman are an essential feature of the rich humanist tradition.

Initially, students are quite shaken with this stress on the fragility of their lives and the inevitability of their own death. Yet as they examine these great texts and see the centrality of death and rebirth, of learning how to die to learn how to live, they are initiated into paideia. I consider this a life-long initiation in deep education, a priceless contribution to their lives and to my life as a teacher. In fact, my enthusiastic teaching itself at my beloved Princeton is a living testimony to the sheer transformative power of paideia.

TEACHABLE MOMENTS DO NOT JUST HAPPEN in the classroom. They are shot through everyday life and take place in a variety of contexts. To be teachable is to muster the courage to listen generously, think critically, and be open to the ambiguity and mystery of life. For example, I began as a fierce critic of black leaders Reverend

Jesse Jackson, Reverend Al Sharpton, Minister Louis Farrakhan, Bishop T.D. Jakes, and Barack Obama. But after breaking bread with all five and spending countless hours in rich dialogue, I realized how short-sighted I had been. All five men had much to teach me, and I certainly had a deep love for each of them. We vowed to continue the conversation for the rest of our lives. Of course, it mattered that we disagreed deeply on many subjects. But what mattered more was the mutual love and respect that came out of those meetings.

THERE WAS ANOTHER IMPROMPTU MEETING that took me by surprise. I was at Reagan Airport in D.C., munching on a hot dog in the waiting area, when I looked up to see Supreme Court Justice Clarence Thomas and his beloved wife standing nearby.

I approached the justice and said, "It's a pleasure to meet you. I just spoke at a school where you had spoken and given encouragement to young students."

"Thank you. It's a pleasure to meet you too, Professor West. I do have to say, though, you've uttered some awfully harsh words about me."

"Yes, they were based on principle and had nothing to do with personal attacks."

"I do welcome criticism and wish we had more time to discuss our differences. Please feel free to visit my home."

With that, we hugged and went our separate ways. It is this spirit of breaking bread that I cherish.

ONE OF MY GRAND MOMENTS of being taught took place during the presidential campaign of my dear brother Bill Bradley. During the Iowa primary, I met the Boston Celtic star, Bill Russell. His wisdom blew me away. I shall never forget his profound and poignant words. He told Brother Bradley and me "to absorb wounds with dignity and turn defiance into determination and to win with integrity." If ever there was a grand bluesman in sports, it was Bill Russell.

I also cherish historical links and historical continuity. Like my favorite philosopher Gadamer, tradition is central to my understanding of vocation. But it is a tradition of critique and resistance. At its best, it is a tradition of bearing witness to love and justice.

AS A FRESHMAN AT HARVARD, I experienced such a historical link in this grand tradition when attending the lectures of Shirley Graham Du Bois, the widow of the W.E.B. Du Bois, the greatest black scholar ever to walk the streets of America.

Yet the story of another such witness both alarmed and troubled me.

It was 1990, and I was walking with John Hope Franklin, the second most famous black scholar, in the hills of Bellagio, Italy. We were attending a conference put together by the prophetic figure, Marian Wright Edelman, for poor black children. Above us, the sky was a baby blue. Below us, Lake Como was comforting and calm. Professor Franklin, a man of quiet dignity with an enchanting smile, was in a reflective mood.

"Cornel," he said, "let me tell you a story that I rarely share. It's about me and W.E.B. Du Bois."

"Wow. Did you know him well?"

"No one knew him *that* well, but my first encounter with him was extraordinary."

"What was it like?"

"I was at a hotel in North Carolina in 1938. I recognized W.E.B. Du Bois sitting in the lobby. He was reading a newspaper. I approached him with great respect and anticipation.

"'Dr. Du Bois,' I said, 'good morning, sir. My name is John Hope Franklin.'

"Du Bois did not react. His eyes remained fixated on the newspaper to the point that he didn't even acknowledge my presence. No matter, I wasn't about to leave. After all, this was the great W.E.B. Du Bois.

'Dr. Du Bois,' I reiterated, 'I am named after John Hope, the president of Atlanta University.'

"Still, no reaction. But, Cornel, I could not imagine leaving without some interaction. So one last time, I said, 'Sir, I am a Harvard graduate student in the same program that awarded you your Ph.D.'

"After several long seconds of silence, Du Bois gave me a quick cursory glance. A glance, mind you, not a word. I slowly walked away."

As I looked into the eyes of John Hope Franklin, I could see inner tears of deep disappointment. The incident might have occurred a half-century earlier, but Professor Franklin made it feel like it happened yesterday.

My gut reaction was, if it had been me, I would have rhetorically slapped Du Bois upside the head and said, "You can at least take a second to say hello." But on further reflection, I recognized that he was who he was—an intellectual freedom fighter and an elitist. I have come to realize that everybody's who they are, and not somebody else. And I believe that Professor Franklin, though his heart was broken, reached the same conclusion. The happy footnote to this story is that years later Du Bois and Franklin became friends. Did Du Bois ever realize whom he failed to acknowledge that morning in North Carolina? We will never know.

What does it mean to be an educated person? Academic accolades and doctoral degrees are one measure of education, but life experience and selfless service are another. One of the most moving experiences I have ever had took place at the 2009 commencements at Morehouse and Spelman. Both events took place on the same day at these historical black institutions where education and empowerment are rooted in the unique brotherhood and sisterhood that comes from a tradition of excellence.

In the morning over 400 young, brilliant black men graduated in pomp and circumstance. At various moments, they placed the academic hoods over each other's heads. As I reflected on my time spent with precious young black men in prisons, on blocks of the 'hood, or just in trouble, tears flowed from my eyes. Listening to the valedictorian's speech and the honoring of those who were graduating was a deeply humbling moment.

In the evening over 500 young, brilliant black women graduated. Just before I was about to give the commencement address, the Spelman College glee club broke into beautiful song filling our hearts with the powerful Negro spiritual, "I Can't Tarry"—"I've got to keep running, running, running as I ascend to the kingdom." Tears again flowed from my eyes. I thought of the powerful new wave of national and global leaders distinctively black and female.

What a blessing to bear witness to these students' glorious achievements. I am their servant and I can't tarry.

Today's graduates are being launched into an uncharted era. The election of the first African American president and the necessity for the nation and the world to discuss issues of race is a profound teachable moment. That is why we must not confuse the empty media category of "post-racial" with the reality of America becoming less racist. The former is an empty illusion, the latter is a grand achievement. For example, when white brothers and sisters in Iowa chose Obama based on his qualifications and not pigmentation, they were not post-racial but less racist than their forebears. In Gary, Indiana, when black voters chose a white mayor over other black candidates, they were not post-racial but rather citizens choosing qualification over pigmentation.

When Obama burst on the scene in Boston at the Democratic National Convention in 2004 proclaiming that America is a magical place, I turned to my dear brother Tavis Smiley and said, "This brother is going to have a Christopher Columbus experience. He's going to discover America!" The greatness of the American democratic experiment has nothing to do with magic but rather the blood, sweat, and tears of ordinary people endeavoring to create a fragile yet noble democracy. And when Obama says his story is only possible in America, he should not forget about the Brazilian president Lula, who dropped out of grade school, or the female heads of state in India, Germany, Chile, and Liberia. By comparison, America lags behind. We need not have Disneyland-like lies about ourselves to acknowledge the grand achievements we have made.

I have a deep appreciation of Obama's brilliance, charisma, and his sense of a fresh start for the nation. In my times with him as a presidential candidate, he struck me as a decent person filled with a sense of destiny. Brother Obama's amiable personality often wants to put a smile on everyone's face and thereby give the impression that he agrees with everyone. My constant worry is that he can be easily mesmerized by fast-talking establishment figures whose braininess lacks wisdom, vision, and commitment.

This dangerous strategy moves toward the center for likeability when often the truth lies not in the middle but beneath the mediocrity of the superficial exchange. The deep tension in Obama's vision and expression of democratic rhetoric and technocratic policies reflects his own divided mind about the crucial role of mobilizing everyday people while satisfying the elite establishment.

I HAVE COME TO APPRECIATE the power that film has to educate, inspire, and entertain. So when I received a call from Brother Larry Wachowski, the co-director of *The Matrix*, I was excited. He said, "Dr. West, my brother and I have been deeply influenced by your writings on philosophy, religion, and race. We have written the role of Councilor West for our next two films, and we would love for you to play the part."

I replied, "Congratulations on your achievement. I salute your genius. I'd love to play the role, but only if it has grace and dignity."

Indeed, it did. The next thing I knew I was on my way to Sydney, Australia. I had never experienced the challenge of being an actor during the filming of a movie. I was deeply encouraged by my neighbor on the set, Laurence Fishburne, as well as fellow actors such as Jada Pinkett Smith, Keanu Reeves, and Anthony Ray Parker.

During one fascinating moment in the middle of a dramatic scene, I shouted, "Cut!" The actors laughed.

Brother Larry said, "Brother West, I'm the director. Only I can say 'Cut!'"

I replied, "But a giant of film and theater just walked in, and we must pay tribute to his presence." I then pointed to Roscoe Lee Browne, and we all broke into spontaneous applause.

Later, even the excitement of filming was eclipsed by the film premieres in Los Angeles and New York. I was honored to escort the beloved mother of Brothers Larry and Andy to the L.A. opening night.

My *Matrix* connection did not end with the initial release of the film. I was also asked to be a major spokesperson to the media. Additionally, religious scholar Ken Wilbur and I were invited to provide scene-by-scene commentary for the *Matrix* Trilogy DVD box set. We spent over two days, buried in the studio with Larry there to encourage us.

I consider *The Matrix* to be a cultural monument marking the turn of the century in America. This is due to its moral vision, technological wizardry, and multicultural embrace. For the first time in American film people of color are at the center of the future.

The teachable moment provided by Tavis Smiley's documentary classic, *Stand*, lays bare the rich humanity of black men in a way unprecedented on screen. It was a great honor and joy to be part of Tavis's visionary and courageous work of art. For the first time in American film, black men were seen praying, crying, holding hands, and hugging, as well as engaging in sophisticated intellectual discussions about politics, religion, culture, and music. Our soul patrol that has existed for years was now made manifest for millions. In this age of Obama, where America is still filled with too many negative stereotypes of black men, the film *Stand* presents the best of who we are.

One of the personally moving moments in the film is our trip to Jubilee Hall at Fisk University, where Mom and Dad first met when they were students. I kissed the exact spot Dad first met Mom. I imagined when he first saw her there, she blew his mind, and the rest is West family history.

At the film's premier in Los Angeles, and at subsequent screenings in Philadelphia, Memphis—and especially my hometown Sacramento at the Irene B. West Elementary School on my fifty-sixth birthday, fifteen years after my father's funeral with my whole family and whole community present—I witnessed an incredible overflow of catharsis, tears, and laughter.

The depths of healing catalyzed by community-sponsored *Stand* screenings was reflected in ritual handshakes, standing ovations, and never-ending, loving embraces that affirmed black manhood. One brother said to me, "*Stand* hit me so hard in my

heart, I hadn't been moved like that since my mother's funeral."
Another brother commented, "This movie changed my life. I'm
now dedicated to being a better person." Participating in *Stand*
with my dear brothers in the film and my dear brothers and sisters
at screenings across the country has been a sublime experience.

"YOU ARE LOVED"

To My Beloved Clifton and Zeytun West:

MY PRIMARY AIM IN LIFE is to be of value to you. This means first and foremost to let you know and feel that you are loved no matter what you do or where you are. To be loved is to be and to be fully human is to cultivate the capacity to give and receive love. It is a gift of grace that you have loving mothers and loving relatives who are willing to support your dreams. Yet it is your choice whether or not you will allow our love to direct and guide you to wisdom and maturity.

The first steps toward wisdom and maturity are to gain self-respect and self-confidence. There can be no quest for wisdom without a healthy regard for one's self. And there can be no advent of maturity without a strong belief in oneself. The benchmark of wisdom is the courage to examine oneself fearlessly just as the hallmark of maturity is the courage to exercise constant humility in the pursuit of a noble cause greater than oneself. The perennial foes of wisdom and maturity are arrogance toward others, manipulation of others, and seizing undue entitlements for oneself.

The most essential lesson I can offer from my twentieth-century life for your twenty-first-century lives is to find and sustain joy every day that you breathe by touching the lives of others and inspiring people through your example to reach higher and serve better. There is no doubt I have fallen short of my lofty goals. But my fallible efforts as a blues philosopher to spread paideia, to make deep education a democratic force for good, and to make the struggle for justice a desirable way of life, have brought me great joy.

I do want you to be happy, but more importantly I want you to seek wisdom. I want you to be so full of self-respect that you cannot but respect others. I want you to be so self-confident that you breed self-confidence in others. I want you to elevate yourselves by uplifting others and to love yourselves by being of service to others. And as a Christian, I beseech you to bear your cross in life with faith, courage, and compassion.

Despite all the hype about globalization and multicultural exchange in the twenty-first century, your crucial tasks in life remain the same as mine—to make it from womb to tomb with grace and dignity such that your contributions leave the world better than you found it. The true measure of your humanity will always rest upon the depth of your love and the quality of your service to others.

I have great hope for you and your life's journeys and I pray you never forget, when we are long gone, the depth of sacrifice made for you, by generations past and those who loved you dearly.

Love,
Dad

GOING AWAY BLUES

"YOU JUST GOT HERE," the lady tells the bluesman. "Can't you stick around?"

"Blues won't let me," the cat says. "Can't stay in one place. Gotta keep moving."

My raw blues—the blues of my life—has to do with voicing the social misery of "the least of these," those less fortunate than myself. And what bluesman doesn't face some unexpected lyrics tied up with women and money? Nothing unusual about that. But the way that I sing my blues—in lectures and books, on hip-hop albums and TV shows, in adult-education classes and prisons, in college auditoriums and church pulpits—well, that *is* unusual.

The fact that my blues have spread to Africa, Central America, Latin America, Europe, the Middle East, and Asia is an international phenomenon that stirs me up even more. It means I just gotta keep on steppin'. What a blessing it was to deliver the Edward Said Memorial Lecture in Cairo, Egypt, the Nelson Mandela Lecture in Pretoria, South Africa, the UNESCO Lecture in Santiago, Chile, and the Albert Einstein Forum Lecture in Berlin, Germany. Benjamin Barber's historic interdependence movement has taken me to Casablanca, Mexico City, Brussels, and Istanbul. Steppin' is my character, my mission, my joy.

As a bluesman, though, I carry the pain that I have caused others. I say my calling comes before my romantic relationships, and surely it does. But are they mutually exclusive or am I someone unable to simply settle down?

I like singing my blues. Like many a bluesman before me, I like my spirits. As a lover of Jesus, I could live without my cognac and Captain Black Gold tobacco in my pipe, but I'd hate to be tested.

I like moving from city to city, country to country, gig to gig, offering up my version of the truth to anyone inclined to listen. I like talking my talk, doing my thing. I like to get paid for my songs, though I sing many for free.

I like seeing *Race Matters* translated into Japanese, Italian, and Portuguese. I like seeing *The American Evasion of Philosophy* translated into Chinese, Spanish, and Italian. I like that there are hundreds of thousands of copies of my book *Democracy Matters* translated into Spanish. There's also an edition that's selling in the French-speaking world. I like the fact that all nineteen of my books are still in print with the exception of the two that won the American Book Award in 1993.

I like being the first black recipient of the James Madison Medal, the highest award given to a graduate of the Graduate School of Princeton University.

I like the fact that seven insightful books, both scholarly and mainstream, have been published on my life and work. I hope that this represents the positive impact of my work on the lives of others.

I like that my only piece of published fiction, "Sing a Song," has been adapted into a play by Andreas Patterson at Alabama State University.

I like that the remarkable young hip-hop artist Lupe Fiasco has honored me by naming his Grammy-nominated album *The Cool* after a lecture I gave in Chicago. Lupe was in the audience when I suggested that we must view intellectual engagement as something cooler than bling bling. My two-hour dialogue with Lupe at Calvin College in Grand Rapids, Michigan forever remains an inspiration to me.

I like learning that my beloved grand niece, Deja, won the Cornel West Distinguished Award at John F. Kennedy High School in Sacramento, the same school attended by me and my brother Cliff, her grandfather.

I like performing with those bebop jazz giants, the Heath Brothers, thanks to the grand Renaissance man James Mtume, the son of Jimmy Heath. And who wouldn't be honored to work on the same stage with Sweet Honey in the Rock, the famous artistic activists with deep gospel roots? I was also honored to collaborate with the renowned dance group of Lula Washington.

I like that on my most recent CD, *Never Forget: A Journey of Revelations*, I collaborated with outstanding artists like Talib Kweli, KRS-One, Jill Scott, Andre 3000, and Cliff West.

I was delighted to be named MTV Artist of the Week and gratified when the album hit the Billboard charts: #1 Spoken Word and #37 R&B/Hip Hop.

I like the thrill of collaborating with the incomparable musical genius of our time, Prince, who had graciously invited me to his Bel Air mansion. When I walked through the door, I was directly approached by a beautiful Latina, who was overflowing with intellectual passion. She wanted to discuss everyone from Nietzsche to Lou Salome. We talked and danced for hours to the live music of Prince, Stevie Wonder, Herbie Hancock, and John Legend. At evening's end, I told the sweet lady that it was a delight. Salma Hayek went her way and I went mine.

I like that I've been invited to perform on the albums of many other good people: Gerald Levert, Rhymefest, Raheem DeVaughn, Dead Prez, John Mellencamp, Cornel West Theory—a prophetic Christian hip-hop group that honored me by adopting my name— jazz icon Terrence Blanchard, and the upcoming artist Ohene. I also cherish my relationship with my dear brother Wynton Marsalis, the reigning icon and exemplar of excellence in contemporary jazz.

I like that these days more people recognize me from my little movie roles than my books. Ironically, I made my film debut in *The Matrix Reloaded*, the movie that broke all existing box office records. At the kind invitation of the incomparable Wachowski brothers, Larry and Andy, I flew down to Sydney, Australia where both *The Matrix Reloaded* and *The Matrix Revolutions* were being shot. When the DVD boxed set trilogy came out I was privileged to do a scene-by-scene commentary, along with religious scholar Ken Wilbur. I've performed in films such as Adam Nemett's *The Instrument*, Astra Taylor's *Examined Life*, Justin Dillon's *Call + Response*, *The Private Lives of Pippa Lee*, directed by Rebecca Miller (daughter of my dear brother, the late great Arthur Miller), and Tavis Smiley's documentary, *Stand*.

I am also pleased to work with Warrington and Reggie Hudlin at the Black Film Foundation—a seminal institution in Hollywood. I was also among the first fellows at the British Film Institute in London, led by my dear brother Colin McCabe.

I like that, although I've been highly critical of dumbed-down TV shows, I've also seized opportunities to use the medium, as the classical poet Horace defined entertainment—to instruct and delight. I can't tell you how many times I've been on C-SPAN, all due to the support of its visionary founder, my good friend Brian Lamb. I am always delighted to appear on Amy Goodman's progressive *Democracy Now* show on a regular basis. When my dear brother Bill Maher calls, as he frequently does, I do my best to hop out to L.A. and work with him on *Real Time*. I revel in his comic brilliance and progressive politics even as I joyfully wrestle with his agnosticism. Furthermore, I have made numerous appearances on my dear brother Tavis Smiley's show on PBS—the best talk show in the business. He has also been kind enough to have me serve as a commentator for seven years on his radio show on PRI brilliantly produced by the late Sheryl Flowers.

I like rereading Alfred North Whitehead on the adventure of ideas, Eric Auerbach on the history of Western literature, Harold Goddard on Shakespeare, Eric Bentley on the life of the drama, Walter Kerr on tragedy and comedy, Ernst Robert Curtius on the Latin middle ages, Eric Voegelin on Plato, M.H. Abrams on romanticism, Harold Bloom on canonical texts, or George Santayana on anything.

I like knowing that the Cornel West Academy of Excellence, founded by Antoine L. Medley of Future Black Men of America in Raleigh, North Carolina, is dedicated to "helping young black boys become responsible black men."

I like the fact that the beautiful Cornel West Wall exists on Martin Luther King Boulevard in Trenton, New Jersey. I am grateful for the illustrious talent of artist Luv One.

I like having public dialogues with leading philosophic thinkers like Alain Badiou, Slavoj Zizek, Simon Crichley, Robert George, and Judith Butler.

I like critically examining and joyfully celebrating the artistic genius of Jane Austen by giving one of the major interviews for the historic exhibition of her written manuscripts and letters at the Morgan Library and Museum in New York City.

I like being one of the inaugurators, along with Darell Fields, Kevin Fuller, and Milton Curry, of the black architectural magazine *Appendx*—the only journal of black architectural theory.

I like using the spotlight of public dialogues to highlight the struggle for love and justice. Teaching, like the preaching I was raised on, can be entertaining without losing an iota of its substance.

I like being a twenty-first-century cosmopolitan open to the cultures of the world and eager to learn from different peoples around the globe.

I like being a free black man who is never afraid or ashamed to be joyously full of gut-bucket sophistication, refined funk, and deep love.

MY STORY, LIKE ALL OF OUR STORIES, is a work in progress. At several junctures and in several ways, it breaks down. That's because, as a cracked vessel, I break down. I try to love my crooked neighbor with my crooked heart. I try to rid myself of prejudices, but always fall short.

I often talk about how all of us live on the edge. Catastrophes are a constant part of our lives on the planet. Disease is always a threat—disease of the body and mind. Staying sane in this world of ours is no easy task. You could lose it. I could lose it. Any of us could. To retain peace of mind and equanimity of spirit is no easy task. As the product of an oppressed, resilient, joyful people, I take refuge in my heritage. My heritage sees life through a tragicomic lens. The comedy is not without dire consequences and the tragedy is not without soul-saving humor.

I am encouraged by the ascendancy of President Barack Obama for whom I worked tirelessly—from campaigning in the cold days of Iowa through over twenty events in a two-day marathon in the swing state of Ohio. As he aspires to be the black Lincoln, I intend to be a blacker Frederick Douglass.

I am encouraged that racism, deep-seated and long-lasting, did not overpower the worthiness of his cause. I am blessed to have lived long enough to see the end of the age of Reagan, the era of conservatism. Barack stepped out on faith and landed on something solid. I hope that the age of Obama is the age of empowering everyday people rather than a recycling of neo-liberal mediocrity. Like all of us, he's got to keep on steppin' too. He'll need all the faith in the world. I believe that faith is that fiduciary dimension in the human condition where we admit that we can't live on doubt. We can't survive on arguments. Logic won't do it. To get up in the morning and do the monumental tasks that face us, our labor is best fueled by love. That's the only way we can move forward—with decency and dignity. That's the only way we can turn our devotion to others.

Meanwhile, the empire continues to wobble and we all continue to waver. There are declines in our culture and decay in our hearts. As the Spinners said, we need a mighty love. We need a mighty healing. I look back at my life, knowing that without that healing love—from my grandparents and parents, from my brother and sisters, from my children and the women I have been blessed to know—I would have spun out a long time ago. This broken vessel would have plain collapsed.

So I say, thank you, Jesus.

I say, thank you, Lord.

I say, thank you for the breath in my lungs and the strength in my loins. May that strength endure so that I can serve you. And in serving you, may I serve others, especially the least of these.

NOTA BENE

GRATITUDE

*At times our own light goes out and is rekindled by a spark
from another person. Each of us has cause to think with deep
gratitude of those who have lighted the flame within us.*

— Albert Schweitzer

I AM ONE GRATEFUL NEGRO. And I must express deep gratitude
for Tavis Smiley. He is the younger brother I never had, and I am
the older brother he never had. Tavis has also become an adopted
brother to my siblings and a son to my mother. In a very real way,
he has been incorporated fully into the West family. He and I are inseparable. Just as Tavis has expressed gratitude for whatever I might
have taught him, I am equally grateful for all he has taught me.

Tavis and I have in common an undying passion for service.
In our friendship, we've pledged to be faithful until death. But our
faithfulness is not based on material or political gain. Our end and
aim are unarmed truth and unconditional love.

On the deepest level, we are connected by our profound commitment to the legacy of Martin Luther King, Jr. That commitment is rooted in our Christian faith. Tavis, a Pentecostal, and I, a
Baptist, meet at the cross. And it is at the cross where we find Dr.
King—a devout disciple of Jesus Christ—whose spirit inspires us to
serve and love a world in need.

The spirit of Martin lives on in Brother Tavis.

I POINT TO THE UNIQUENESS OF MY journey with the certain knowledge that all our journeys are unique.

In the case of intellectuals, we follow different paths, encounter different teachers and, if we do our job well, nurture students who themselves will carry on a tradition of loving service to others.

When I think back to the uniqueness of my journey, I'm amazed. I was strongly supported by the Ford Foundation during my graduate years and received the Prize for Cultural Freedom from the Lannan Foundation in recent years.

As a professor, it has been my policy to never apply for any money in regard to sustaining my work. I have never received any fellowship or subsidies. In fact, I have never even solicited one letter of recommendation in my thirty-two years of teaching, even though I've written thousands of them for others. My attitude may appear a bit crazy, but this is how I remain a free black man in the predominantly white academy.

I've also been blessed to teach and be taught in an incredibly wide variety of circumstances. There's the on-the-ground teaching at prisons and churches and public schools. There's Harvard, Princeton, Union, and Yale. There's the University of Paris. And there's a list of world-class academic figures with whom I studied closely as an undergraduate and graduate student. And because I dare to resist the condition of namelessness for those who have made such a rich contribution to my life, I take great joy in calling the roll.

John Rawls, Hilary Putnam, Stanley Cavell, Roderick Firth, Israel Scheffler, Hans-Georg Gadamer, Bernard Williams, Robert Nozick, Samuel Beer, H. Stuart Hughes, Talcott Parsons, Richard Rorty, Thomas Kuhn, Carl Hempel, Paul Benacerraf, Walter Kaufmann, Thomas Scanlon, Peter Gomes, Malcolm Diamond, Thomas Nagel, Sir Arthur Lewis, Gregory Vlastos, Terry Irwin, Sheldon Wolin, Richard Grandy, Raymond Geuss, David Hoy, G.A. Cohen, Joel Porte, Daniel Aaron, Thorkild Jacobsen, Paul Hanson, G. Ernest Wright, and, above all, Martin Kilson and Preston Williams.

At Union, the blessings mounted: my dear brother James Washington deepened my spiritual faith as did James Cone, James Forbes, Beverly Harrison, Donald Shriver (the president who hired me), Roger Shinn, Bob Seaver, Christopher Morse, Robert Handy,

Ann Ulanov, and Tom Driver. I also received great wisdom and support from colleagues at Columbia: Edward Said, Paul Bové, Jonathan Arac, Sidney Morgenbesser, Anders Stephanson, Stanley Aronowitz, and Margaret Ferguson.

In the spirit of call-and-response, it's also been a sheer delight to co-teach in dialogical form courses in philosophy and the arts with magnificent colleagues like Eddie Glaude, Jr., James Cone, Nell Irvin Painter, Wahneema Lubiano, Eduardo Cadava, Elisabeth Schüssler Fiorenza, Ronald Thiemann, Robert George, Peter Guralnick, Guthrie Ramsey, Serene Jones, Gary Dorrien, Constanze Güthenke, Leora Batnitzky, and especially Jeff Stout, the best teaching partner imaginable. Those Monday night dinners at the Stout house with Jeff and his lovely wife Sally were grand reprieves from my daily diet of hot dogs and potato chips. And for the remainder of my life, I will relish the precious memory of co-teaching at Harvard the last course in the distinguished career of Hilary Putnam, one of the few philosophic geniuses alive. However, the memory of giving one of the eulogies at Stanford for my beloved mentor Richard Rorty—the most influential American philosopher of our time—remains a moment I will forever cherish.

It was Daphne Brooks, my colleague at Princeton, who came up with the concept of celebrating one of the musical geniuses of our time, James Brown. Thanks to Daphne's brilliant mind and profound scholarship, the James Brown Conference, the first of its kind, was a triumphant success and a beautiful way to honor a man the academy had both dismissed and demeaned.

My intellectual fire also was fueled by my humanist colleagues at Princeton: my dear brothers and sisters Peter Brown, Anthony Grafton, Kwame Anthony Appiah, Alexander Nehamas, Caryl Emerson, Sean Wilentz, Eric Gregory, D. Graham Burnett, and Danielle Allen. Needless to say, the sheer presence of the prophetic economist and Nobel Prize laureate Paul Krugman is an intellectual delight.

My friends have also meant the world to me.

Michael Pfleger is one of the grand prophetic voices in contemporary Christendom. I am blessed to preach every February in his Chicago church, St. Sabina. How could I not love a white Catholic brother who has devoted his life to ministering in the black South Side of Chicago with such love and commitment to justice?

My two dear brothers with whom I shared rooms at Harvard College remain an active part of my life. Robert Gerrard and Neil Brown are exemplary human beings whose fusion of mind, heart, and soul inspire me. And we shall never forget Brother Roberto Garcia, our valiant Puerto Rican comrade and friend.

Even earlier, my friendship with Glenn Jordan, distinguished professor at the University of Glamorgan in Cardiff, Wales, changed my life.

Professor David L. Smith, the first black dean at Williams College, has been such a loyal and loving friend.

Reverend Michael Horton, novelist and pastor of two major Seventh Day Adventist churches in Chicago, and Lovell Jackson have been pillars of my spiritual life.

In the spirit of piety—my reverent attachment to those who sustain me—let me testify to two noteworthy young black intellectuals who died before their time: James Snead and Ulysses Santamaria. Snead, a literary scholar and jazz musician, carved new wood when it came to black intellectualism. He wrote on Faulkner, Mann, Joyce, Proust, and Baldwin. I was honored to co-edit, with Colin MacCabe, Snead's classic texts, *White Screens, Black Images: Hollywood from the Dark Side and Racist Traces and Other Writings*, on which we were joined by co-editor Kara Keeling. When Brother James died, he and I were working on a joyous and serious book, a semiotic analysis of black culture beginning with a close reading of Melville's *Benito Cereno*.

Ulysses Santamaria was born in Mississippi, educated in Spain, trained in Paris and Frankfurt, and wound up teaching in Tel Aviv. He and I worked together in Paris on a special issue of *Les Temps Modernes*, the magazine of Jean-Paul Sartre and Simone de Beauvoir. He's the most cosmopolitan brother since Paul Robeson. Snead and Santamaria were new kinds of black intellectuals. They didn't have a trace of self-hatred or self-doubt. Had they lived, their reputations would have rivaled Stuart Hall, Orlando Patterson, Adolph Reed, Jr., bell hooks, Stanley Crouch, Gerald Horne, Dwight McKee, Manning Marable, Henry Louis Gates, Jr.,

Kwame Anthony Appiah, June Jordan, Audre Lorde, Isaac Julien, Kobena Mercer, Toni Cade Bambara, Michael Hanchard, Kimberly Crenshaw, Peter Paris, Robin D.G. Kelley, Maulana Karenga, Molefi Kete Asante, Patricia Williams, Hortense Spiliers, Glenn Loury, Robert O'Meally, Carlos Broussard, Tricia Rose, Cheryl Townsend Gilkes, Sonia Sanchez, Darryl Pinckney, Houston Baker, Lewis Gordon, Haki Madhubuti, Paul Gilroy, Albert Raboteau, Farah Jasmine Griffin, Eddie Glaude, Jr., and Lamine Sagna.

Then there's Brother Mark Ridley-Thomas. He and I met in 1980 when he was on the verge of becoming the executive director of the Southern Christian Leadership Conference of Greater Los Angeles. When Mark and I connected, we dedicated our lives to let suffering speak. Mark has been someone who keeps the focus on the folks whose needs are urgent and real. He became an L.A. city councilman, then a state senator, then the first black man elected to the powerful L.A. County Board of Supervisors. I'm always blessed to spend time with Mark, his lovely wife Avis, and their twin sons, Sebastian and Sinclair.

Another dear friend from L.A., Wren Brown, is a national treasure, a highly gifted actor and brilliant orator who singlehandedly created the Ebony Repertory Theater right in the neighborhood where he grew up, creating a model of community service in the world of the arts.

In the same world, I'm grateful for having worked with Steve McKeever, visionary founder of Hidden Beach Records.

It's hard to find words to praise those brave and good souls who travel with me week in and week out. Let me just say this: when it comes to facilitating my public appearances, I turn to Brother Raymond Ross, the grand master of the art form. He also taught my dear brother Whirlington Anderson well. Together, we have wonderful fellowship. And without my dear brother Jani Hameed I would never reach my destination.

I also want to thank the three agencies who have facilitated my speaking engagements—those led by Carlton Sidgeley, Charles Davis, Perry Steinberg, Tavis Smiley, and the inimitable Denise Pines. And I salute my dear sister, Kimberly McFarland, Tavis Smiley's superb assistant, who keeps chaos at bay.

My life has been enriched by my friendships with Eleni Mavromatidou, Becky Fisk, Paula Mann, Susannah Cjernovitch, Yun Ja Lasser, Leslie Leventman, Kumkum Sangari, Christa Buschendorf, Margaret Haugwitz, Val Moghadam, Lulie Haddad, Eida Berrio, Maxine Leighton, Terri Reed, Kate Gillespie, Ann Bergren, Samuel Scheffler, Joshua Cohen, Susan Neiman, Leon Watts, Cecelia Rio, Christina Lopes, Rachel Emerick, Melanie Mashburn, Sacvan Bercovitch, Dwight McKee, Charles Ogletree, Anna Kirkland, Monika Lavkova, Karen Jackson-Weaver, Alexandra Buresch, Carla Hailey Penn, Valerie Smith, Petra Azar, Noliwe Rooks, Jonathan Demme, Joseph Buttigieg, Elnora Tina Webb, Linda Jamison, Philip Angelides, Russell Banks, Alicia Brown, Martha Rosler, Reverend Bill Howard, Peter Harvey, Richard Roper, and Harry Belafonte.

The noble calling of teaching sometimes invokes the parable of the sower who plants the seeds but dies before seeing his crops. I've been blessed, though, to witness a magnificent harvest. So many of my students have succeeded in spectacular fashion. Among hundreds, I cite only a few: the creative and courageous Farah Jasmine Griffin, director of African American Studies and professor of English at Columbia; David Kyuman Kim, the leading philosopher of religion and culture of his generation and one of my dearest friends, who teaches at Connecticut College; Professor Eddie Glaude, Jr., the leading public intellectual of his generation (with whom I co-edited the canonical text *African American Religious Thought: An Anthology*), who is my supportive and visionary boss who serves as the director of the African American Studies program at Princeton; Serene Jones, the first female president of Union Theological Seminary and the pre-eminent reform theologian who taught at Yale for twenty years; Michael Eric Dyson, unadulterated rhetorical genius and University Professor at Georgetown; Professor Dwight McBride, the young visionary dean at the University of Illinois at Chicago, Chicago Circle; Matthew Briones, professor of American Studies at the University of Chicago; Andre Willis, professor of religion at Yale Divinity School; John Bowlin, professor of theology at Princeton Theological Seminary; Reverend Carolyn Knight, professor of preaching at the Interdenominational Theological Seminary;

Reverend Mark Taylor of the Church of the Open Door in Brooklyn; Reverend Dr. Sujay Johnson, a renowned figure; Reverend Victor Hall of Calvary Baptist Church in Queens; Reverend Gary Simpson of Concord Baptist Church in Brooklyn; Professor Julius Bailey of Central State University; April Garrett, a visionary leader of Civic Frame in Baltimore; Karen Hse, a pioneering human rights activist in China and Cambodia; JoAnne Terrell, Professor of Ethics and Theology, Chicago Theological Seminary; Joy James, professor of humanities, University of Texas at Austin; Salim Washington, a jazz musician and professor of music studies at Brooklyn College; Martha Nadell, a professor of English, also at Brooklyn College; Steve Marshall, political theorist and professor of American Studies at the University of Texas in Austin; Imani Perry, professor of Afro-American Studies, Princeton University; Temitayo Ogunbiyi, superb artist and teacher; Dr. Cynthia Biggs, scholar and renowned songwriter; Bennett Ramsey, professor of religion, University of North Carolina, Greensboro; William Hart, professor of religion, University of North Carolina, Greensboro; Joseph Winters, professor of religion, University of North Carolina, Charlotte; Josiah Young, professor of theology, Wesley Theological Seminary; Anthony Cook, professor of law, Georgetown Law School; Professor Jonathan Walton of University of California Riverside; Verna Myers, head of her legal consulting firm; Philip Goff, professor of psychology, University of Michigan; Victor Anderson, Professor of Christian Ethics and Religious Studies, Vanderbilt University; Saidiya Hartman, professor of English, Columbia University; Christopher Tirres, professor of religion at DePaul University; Leora Batnitzky, professor of religion at Princeton; A.G. Miller, professor of religion at Oberlin College, Jim Wetzel, professor of theology at Villanova University; Gabriel Mendes, professor in the Department of Ethnics Studies at University of California, San Diego.

I am also exceedingly proud of Anthony Edwards, whom I taught when he was incarcerated at Green Haven Correctional Facility in Stormville, New York. Anthony went on to get his Ph.D. and is now a professor of philosophy.

I also was especially pleased to teach in a doctoral program at United Theological Seminary in Dayton, Ohio, that trained hundreds of black preachers under the leadership of the legendary Reverend Dr. Samuel Proctor.

I was blessed to teach many summers at the Governors' Schools in Wake Forest, North Carolina and Conway, Arkansas—teaching centers for talented high school students, most of whom came from poor rural areas.

Once again as with *Hope on a Tightrope*, the editorial genius of Cheryl Woodruff and wise scrutiny of B. Colby Hamilton has greatly contributed to the quality of this book. They are the grand pride of SmileyBooks, especially the indefatigable and visionary leadership of president Cheryl Woodruff.

Mary Ann Rodriguez is not my student, but there is no way I could teach, lecture, write, travel, or endure without her vision, patience, and wisdom. Others call her my assistant, but she is really my guardian angel. She's the gentle gatekeeper in an office where people from every walk of life pass through. Her inner sunshine warms all who come her way and keeps me sane. She is deeply loved and respected by everyone. I thank God she came my way.

When I consider the epic nature of my journey—the toils and snares, the joys and blessings—I am truly humbled. If I had three lifetimes, I could never express enough gratitude. So much of it comes down to Mom's love, Dad's devotion, and the life-sustaining support of my brother and sisters. I wish everyone could experience such grace. Each breath is a breakthrough, each day a gift, each life a miracle.

Living and loving out loud is a beautiful thing.

OUR COLLABORATIVE SPIRIT

I'D LIKE TO OFFER A BRIEF EXPLANATION of the authors' credit, *"Cornel West with David Ritz"*:

I've done a number of books with other people based on conversations and spontaneous give-and-take. I'm a collaborator by nature. In my life it's always been call-and-response.

This book is certainly a collaboration, but one with a difference. David Ritz and I have worked together to sculpt a voice that I hear as my own. Many of my other books were written in what I consider an "academic" voice. *Brother West* is rendered in a "conversational" voice.

That's Ritz's specialty, bringing out the intimate conversational cadences of a living language. He did it, to name a few, with Ray Charles, Marvin Gaye, B.B. King, Smokey Robinson, Grandmaster Flash, Aretha Franklin, Etta James, the Neville Brothers, Tavis Smiley—and I think he's done it with me.

The process is based on friendship, empathy, and a common spirituality. Those readers familiar with Ritz's other books will certainly hear echoes of his own voice in mine. At the same time, those who know me well will hear my distinct voice. It's a melding that borders on the mystical. I'm convinced it's also based on our spiritual bond. The process of writing with David has gone on for well over a year without a single disagreement or uncomfortable moment. How can two men understand each other so deeply that they are able to forge an authentic voice as seamless as Sam and Dave? The answer, I believe, is our Christian orientation and Christian faith. Of course it helped enormously that David's passion for music and Jewish intellectual background made him comfortable with the ideas and sounds that shaped my life. But it is as believers that we have become collaborators. It is at the cross where we meet. And it is at the cross where we write together, brothers in Jesus Christ.

What a wonderful adventure it has been to work with such a master of language and story—my dear brother David Ritz!

ACKNOWLEDGMENTS

DAVID RITZ WOULD LIKE TO THANK . . .

Cornel, for what has been one of the great literary jam sessions of my life. I love James Brown, but, for my money, you're Soul Brother Number One.

Tavis, for hooking us up.

Cheryl Woodruff

Kimberly McFarland

David Vigliano

Gloria Loomis

My loving family: Pops Ritz, Roberta, Alison, Jessica, Jim, Henry, Charlotte, Alden, James, Elizabeth, Esther, all nieces and nephews, my friends Alan Eisenstock and Harry Weinger, my pastor Skip Smith, my fellow parishioner Brother Herb Powell.

MUSIC CREDITS

INDEX

ABOUT THE AUTHORS

EDUCATOR AND PHILOSOPHER CORNEL WEST is the Class of 1943 University Professor at Princeton University. Known as one of America's most gifted, provocative, and important public intellectuals, he is the author of the contemporary classic *Race Matters,* which changed the course of America's dialogue on race and justice; and the *New York Times* bestseller *Democracy Matters.* He is the recipient of the American Book Award and holds more than 20 honorary degrees.

AWARD-WINNING DAVID RITZ is the author of *Divided Soul: The Life of Marvin Gaye;* and the co-author of the autobiographies of Ray Charles, Aretha Franklin, B.B. King, Smokey Robinson, Etta James, Grandmaster Flash, and the Neville Brothers.

We hoped you enjoyed this SMILEYBOOKS publication.
If you would like to receive additional information, please contact:

SMILEYBOOKS

Distributed by:

Hay House, Inc.
P.O. Box 5100
Carlsbad, CA 92018-5100

(760) 431-7695 or (800) 654-5126
(760) 431-6948 (fax) or (800) 650-5115 (fax)
www.hayhouse.com® • www.hayfoundation.org

Published and distributed in Australia by: Hay House Australia Pty. Ltd.
18/36 Ralph St. • Alexandria NSW 2015 • *Phone:* 612-9669-4299
Fax: 612-9669-4144 • www.hayhouse.com.au

Published and distributed in the United Kingdom by: Hay House UK, Ltd.
292B Kensal Rd., London W10 5BE • *Phone:* 44-20-8962-1230
Fax: 44-20-8962-1239 • www.hayhouse.co.uk

Published and distributed in the Republic of South Africa by: Hay House SA
(Pty), Ltd., P.O. Box 990, Witkoppen 2068 • *Phone/Fax:* 27-11-467-8904
info@hayhouse.co.za • www.hayhouse.co.za

Published and Distributed in India by: Hay House Publishers India, Muskaan
Complex, Plot No. 3, B-2, Vasant Kunj, New Delhi 110 070 • *Phone:* 91-11-4176-
1620 • *Fax:* 91-11-4176-1630 • www.hayhouse.co.in

Distributed in Canada by: Raincoast • 9050 Shaughnessy St., Vancouver, B.C.
V6P 6E5 • *Phone:* (604) 323-7100 • *Fax:* (604) 323-2600